D0706955

Native America, Discovered and Conquered

Native America: Yesterday and Today
Bruce E. Johansen, Series Editor

Recent Titles in This Series

Native America, Discovered and Conquered

Thomas Jefferson, Lewis & Clark, and Manifest Destiny

Robert J. Miller

Foreword by Elizabeth Furse

NATIVE AMERICA: YESTERDAY AND TODAY
Bruce E. Johansen, Series Editor

Westport, Connecticut
London

Library of Congress Cataloging-in-Publication Data

Miller, Robert J.
    Native America, discovered and conquered : Thomas Jefferson, Lewis & Clark, and Manifest Destiny / Robert J. Miller.
        p. cm.—(Native America, ISSN 1552–8022)
    Includes bibliographical references and index.
    ISBN 0–275–99011–7
    1. Indians of North America—Government relations. 2. Indians of North America—Government policy. 3. Lewis and Clark Expedition (1804–1806) 4. Jefferson, Thomas, 1743–1826—Relations with Indians. 5. United States—Territorial expansion. 6. United States—Discovery and exploration. 7. United States—Race relations. I. Title.
    E93.M582 2006
    973.04'97—dc22   2006021772

British Library Cataloguing in Publication Data is available.

Library of Congress Catalog Card Number: 2006021772
ISBN: 0–275–99011–7
ISSN: 1552–8022

First published in 2006

Praeger Publishers, 88 Post Road West, Westport, CT 06881
An imprint of Greenwood Publishing Group, Inc.
www.praeger.com

Printed in the United States of America

The paper used in this book complies with the Permanent Paper Standard issued by the National Information Standards Organization (Z39.48–1984).

10 9 8 7 6 5 4 3 2

Contents

Series Foreword

As the Earth's most powerful nation-state in its time, the United States of America has matured quickly—barely more than two centuries from genesis, in the late eighteenth century, to long-in-the-tooth oligarchy in our time. Robert J. Miller, in *Native America, Discovered and Conquered: Thomas Jefferson, Lewis & Clark, and Manifest Destiny,* delineates how the language of empire was spoken in the cradle of our nation-state, as Thomas Jefferson adapted the Doctrine of Discovery's European-centric assumptions to the ideology of Manifest Destiny, propelling the United States' expansion across North America. Following the Louisiana Purchase, the size of the United States doubled. Jefferson sent Lewis and Clark, who have become the country's signature explorers, to report on what the United States had acquired, under European law, from France.

The new United States was assembled on land occupied by other peoples, the tasking of which required justification to protect the self-image of the country's founders as decent (and even heroic) people. This rationale stemmed from the European Doctrine of Discovery, by which an old-world sovereign could assume ownership of New World land by laying eyes upon it, mumbling a few ritual words about God and country, and compensating the Natives with presents and a piece of paper laced with words they usually couldn't read. (Imagine the reaction in Paris if an English sailor had planted the Union Jack on Normandy, said a few words in English, and thereby claimed all of France for the United Kingdom.)

Miller's assay into the records of the Lewis and Clark expedition in the context of Jefferson's thoughts, words, and actions breaks new ground because it provides a critical review of the ethnocentric assumptions of U.S. nation-building from an indigenous point of view, one that has been sorely lacking in the recent national remembrance of Lewis and Clark's transcontinental journey.

Jefferson was a complex man—an intellectually kind way of saying that he displayed some rather stark contradictions. Jefferson's writings sang of freedom (best known in the Declaration of Independence), even as he owned 300 slaves at Monticello. The slaves' shanties made up an entire village. He invoked Native Americans as exemplars of individual freedom in some of his letters as his statecraft led Jefferson to invoke doctrines that assumed European-American property rights, and largely ignored (or did their best to usurp by treaty) the fact that the land on which his feet were planted was owned and occupied by Native peoples with societies and governments of their own.

Jefferson, who is remembered today mainly as a kind and gentle man of letters, architect and scientist, also was one of the most aggressive and expansionist presidents to hold the office, Miller argues. Even as Jefferson wrote that all men were created equal, the legal rules by which property was held were not the least bit equal; Miller traces with a Native eye (he is a citizen of the Eastern Shawnee Tribe of Oklahoma) the ways in which European assumptions laid the legal framework for conquest. Jefferson also advocated removal as early as 1776 of American Indians whose nations stood in the way of Anglo-American expansion. In the world of ideas he held forth in favor of Indians' equality with the immigrants from across the ocean; however, he also used the words "exterminate" and its synonym "extirpate," as a putative solution to "troubles" with Indians who presented violent opposition to the assemblage of empire.

Miller provides an insightful analysis of Manifest Destiny and its roots in the Doctrine of Discovery that may strike some readers as reminiscent of today's news. Manifest Destiny was divinely inspired, so it was said—in much the same manner as George W. Bush has claimed his God's approval for his invasion of Iraq. The messianic aspects of Manifest Destiny also have roots in older forms of European empire-building, which since have echoed down the halls of our history to Vietnam, Iraq, and other points around the world. The stated ambition of Manifest Destiny to spread a "democratic" way of life similarly echoes in U.S. statecraft of recent years, most recently in the presidential rhetoric of G.W. Bush's desire to spread this sort of political manna throughout the Middle East. Self-defined, "civilization" thus seeks to replicate itself, whether the "savages" appreciate the gift or not.

The Lewis and Clark expedition was both a scientific expedition and an imperial mission meant to plant the U.S. flag (and seeds of commerce) on the Pacific shore. Jefferson instructed Lewis and Clark to collect vocabularies of Native languages as he built the empire that would contribute to those people's widespread demise. He also ordered the explorers to name natural features they encountered to provide landmarks to which immigrants could return and claim property.

Although Jefferson studied Native languages and theories of their origins, he also portrayed the United States as a "rising nation … advancing rapidly to destinies beyond the reach of the mortal eye." During 1809, he wrote to President James Madison, saying of the U.S. Constitution, "No constitution was ever before so well calculated as ours for extensive empire." He advocated invasion of Canada in a letter to James Monroe in 1813 and, four years later, set his eyes on Texas.

Jefferson was, in Miller's analysis, a practitioner of ethics bent to serve political convenience. Compared with the myths of Jefferson with which we sometimes comfort ourselves, Miller's is sometimes not a pretty picture. Jefferson has his epic qualities, but the myth is hardly the whole picture. Miller shines a light of historical veracity on the mythical Jefferson from a Native point of view, and he does it with uncommon precision.

Bruce E. Johansen
Frederick W. Kayser Research Professor
School of Communication
University of Nebraska at Omaha

Foreword

History is an elusive and misleading discipline. It is practically impossible to find unbiased history, one not filtered through preconceived ideas. That is why this book, *Native America, Discovered and Conquered,* is so important. This history strips away so much cultural clutter and brings us information that until now has been practically impossible to find. Search the "history books" of American schools and I challenge you to learn that there are over 550 Indian tribes in the United States with governmental powers over land and people. Nowhere will you learn that the U.S. Constitution recognizes treaties as the "supreme Law of the Land" or that the U.S. Supreme Court has stated that a "treaty was not a grant of rights to the Indians, but a grant of rights from them—a reservation of those not granted." (U.S. Const. art. VI; United States v. Winans, 198 U.S. 371 (1905)).

Through great good luck, I was educated about these issues over 38 years ago. I went down to the Nisqually River in Washington State to find out why there was a war being waged on the state's rivers, with all jurisdictions and the majority of people opposing Indian fishing. The newspapers (the present history tellers), all portrayed the Indian fishers as renegades and they were being arrested over and over again, despite that the tribal fishers were maintaining that they were fishing under treaty-guaranteed rights. I read a book called *Uncommon Controversy,* published by the American Friends Service Committee, which gave a totally different explanation of the situation than that presented by the press and the federal, state and county authorities. *Uncommon Controversy* was the wake-up call for me that Professor Miller's book will be for generations to come—the clear light of reason, unfogged by prejudice and, dare I say, racism?

When I went to the Nisqually River that day, I met a most extraordinary man, Billy Frank Jr., a Nisqually Indian, just out of prison that morning, after more than 30 arrests for fishing under the Medicine Creek Treaty. Billy did the most wonderful thing—he educated me and my husband on treaties, treaty rights and tribal fishing. How amazing to have been educated that way, and, of course, there was no other way to find that information, as it certainly wasn't available through the local media or taught in schools.

My husband Dr. Richard Briggs and I started Citizens for Indian Rights to expand this education to other non-Indians—the Indians had their hands full already in their fight for their treaty rights. For years I learned all I could and the information was hard to come by. How useful Robert Miller's brilliant book would have been to me and countless people working to right the century-old wrongs done to tribes and tribal people. Information such as this is liberating and empowering.

The U.S. Constitution has designated that the United States Congress shall have the sole power to treaty and trade with the Indian tribes—not states and counties: the U.S. Congress. And yet, the majority of the members of the House and Senate are just as uneducated about tribes and treaties and treaty rights as the rest of the population because they are the product of the same education system. All branches of the federal government share a trust responsibility to tribes, and yet they are equally ill-informed.

The education system has ignored Indian issues, laws, governmental powers and the unique government-to-government relationship with the federal government. It is shocking that the members of Congress with awesome powers over the tribes should be so ill informed and that tribes are forced to spend huge amounts of time trying to educate their representatives.

When I was in the U.S. Congress, I had a startling example of the danger of the lack of education on Indian affairs in our system. I received a call from the tribal chairman of the Umatilla Tribe in Eastern Oregon. There is a chemical weapons dump on the banks of the Columbia River that impacts the tribe. This dump has been of great concern to the Army and the citizens of Oregon and Washington because it is unstable. Chairman Don Sampson told me that the tribe had received word over the "grapevine" that the U.S. Army had developed an evacuation plan should the dump go critical. This plan was to evacuate the residents of the four surrounding counties onto the Umatilla Indian Reservation. But no one had informed the tribal government of this plan. I asked the Secretary of the Army if he could come to my office to explain this, as the tribe was getting no response to its inquiries. The Secretary came accompanied by two generals and we had a long discussion about the problem. Finally in frustration I said, "But Mr. Secretary, why did you not inform the Tribe and the tribal chairman?" His answer was, "Congresswoman, we didn't know how to reach them." My response was, "Mr. Secretary, they have telephones, they are listed in the phone book, and they speak English."

When I was elected to the U.S. House of Representatives (OR1) in 1992, I went with all my fellow freshmen and women to a week-long training at the Kennedy School of Government at Harvard University. There we learned our new duties. It was that experience that led me to develop the Institute for Tribal Government at

Portland State University upon my retirement in 1999. It seemed to me that tribal governments would benefit from such training and we have provided training to over 30 tribes nationwide. The board of directors, a fully tribal board, urged us to also develop a project to interview tribal leaders across the country. These interviews are on-going with over 40 tribal leaders video-taped and edited, with an entire curriculum developed for university level teaching presently being adapted for high school classes. Professor Miller serves on the Board of the Institute for Tribal Government and has assisted us with trainings for tribal governments. He is able to do a one-day class on Federal Indian Law which covers fourteen weeks of law school and, most amazingly, keeps the audience awake, eager and begging for more.

Professor Miller's fine book is so important and so relevant to all Americans who care about the truth and want their history to be accurate and unbiased. As a former Congresswoman, I will recommend it to the co-chairs of the Native American Caucus of the U.S. House and Senate for basic reading and will also make it required reading for the students in my Great Tribal Leaders of Modern Times classes. Professor Miller is to be congratulated—he has done a great service to Indian and non-Indian Country in writing this book.

The Honorable Elizabeth Furse
Director, Institute for Tribal Government
Hatfield School, Portland State University

Acknowledgments

I thank Professor Peter Onuf, Steve Bahnson, and Andria Joseph for reading my draft manuscript and providing excellent suggestions and my research assistants John Ptacin, Andria Joseph, and Michael Lopez for their diligent assistance over the past three and a half years. I also thank Lynn Williams of the Lewis & Clark Law School Library who endured countless requests from me for the most obscure resources. She always delivered them expeditiously and with a smile.

Professors John Grant, Ed Brunet, and Mike Blumm of Lewis & Clark Law School also deserve my thanks. John encouraged me to publish this work and helped me navigate the world of publishing, and Ed and Mike read my earlier writings on this subject and provided excellent advice.

I appreciate Lewis & Clark Law School in Portland, Oregon, and my dean, Jim Huffman, for granting me the time and resources to undertake this project.

I thank my tribal council, the Eastern Shawnee Tribe of Oklahoma, for appointing me to the Circle of Tribal Advisors in 2003 to work with the National Lewis & Clark Bicentennial Committee.

Finally, I am very grateful to Hilary Claggett, my acquisitions editor at Praeger Publishers; my series editor, Professor Bruce Johansen; and the staff of Praeger Publishers.

Preface

This book grew out of my involvement with the two hundred year anniversary of the Lewis and Clark expedition. In 2002, I replied to a call for presentations at a conference on Lewis and Clark and the Indian Nations at the Buffalo Bill Historical Center in Cody, Wyoming. Since I am a law professor, I naturally asked myself what legal issues were involved in the expedition and what law governed President Thomas Jefferson's dispatch of the expedition to the Pacific coast and Lewis and Clark's conduct during the voyage. The Doctrine of Discovery immediately sprang to mind because this is the international law that governed European exploration and discovery of new lands around the world for centuries. I asked myself "what did Jefferson know about the Doctrine of Discovery" and "did Lewis and Clark use the principles of the Doctrine during their expedition?"

I am very familiar with Discovery because I have taught the subject in American Indian Law classes since 1993 at Lewis & Clark Law School. The Doctrine of Discovery is an international legal principle that allegedly granted Euro-Americans property and sovereignty claims over native peoples and native lands as soon as Euro-Americans "discovered" these lands. The Doctrine is also an important part of American history and modern day Indian Law. Every year my class studies the seminal United States Supreme Court case, *Johnson v. M'Intosh,* in which the Supreme Court adopted the Doctrine of Discovery as federal case law in 1823. I was eager to see what, if anything, the Doctrine had to do with Thomas Jefferson and the Lewis and Clark expedition of 1803-06.

I then began reading and researching the journals of Lewis and Clark and other materials about the explorers and Thomas Jefferson and quickly realized that I had stumbled onto something new. I could not find any discussion by legal or non-legal sources on this topic; yet I found a wealth of information demonstrating that Jefferson accurately understood the Doctrine of Discovery and utilized it during his entire legal and political career from 1767 forward and that the Lewis and Clark expedition used Discovery principles in the Louisiana Territory and the Pacific Northwest. I then began speaking on this topic across the country, and in late 2003 my tribal council, of the Eastern Shawnee Tribe of Oklahoma, appointed me to the Circle of Tribal Advisors to work with the National Lewis and Clark Bicentennial Committee.

My tribe, and many other American Indian tribes and Indian people, were conflicted by the observance of the Lewis and Clark anniversary. Similar to how Indian tribes had viewed the five hundred year anniversary of Christopher Columbus' "discovery" of the New World, the vast majority of Indians and tribes did not want to "celebrate" the Lewis and Clark expedition. Instead of something to celebrate, Indians saw the expedition as the forerunner of centuries of conquest, oppression, and destruction. Understandably, tribes were very cautious about becoming involved with the anniversary. Consequently, tribal representatives and Indian members of the National Lewis and Clark Bicentennial Committee communicated this concern. The Committee came to understand this issue and expressly decided not to call the Lewis and Clark anniversary a "celebration" because it realized that this was not the case for American Indians. The National Committee called the event a "commemoration," a remembrance of an important event in America's history. This was accurate because the Lewis and Clark expedition was an important event in American history. But the only aspect of this anniversary that Indian people and nations wanted to celebrate was that they were still in existence even after the Lewis and Clark expedition and American Manifest Destiny had rolled over them. The Indian nations are still here, as they had been for thousands of years before Lewis and Clark, and as they will be for thousands of years into the future. That is something worth celebrating.

My book shines new light on American history by demonstrating how the Doctrine of Discovery, President Thomas Jefferson, Lewis and Clark, and Manifest Destiny led to the domination and conquest of the Indian nations, and how the Doctrine remains part of American Indian Law today.

This book is important because it will open the eyes of Americans to how "law" was used by Europeans, the American colonists, and the American state and federal governments to dominate Indian people and nations and to dispossess them of much of their sovereignty, self-determination rights, and their property rights. This book is also important because it demonstrates clearly that Discovery is not just a relic of America's past. The Doctrine of Discovery still has a major impact in federal Indian law and the lives of Indians and their tribal governments today. We can and should work to eliminate this medieval, ethnocentric, religious, and racial doctrine from the lives of modern day American Indians.

This book fits perfectly into many important areas of American history and American Indian history and the question of native rights in the modern era because it helps to explain why certain things are the way they are today. We will see that the Doctrine of Discovery was brought to this continent from 1492 forward and was applied to limit the human and property rights of indigenous peoples by Spanish, French, and English explorers and colonists. And, remarkably, we will see that the Doctrine still limits native rights today. Thus, it behooves Americans to learn about their history and it is important for Americans and American Indians to identify the vestiges of the Doctrine of Discovery in American law and to work to eliminate these ethnocentric, racial, and feudal ideas from American law and life.

Introduction

T he New World was colonized under an international legal principle that is known today as the Doctrine of Discovery. When Europeans and Americans set out to explore and exploit new lands in the fifteenth through the twentieth centuries, they justified their governmental and property claims over these territories and over the indigenous inhabitants with the Discovery Doctrine. This legal principle was created and justified by religious and ethnocentric ideas of European and Caucasian superiority over the other cultures, religions, and races of the world. The Doctrine provided, under established international law, that newly arrived Europeans immediately and automatically acquired property rights in native lands and gained governmental, political, and commercial rights over the inhabitants without the knowledge nor the consent of the indigenous peoples. When Europeans and Americans planted their national flags and religious symbols in these "newly discovered" lands, they were not just thanking Providence for a safe voyage. Instead, they were undertaking the well-recognized legal procedures and rituals of Discovery designed to demonstrate their country's legal claim over the "newly discovered" lands and peoples. Needless to say, indigenous peoples objected to the application of this international law to them, their governments, and their property rights. Surprisingly, perhaps, the Doctrine is still international and American law today. In fact, Canadian and Australian courts have struggled with questions regarding Discovery, native title, and native ownership of land just in recent decades, and the United States Supreme Court was faced in 2005 with a case that raised Discovery issues.[1]

This book undertakes an original analysis of the legal and historical evidence that demonstrates the application of the Doctrine of Discovery by Euro-Americans against the native peoples and their governments in the areas that now make up the United States. We will see that the English/American colonists and then the American state and federal governments all utilized the Doctrine of Discovery and its religiously, culturally, and racially based ideas of superiority and preeminence over Native American peoples in staking legal claims to the lands and property rights of the indigenous people. The United States was ultimately able to enforce the Doctrine against the Indian Nations as Manifest Destiny led the United States across the North American continent and almost totally swept the Indian Nations from its path. Discovery is still the law today, and it is still being used against American Indians and their governments. Thus was Native America "discovered."[2]

The legal and factual evidence of American history proves that the expansion of the United States from the 13 original colonies, or states, in 1774 until 1855, when the Pacific Northwest was acquired by the United States, was rationalized on the basis of the Doctrine of Discovery. Our Founding Fathers were well aware of the Doctrine and utilized it while they were part of the colonial English system. They then naturally continued to use Discovery under the flag of the new United States. From George Washington and Benjamin Franklin on, American leaders utilized this legal principle to justify making claims of property rights and political dominance over the Indian Nations and their citizens. Thomas Jefferson, in particular, demonstrated a working day-to-day knowledge of Discovery and used its legal principles against the Indian Nations within the original 13 colonies, in the trans-Appalachia area, the Louisiana Territory, and the Pacific Northwest. In fact, Jefferson's dispatch of the Lewis and Clark expedition in 1803 was directly targeted at the mouth of the Columbia River in the Pacific Northwest because the expedition was expressly designed to strengthen the United States Discovery claim to ownership and dominance of that area. Meriwether Lewis and William Clark and their "Corps of Northwestern Discovery" complied with Jefferson's instructions and desires to solidify the United States' claim to the Pacific Northwest. The United States then argued with Russia, Spain, and England for four decades that it owned the Northwest under the principles of international law because of its first discovery of the Columbia River by the American sea captain Robert Gray in 1792, the first inland exploration and occupation of the territory by Lewis and Clark in 1805–1806, and then the building of Astoria in 1811, the first permanent settlement in the Northwest.[3]

After the Lewis and Clark expedition in 1804–1806, American history was dominated by an erratic but fairly constant advance of American interests and empire across the continent under the principles of the Doctrine of Discovery. This was not an accident but was instead the expressed goal of Thomas Jefferson, James Madison, James Monroe, John Quincy Adams, and a multitude of other American politicians and citizens. "Manifest Destiny" is the name that was ultimately used in 1845 to describe this relentless, predestined, and divinely inspired advance across the continent. We will see that Manifest Destiny was fueled by the Doctrine of Discovery and was created by the rationales and justifications of Discovery.

Manifest Destiny was exemplified by three basic aspects that characterized the rhetoric of an American continental empire. These ideas had pervaded American political and cultural thinking long before the definition of the ideas as Manifest Destiny in 1845. The three aspects that composed Manifest Destiny arose from the same elements as the Doctrine of Discovery. Manifest Destiny first assumed that the United States had some unique moral virtues that other countries did not possess. Second, Manifest Destiny asserted that the United States had a mission to redeem the world by spreading republican government and the American way of life around the globe. Third, Manifest Destiny had a messianic dimension because it assumed a faith in America's divinely ordained destiny. This kind of thinking could only arise, it seems, from an ethnocentric view that one's own culture, government, race, religion, and country are superior to all others. This exact kind of thinking justified and motivated the development of the Doctrine of Discovery in the fifteenth century and then helped develop Manifest Destiny in the nineteenth century.

In the chapters to follow we will trace the legal and historical evidence that demonstrates the development of the Doctrine of Discovery in America and its metamorphosis into Manifest Destiny. By "legal history," I do not mean that we will be looking at only court cases and laws. We will look at far more evidence than just the actions of state and federal courts. We will instead examine how the legal principle of Discovery and its elements were used by politicians, newspapers, governments, courts, and common Americans to justify and prod American expansion across our continent. We will see how Native America came to be "discovered."

We need to clearly define the elements of the Doctrine of Discovery at the outset so that we can observe their historical and legal development and application in Europe in the 1400s. We can then more easily follow the adoption and use of Discovery in North America by European colonists and by the United States to create Manifest Destiny.

There are 10 elements to Discovery:

1. *First discovery.* The first European country to "discover" new lands unknown to other Europeans gained property and sovereign rights over the lands. First discovery alone, without a taking of physical possession, was often considered to create a claim of title to the newly found lands, but it was usually considered to be only an incomplete title.

2. *Actual occupancy and current possession.* To fully establish a "first discovery" claim and turn it into a complete title, a European country had to actually occupy and possess newly found lands. This was usually done by actual physical possession with the building of a fort or settlement, for example, and leaving soldiers or settlers on the land. This physical possession had to be accomplished within a reasonable amount of time after the first discovery to create a complete title to the land in the discovering country.

3. *Preemption/European title.* The discovering European country gained the power of preemption, the sole right to buy the land from the native people. This is a valuable property right. The government that held the Discovery power of preemption prevented or preempted any other European or American government or individual from buying land from the discovered native people.

4. *Indian title.* After first discovery, Indian Nations and the indigenous peoples were considered by European and American legal systems to have lost the full property rights and ownership of their lands. They only retained rights to occupy and use their land. Nevertheless, this right could last forever if the indigenous people never consented to sell their land. But if they ever did choose to sell, they could only sell to the government that held the power of preemption over their lands. Thus, Indian title was a limited ownership right.

5. *Tribal limited sovereign and commercial rights.* After first discovery, Indian Nations and native peoples were also considered to have lost some of their inherent sovereign powers and the rights to free trade and diplomatic international relations. Thereafter, they could only deal with the Euro-American government that had first discovered them.

6. *Contiguity.* The dictionary definition of this word means the state of being contiguous to, to have proximity to, or to be near to. This element provided that Europeans had a Discovery claim to a reasonable and significant amount of land contiguous to and surrounding their settlements and the lands that they actually possessed in the New World. This element became very important when different European countries had settlements somewhat close together. In that situation, each country held rights over the unoccupied lands between their settlements to a point half way between their actual settlements. Most importantly, contiguity held that the discovery of the mouth of a river gave the discovering country a claim over all the lands drained by that river; even if that was thousands of miles of territory.

7. *Terra nullius.* This phrase literally means a land or earth that is null or void. The term *vacuum domicilium* was also sometimes used to describe this element, and this term literally means an empty, vacant, or unoccupied home or domicile. According to this idea, if lands were not possessed or occupied by any person or nation, or were occupied by non-Europeans but not being used in a fashion that European legal systems approved, the lands were considered to be empty and waste and available for Discovery claims. Europeans and Americans were very liberal in applying this definition to the lands of native people. Euro-Americans often considered lands that were actually owned, occupied, and being actively utilized by indigenous people to be "vacant" and available for Discovery claims if they were not being "properly used" according to European and American law and culture.

8. *Christianity.* Religion was a significant aspect of the Doctrine of Discovery and of Manifest Destiny. Under Discovery, non-Christian people were not deemed to have the same rights to land, sovereignty, and self-determination as Christians because their rights could be trumped upon their discovery by Christians.

9. *Civilization.* The European and later American definition of civilization was an important part of Discovery and the idea of Euro-American superiority. Euro-Americans thought that God had directed them to bring civilized ways and education and religion to indigenous peoples and often to exercise paternalism and guardianship powers over them.

10. *Conquest.* We will encounter two different definitions for this element. It can mean a military victory. We will see this definition reflected in Spanish, English, and American ideas that "just wars" allegedly justified the invasion and conquest of Indian lands in certain circumstances. But that is not the only definition we

will encounter. "Conquest" was also used as a "term of art," a word with a special meaning, when it was used as an element of Discovery.

The Discovery element of conquest was defined in *Johnson v. M'Intosh* in 1823 by the United States Supreme Court. The Court used the word "conquest" to describe the property rights Europeans gained over the Indian Nations after their first discovery. By analogy, the Court considered first discovery to be in essence like a military conquest because the European discovering country claimed political, real property, and commercial rights over the native people. In European law, when the word "conquest" was used as a term of art, it defined the effect that an actual military conquest had on the property rights of the inhabitants of the conquered country. In Europe, the U.S. Supreme Court explained, the property rights of the conquered people were not taken away, and the people were ultimately absorbed into the culture and life of the conquering country. But the Court said that this European property theory of "conquest" could not be directly applied in America. The Supreme Court instead modified the standard definition of European conquest because of the different cultures, religions, and "savagery" of Native Americans. The Court said that "conquest" in America defined the restricted property rights Indians retained after their first discovery by Europeans. The Court claimed it had to develop a modified theory of the European principle of "conquest" because the Indian Nations could not be left in complete ownership of the lands in America.[4]

We will see all these elements of the Discovery Doctrine adopted into American law and Manifest Destiny as the United States ambitions grew to control and dominate North America. We will watch these elements develop throughout American law and history and observe how they were used against American Indians and their governments and how they are still being used today.

In chapter 1, we examine the development of Discovery in the fifteenth and sixteenth centuries by Spain, Portugal, England, France, and the Church.

Chapter 2 describes how the Discovery Doctrine was adopted into American colonial and state law, then into the U.S. Constitution, federal laws, and executive branch actions, and finally by the Supreme Court in *Johnson v. M'Intosh* in 1823.

Chapter 3 breaks new ground by proving from Thomas Jefferson's own words and actions that he fully understood the Doctrine and utilized that international legal principle against American Indians. Jefferson also relied on Discovery principles in conceiving and launching the Lewis and Clark expedition with the goal of securing America's first discovery claim to the Pacific Northwest and extending his idea of an American "empire of liberty" over the entire North American continent.[5]

Chapter 4 analyzes the contradictory ideas and goals Jefferson had about the Indian Nations and their people and their futures, as well as the strategies he used to manipulate Indians to serve American Manifest Destiny. Jefferson's actual conduct regarding Indians and the Indian Nations demonstrates a serious contradiction between his words and his actions.

Chapter 5 also establishes a new concept by demonstrating emphatically that Indian political, legal, and commercial affairs were Jefferson's primary motivations for the Lewis and Clark expedition and that Lewis and Clark's interactions with the Indian Nations and their use of the well-known rituals and formalities of Discovery strengthened America's first discovery claim to the Pacific Northwest. Lewis and Clark were clearly part of the application of Discovery and American Manifest Destiny to the indigenous people of North America. In addition, analyzing Lewis and Clark's conduct under the microscope of Discovery proves that they were more important to American expansion and the acquisition of the Pacific Northwest under the legal principles of the Doctrine than most historians give them credit for today.

Chapter 6 explains a new theory about American Manifest Destiny: Manifest Destiny grew out of the legal elements and justifications of the Doctrine of Discovery.

Chapter 7 surveys the impact of the adoption of Discovery into American law on Indian people and their governments from 1774 to 2005 and the resulting loss of tribal and individual Indian property rights, human rights, and sovereign powers.

Finally, we conclude our discussion with the idea that it is time for the United States to try to undo more than 200 years of the application of the ethnocentrically, racially, and religiously inspired Doctrine of Discovery to American Indians and nations.

It is my hope that presenting and analyzing these new ideas regarding Thomas Jefferson, the Lewis and Clark expedition, Manifest Destiny, and the Doctrine of Discovery will assist readers in achieving a fuller and more diverse understanding of these crucial aspects of American history and their continuing impact today. This discussion shows the modern-day relevance of Discovery and the amazing fact that the Doctrine is still an active part of American law. In fact, the deed to almost all real estate in the United States originates from an Indian title that was acquired by the United States via Discovery principles. In addition, it continues to play a very significant role in American federal Indian law and Indian policies today because the Doctrine is still being actively applied against American Indian people, Indian Nations, and their lands today, and it still restricts their property, governmental, and self-determination rights. The United States government and the American people need to carefully reexamine their continuing use of Discovery against our Indian citizens and Indian Nations. The cultural, racial, and religious justifications that led to the development of Discovery raise serious doubts about the validity of continuing to apply the Doctrine of Discovery in modern-day Indian affairs and federal Indian law. Discovery is *not* an esoteric relic of history or a mistake of our past that we can do nothing about today.[6]

Five brief points need to be made before we begin.

1. We will encounter the word "discovery" being used in two different ways. We will see the word used to denote the act of uncovering or finding new lands and

new things. But we will also see it used as a term of art—that is, as a word with a specialized meaning. When the word "discovery" is used as a term of art, it is being used to define a legal claim under the Doctrine of Discovery. It is not always certain in the quotations that we will examine which way the word was being used, to describe the act of discovering or as a term of art. Thus, we will be conservative and only interpret the word "discovery" to be a term of art and to mean the legal act of claiming newly discovered territory and rights when that is clearly the case. I will capitalize the word "discovery" when I use it as a term of art. There is ample evidence to prove that the legal Doctrine of Discovery and the principles of "Discovery" were used by France, England, Spain, Portugal, Holland, Sweden, Russia, and the United States to claim lands in the New World. The evidence is overwhelming on this point. The United States, Spain, Russia, and England then used the elements of Discovery and the word "Discovery" to try to prove their ownership claims to the Pacific Northwest. The United States ultimately prevailed to make the Oregon country its own, and in the process it turned Discovery into Manifest Destiny.

2. We need to define several aspects of real property law. Real property is just another term for real estate or land. I will briefly define here most of the specific terms we will encounter. These short definitions and the context in which we will see the terms used will make their definitions clear.

   The American property system is primarily inherited and adapted from English law and its medieval roots. We will encounter words from feudal times such as "fee," "fee simple," "fee simple absolute," "seisin," "seised in fee," and "livery of seisin." All of these words apply to the ownership of land. The word "fee" means an ownership interest in land. The phrase "fee simple absolute" means that there are no conditions on the ownership right. These ownership rights can last forever and can be left to a person's heirs, or they can be sold at the choice of the owner to whomever they wish and for whatever amount of money they can get. Fee simple absolute is the largest possible estate, or ownership interest, a person can possess in land. There are several lesser forms of estates or ownership interests in land that we do not need to worry about.

   "Seisin" means the possession of real property under one of the different types of ownership claims to an estate in land. To be "seised in fee" means that a person possesses land under a claim of unconditional ownership rights. "Livery of seisin" means the delivery of the seisin, the delivery of the possession of land, to a new owner. This was accomplished in feudal times, in the days before written deeds and county title offices, by a ritual or formality in which the old owner and the new owner would go onto the land and turn over a shovelful of dirt. The old owner would then hand a dirt clod or a twig or branch from the property to the new owner in the presence of witnesses and neighbors. This ritual demonstrated the delivery, "livery," of the possession, "seisin," of the land to the new owner.[7]

3. We will only address Manifest Destiny in regard to the Pacific Northwest, the Oregon country. This is because the Pacific Northwest was the only part of today's 48 contiguous states where no European or American government had already established a Discovery ownership claim in the time period we are considering. The Pacific Northwest was the primary part of North America where the United States government applied the Discovery Doctrine to native governments and peoples through Manifest Destiny.

4. I am not a historian. I am an attorney, a tribal judge, and a law professor who has practiced and taught Indian law for over 14 years. This book does not claim to be an analysis or interpretation of a particular set of historical events in a certain time period. Instead, this book is a survey of legal history. It is a search for historical evidence of legal significance that demonstrates the development and use of the international Doctrine of Discovery throughout American history and proves how Discovery was converted into American Manifest Destiny. We will see that there is an enormous amount of legal/historical evidence that proves that the United States used the Doctrine of Discovery to its advantage to claim and exercise property rights and sovereign control over lands and rights owned and used by native peoples and their governments.

I believe that being an attorney and law professor and *not* being a historian actually increases the value of this review of the historical facts about Discovery and Manifest Destiny. This book demonstrates one of the valuable aspects of interdisciplinary research. In writing this book I have researched and examined information that for the most part has been reviewed and written about already by numerous historians. But I looked at this information through the eyes of a lawyer and law professor with an intimate knowledge of the Doctrine of Discovery. I saw these "historical" facts in a new light, a "legal light." In tracing the legal history and justifications of Discovery and Manifest Destiny, I detect different meanings and reach different interpretations regarding the identical documents and events that have already been analyzed by many historians.

5. In attempting to prove my thesis that the Doctrine of Discovery was used to settle this continent and ultimately became Manifest Destiny, I am confident that in more than three and a half years of research, my research assistants and I have found only a small fraction of all the evidence on Discovery that there is to find in European and American colonial, state, and federal archives. Notwithstanding that fact, the evidence we have uncovered is overwhelming that the United States used the Doctrine of Discovery to gain the Pacific Northwest and used the elements of Discovery to create the concept of an American Manifest Destiny to sweep over the North American continent.

CHAPTER 1

The Doctrine of Discovery

In 1823, in *Johnson v. M'Intosh*, the United States Supreme Court decided that the Doctrine of Discovery, the established international legal principle of European and American colonial law, had also become the law of the American state and federal governments. We examine the *Johnson* case in detail in chapter 2. It is beneficial at this point, however, before we start analyzing the historical and legal evidence, to understand how the United States Supreme Court defined the Doctrine of Discovery in 1823. We can then better understand the evidence demonstrating the development of the Doctrine in Europe and its adoption into American law and Manifest Destiny.

In a nutshell, the Supreme Court said that, under Discovery, when European, Christian nations discovered new lands, the discovering country automatically gained sovereign and property rights in the lands of non-Christian, non-European peoples, even though, obviously, the native peoples already owned, occupied, and used these lands. The property right Euro-Americans gained in North America was defined as a future right, a kind of limited fee-simple title or ownership right. This "European title" was the exclusive right to buy the newly discovered lands whenever natives consented. The right held by the discovering European country was limited by and subject to the natives' right to occupy and use the land. In reality, the Euro-Americans had acquired an exclusive option to buy American Indian lands if ever the tribal nation chose to sell. This was called the power of preemption. The discovering country owned the property right of the power to exclude any other Euro-American country from buying the lands it had discovered. In addition, the discovering country also automatically gained some sovereign governmental rights over the native peoples and their governments, which restricted tribal international political and commercial relationships. This transfer of political, commercial, and property rights was accomplished without the knowledge or the consent of the Indian people or their governments.[1]

The U.S. Supreme Court expressly relied on all of the Discovery elements that are defined in this book's introduction: (1) first discovery, (2) actual occupancy and current possession, (3) preemption and European title, (4) Indian title, (5) limitations on tribal sovereign and commercial rights, (6) contiguity, (7) *terra nullius,* (8) Christianity, (9) civilization, and (10) conquest. We only need to quote a few short statements from the *Johnson* Court to see its use of all ten Discovery elements. "The United States ... [and] its civilized inhabitants now hold this country. They hold, and assert in themselves, the title by which it was acquired. They maintain, as all others have maintained, that discovery gave an exclusive right to extinguish the Indian title of occupancy, either by purchase or by conquest; and gave also a right to such a degree of sovereignty, as the circumstances of the people would allow them to exercise." The Court continued, "discovery gave title to the government by whose subjects, or by whose authority, it was made against all other European governments, which title might be consummated by possession." A discovering European country gained exclusive property rights that were to be respected by other Europeans and that preempted other Europeans from the same rights.[2]

Accordingly, the European discovering nation gained real property rights to native lands and sovereign powers merely by walking ashore in the New World and planting a flag in the soil. The Court defined this property right as being an "absolute ultimate title ... acquired by discovery." Native rights, however, were "in no instance, entirely disregarded; but were necessarily, to a considerable extent, impaired." This was so because although the Doctrine recognized that natives still held the legal right to possess, occupy, and use their lands as long as they wished, "their rights to complete sovereignty, as independent nations, were necessarily diminished, and their power to dispose of the soil at their own will, to whomsoever they pleased, was denied by the original fundamental principle, that discovery gave exclusive title to those who made it." This loss of native property and sovereignty rights was justified, the Court said, by "the character and religion of its inhabitants ... the superior genius of Europe ... [and] ample compensation to the [Indians] by bestowing on them civilization and Christianity, in exchange for unlimited independence." The superior European civilizations and religions justified Discovery claims in the Americas and the loss of rights for native people and their governments. The Court also referred to contiguity when it discussed England's Discovery claim across the entire continent, "from sea to sea," and the French claim to "vast territories ... on discovery ... [even to] country not actually settled by Frenchmen." Finally, the Court relied on the principle of *terra nullius* when it discussed the English "title ... to vacant lands." Here, then, we see the Supreme Court's express use of all the Discovery elements.[3]

In considering just the real estate or real property right, the U.S. Supreme Court said that the discovering nation gained, among other rights, the right to preempt or preclude other European nations from buying the newly discovered Indian lands. In other words, the discoverer acquired an exclusive option to purchase tribal lands whenever tribes consented to sell. The discovering European country gained a current property right, a current "title" in the lands of the indigenous people—the exclusive right to buy the native's real property and their occupancy and use rights at some later date. European countries could even sell or grant this interest, this "title" in the property, to others while the lands were still in the possession and use of the natives. Euro-American governments did this many times in treaties. That is exactly how the United States acquired the Louisiana Territory, for instance. This European title, the power of preemption, limited the real property rights of natives and their governments to freely sell their lands to whomever they wished and for whatever price they could obtain because Discovery granted to the discovering European country the right of preemption. Obviously, preempting the Indian Nations from selling their lands as they wished diminished the economic value of native land assets and greatly benefited the European countries and settlers. Consequently, indigenous real property rights and values were severely injured immediately and automatically upon their "discovery" by Europeans. Tribal sovereign powers were also greatly affected by the Doctrine because their national sovereignty and independence were diminished by Discovery's restriction of the Indian Nations' international diplomacy, commercial, and political activities to only their "discovering" European country.[4]

On one esoteric level, Discovery was a legal principle designed only to control the European nations. Clearly, however, the native peoples and nations felt most heavily its onerous burdens. The political and economic aspects of the Doctrine were developed to serve the interests of European countries in an attempt to control European exploration and conflicts in non-European areas. The Doctrine was motivated by greed and by the economic and political interests of European countries to share, to some extent, the lands and assets to be gained in the New World instead of engaging in expensive wars fighting over them. This is not to say that European countries did not fight over land in the New World, but they did try to develop a legal principle that would control exploration and colonization and make it as profitable for Europeans as possible. Although they occasionally disagreed over the exact definition of the Doctrine and sometimes fought over discoveries in the New World, one thing they never disagreed about was that native people lost significant property and governmental rights immediately upon their first discovery by a European country.

One Supreme Court justice from the *Johnson* case later demonstrated his clear understanding of the advantages that the Doctrine granted Europeans. Justice Joseph Story wrote that Discovery avoided conflicts for European countries and was a "most flexible and convenient principle [because] the first discovery should confer upon the nation of the discoverer an exclusive right to the soil, for the purposes of sovereignty and settlement."[5]

The Doctrine has been severely criticized as a fictional justification for the European colonization and subjugation of the New World. A close look at the origins and development of this legal doctrine does leave one thinking more of the saying "might makes right" than of the principled development of law in a singular society where all people share the rights and obligations of a law. In fact, a "cynic" might conclude that the legalistic international law Doctrine of Discovery was nothing more than an attempt to put a patina of legality on the armed confiscation of almost all the assets of the people of the New World. Chief Justice John Marshall, the author of *Johnson v. M'Intosh,* and his colleague Justice Story both recognized that the "rights" of discovery were required to be "maintained and established ... by the sword" as "the right of the strongest."[6]

THE EUROPEAN FORMULATION OF THE DOCTRINE

The Doctrine of Discovery is one of the earliest examples of international law, that is, the accepted legal principles that apply to the conduct of nations vis-à-vis other nations. The Doctrine was developed by European, Christian countries to control their own actions and conflicts regarding exploration, trade, and colonization in non-European countries and was used as a justification for the domination of non-Christian, non-European peoples. European nations and their legal systems have a long history of developing, refining, and applying Discovery theories to non-Europeans.

The Doctrine has been traced as far back as medieval times and the Crusades to recover the Holy Lands in 1096–1271. Even before that time, the Roman Catholic Church and various popes had established the idea of a worldwide papal jurisdiction, which created a legal responsibility for the Church to work for a universal Christian commonwealth. This papal responsibility and especially the Crusades led to the idea of holy war by Christians against infidels.[7]

In particular, Pope Innocent IV's writings in 1240 influenced the famous sixteenth- and seventeenth-century legal writers Franciscus de Victoria and Hugo Grotius when they began writing about the Discovery Doctrine. Pope Innocent considered whether it was legitimate for Christians to invade infidel lands. He answered yes because the Crusades were "just" wars fought for the "defense" of Christians. Pope Innocent focused on the legal question of the authority of Christians to dispossess infidels of their *dominium,* their governmental sovereignty and their property. The pope's answer was that the non-Christian's natural law rights to elect their own leaders and to own property were qualified by the papacy's divine mandate to care for the entire world. Because the pope was entrusted with the task of the spiritual health of all humans, that necessarily meant the pope had a voice in all the affairs of all humans. It was the duty of the pope to intervene even in the secular affairs of infidels when they violated natural law, as that natural law was defined by Europeans and the Church.[8]

The European and Church development of the ideas behind Discovery continued most significantly in the early 1400s in a controversy between Poland and the Teutonic Knights to control non-Christian Lithuania. This conflict again raised the question of the legality of the seizure of infidels' lands by papal sanction because infidels lacked lawful *dominium,* that is, sovereignty and property rights. In the Council of Constance in 1414, the Teutonic Knights argued that their territorial and jurisdictional claims to Lithuania were authorized by papal proclamations from the time of the Crusades, called papal bulls, that allowed the outright confiscation of the property and sovereign rights of heathens. The Council, which had been called to consider this question, disagreed and accepted Poland's argument based on Pope Innocent IV's writings that infidels possessed the same natural law rights to sovereignty and property as Christians but that the pope could order invasions to punish violations of natural law or to spread the gospel. Consequently, all future crusades, discoveries, and conquests of heathens would have to proceed under Innocent IV's legal rules that pagans had natural rights, but that they also had to comply with European concepts of natural law or they risked a "just war" of conquest and subjugation. The Council of Constance in 1414 had now placed a formal definition on the Christian Doctrine of Discovery. The Church and the secular Christian princes had to respect the natural rights of pagans but not if heathens strayed from the European definition of natural law. Commentators have argued that this meant that to be considered civilized, a country had to be Christian because "Christians simply refused to recognize the right of non-Christians to remain free of Christian dominion."[9]

After this very brief overview of the development of the Discovery Doctrine up to the early 1400s, we will now examine the specific application and interpretations of Discovery by various European countries.

SPAIN AND PORTUGAL

By the mid-1400s, Spain and Portugal had developed the technology and experience needed for long-range ocean travel. They soon began to clash over explorations and trade in the Atlantic island groups off the Iberian coast in Europe. The Church became involved and in 1434 Pope Eugenius IV issued a papal bull, or proclamation, banning all Europeans from the Canary Islands as a protective measure for both the converted and infidel Canary Islanders. In 1436 the King of Portugal appealed this ban on colonizing the Canaries. He based his argument on the fact that Portugal's explorations were conquests on behalf of Christianity. The conversion of the infidel natives was justified, he said, because they allegedly did not have a common religion or laws; lacked normal social intercourse, money, metal, writing, and European-style clothing; and lived like animals. The king claimed that the Canary converts to Christianity had made themselves subjects of Portugal and had now received the benefits of civil laws and organized society. Moreover, the king argued that the pope's ban interfered with this advance of civilization and Christianity that the king had commenced out of the goodness of his heart; "more indeed for the salvation of the souls of the pagans of the islands than for personal gain." The king appealed to the pope to grant the islands to Portugal out of the Church's sense of guardianship duties towards the infidels.[10]

This dialogue led to a revision of the Doctrine of Discovery. The new argument for European and Christian domination was not based on the infidels' lack of dominion or natural rights, but instead based Portuguese rights of discovery on the perceived need to protect natives from the oppression of others and to lead them to civilization and conversion under papal guidance. Pope Eugenius IV's legal advisors agreed that under the Roman law of nations (*jus gentium,* a Latin phrase Thomas Jefferson used several times), infidels had a right to *dominium* even though the papacy maintained an indirect jurisdiction over their secular activities. They cited Pope Innocent IV's writings from 1240 that said the Church had the authority to deprive pagans of their property and sovereignty if they failed to admit Christian missionaries or if they violated European defined natural law. Pope Eugenius agreed with this extension of papal and Discovery authority and issued another bull in 1436, *Romanus Pontifex,* which authorized Portugal to convert the Canary Island natives and to manage and control the islands on behalf of the pope. This bull was reissued several times in the fifteenth century by various popes. Each new bull significantly extended Portugal's jurisdiction and geographical rights over infidels and their lands down the West Coast of Africa as Portugal extended the scope of its discoveries. The bull of Pope Nicholas in 1455 was significantly more aggressive because it authorized Portugal "to invade, search out, capture, vanquish, and subdue all Saracens and pagans" and to place them into perpetual slavery and to take all their property. These papal bulls demonstrated the meaning of the Doctrine of Discovery at that time because they recognized the pope's interest to bring all humankind to the one true religion, authorized Portugal's work toward Christian conversion and civilization, and recognized Portugal's title and sovereignty over lands "which have already been acquired and which shall be acquired in the future."[11]

Under the threat of excommunication for violating these papal bulls, Catholic Spain had to look elsewhere for lands to explore and conquer. Thus, Christopher Columbus's idea of a westward passage to the Indies struck a resonant chord with King Ferdinand and Queen Isabella. After studying the legal and scriptural authority for such a mission, Isabella agreed to sponsor the venture, and Spain sent Columbus forth under a contract that declared he would be the Spanish Admiral of any lands he would "discover and acquire." Under the precedent of Discovery, the papal bulls, and this contract, it is no surprise that he claimed that his "discovery" of already-inhabited islands in the Caribbean meant that the islands had become Spanish possessions. Ferdinand and Isabella wasted no time in seeking papal ratification of these discoveries. They dispatched ambassadors to the pope to confirm Spain's title to the islands Columbus had discovered. In 1493, Pope Alexander VI issued three bulls that confirmed Spain's title to Columbus's discoveries. Specifically, in May 1493 he issued *Inter caetera divinai,* which stated that the lands found by Columbus, because they had been "undiscovered by others," belonged to Ferdinand and Isabella. Pope Alexander VI also granted Spain any lands it might discover in the future, provided they were "not previously possessed by any Christian owner." Consequently, the Doctrine of Discovery arrived in the New World. The idea that the Doctrine granted European monarchs ownership rights in native lands and sovereign and commercial rights over native people due to a "first discovery" by European Christians was now established international law.[12]

Both Spain and Portugal were concerned with the geographical limits of their possibly conflicting papal bulls. So Spain requested another bull that would clearly delineate its ownership of the islands and landmasses that Columbus discovered or would discover in the New World. In 1493, Pope Alexander VI obliged and issued *Inter caetera II*. The pope now drew a line of demarcation from the North Pole to the South Pole, 100 leagues (roughly 300 miles) west of the Azore Islands off the coast of Europe, and granted Spain title under the authority of God to all the lands discovered or to be discovered west of the line. This bull also stated that Spain was assigned this "holy and laudable work" to contribute to "the expansion of the Christian rule." The pope had divided the world for Christian exploration and domination between Spain and Portugal. In 1494, to reduce their rivalry, these countries signed the Treaty of Tordesillas and adjusted the papally drawn line further west to 370 leagues (roughly 1,100 miles) west of the Cape Verde Islands. This new line now gave Portugal Discovery rights in part of the New World. Thus, Portugal's right to colonize and control what is today Brazil was recognized by Spain because that landmass lies east of the line agreed upon in the Treaty of Tordesillas. Today, Portuguese is still the official language of Brazil, whereas Spanish is the official language for the rest of South and Central America and Mexico.[13]

The Church's interest in expanding Christendom and Spain and Portugal's economic and political interests in colonization had solidified by 1493 under the existing canon and international law of the Doctrine of Discovery to stand for four basic points. First, the Church had the political and secular authority to grant to Christian kings some form of title and ownership rights in the lands of infidels. Second, European exploration and colonization was designed to assist the pope's guardianship duties over all the earthly flock, including infidels. Third, Spain and Portugal held exclusive rights over other European, Christian countries to explore and colonize the unknown parts of the entire world. Fourth, the mere sighting and discovery of new lands by Spain or Portugal in their respective spheres of influence and the symbolic possession of these lands by undertaking the Discovery rituals and formalities of possession, such as planting flags or leaving objects to prove their presence, were sufficient to pass rights in these lands to the discovering European country. The law of Discovery, as it applied between Europeans, was thus well settled by the Church, Portugal, and Spain by 1493.[14]

It is worth noting that Portugal and Spain usually claimed that their rights of Discovery arose from merely seeing non-Christian lands first and by performing the formalities and rituals of symbolic possession. Even as late as the 1790s, a Spanish expedition in North America seeking a route to the Pacific still utilized the traditional rituals of Discovery and the taking of symbolic possession of territory by marking notches on trees and engraving stones with the name of the Spanish king, Charles IV. These countries claimed that this ritual of symbolic possession was sufficient to establish their legal rights to newly found non-Christian lands. Spain and Portugal were delighted with this argument because the papal bulls and first discovery gave them an almost exclusive right to explore and claim new parts of the world. England, France, and Holland, as will be discussed, saw things differently, although even these countries sometimes engaged in making Discovery claims based only on their first discovery of new territory and performing Discovery formalities and rituals.[15]

Notwithstanding these well-established ideas about Discovery, a serious debate arose within Spanish legal and religious circles as to the authority for the Crown's rights against the native people in the New World. This uproar led the Spanish king to ask for legal opinions on the legitimacy of papal authority as the sole basis of Spain's New World titles. He even convened a group to draft regulations to control future discoveries and conquests. Into this discussion stepped the priest Franciscus de Victoria. Victoria was the King's lead advisor, held the first chair in theology at the University of Salamanca for 20 years, and is considered to be one of the earliest writers in international law. In 1532, Victoria delivered lectures "On the Indians Lately Discovered" in which he accepted the idea that indigenous people had natural rights and that title to their lands could not pass to Europeans by Discovery alone because the Indians were free men and the true owners of the lands they possessed under their natural law rights. This principle led him to three conclusions regarding Spanish explorations in the New World. His conclusions have been "adopted essentially intact as the accepted European Law of Nations on American Indian rights and status." First, the natives of the Americas possessed natural legal rights as free and rational people. Second, the pope's grant of title to lands in America to Spain was invalid and could not affect the inherent rights of the Indians. Third, violations by the Indians of the natural law principles of the Law of Nations (as determined by European Christian nations) might justify a Christian nation's conquest and empire in the New World.[16]

Victoria's first two conclusions sound like treason given that they rejected Spain's title to lands in the New World if the titles were based solely on papal grants. It sounds like Victoria was dismissing the Doctrine of Discovery. But what Victoria actually did was strengthen the justification for Spain's empire and rights against other Europeans and against the indigenous peoples in the New World from being solely based on papal authority to a firmer foundation based on the "universal obligations of a Eurocentrically constructed natural law." In fact, in applying this European natural law to the New World, Victoria greatly benefited Spain. No wonder the king retained him as his advisor! Victoria reasoned that natives were required to allow Spaniards to exercise their natural law rights in the New World. These rights included Spanish travel to foreign lands, Spanish trade and commerce in native lands, the taking of profits from items the natives apparently held in common, such as minerals for example, and the Spanish right to send missionaries to preach the gospel. Victoria's conclusion, which would have placed him firmly in the King's good graces, was that if infidels prevented the Spanish from carrying out any of their natural law rights, then Spain could "protect its rights" and "defend the faith" by waging lawful and "just wars" against the natives. It is striking how similar this definition is to the justifications for the holy wars of the Crusades.[17]

Moreover, although Victoria rejected the idea of the sole authority of the pope to grant Spain title in the first two steps of his analysis, the third step created an enormous loophole for Spain. The reasoning that natives were bound by the European definition of the natural-law rights of the Spanish was an ample excuse to dominate, defraud, and then engage in "just wars" against native nations that dared to stop the Spanish from doing whatever they wished. Consequently, Victoria limited the freedom and rights of the natives of the Americas by allowing Spain's natural law rights to trump native rights. The legal regime envisioned by Victoria was just as destructive to native sovereignty and property interests, if not more so, than the earlier definition of Spain's authority in the New World that had been based solely on papal authority.

An interesting example of Spanish natural law rights at work in the New World was demonstrated by the regulations drafted by the group ordered to consider Spain's future discoveries in the New World. The most well known regulation this group created was the *Requerimiento*. This document informed New World natives that they must accept Spanish missionaries and sovereignty or be annihilated. It was required to be read aloud to natives before hostilities or "just war" could legally ensue. The *Requerimiento* informed the natives of their natural-law obligation to hear the gospel and told them that their territory had been donated to Spain. If the natives refused to acknowledge the Catholic Church and the Spanish King and to admit priests, then Spain was justified in waging "just war" on them. Many conquistadors must have worried that even this preposterous document might convince some natives to change religions and accept Spanish rule, thus preventing the explorers from gaining conquests and riches, because they took to reading the document aloud in the night to the trees, or they read it to the land from their ships. They considered this adequate notice to the natives of the points in the *Requerimiento*. So much for the free will and natural-law rights of New World natives.[18]

ENGLAND AND FRANCE

England and France were also strong advocates of the Doctrine of Discovery. Both countries utilized the international law to claim the rights and powers of first discovery and title in North America. One English author, for example, wrote in 1609 that James I's rights in America were by "right of discovery." England claimed for centuries that John Cabot's 1496–1498 explorations and first discoveries of the coast of North America, from Newfoundland to Florida, gave England priority over any other European country, even including Spain's claim of first discovery of the New World via Columbus in the Caribbean in 1492. England later contested Dutch settlements and trade activities in North America according to England's claim of "first discovery, occupation, and the possession" of its colonial settlements.[19]

France vigorously contested England's claims of first discovery in North America. The French pointed to their alleged first discoveries of what are now parts of Canada and the United States as establishing their Discovery claim to ownership and sovereignty. In 1627, Louis XIII discussed France's "newly discovered lands" in the New World. Furthermore, the detailed accounts of Jesuit activities in the New World demonstrate the common understanding of the ideas of first discovery and possession of territory inhabited by non-Christians as being the grounds for legal claims by European kings to sovereignty and jurisdiction. In 1670–1672, for example, Jesuits wrote that they had taken possession of land near the Great Lakes by "observing all the forms customary on such occasions." They were performing the accepted Discovery rituals to prove France's claim. Other Jesuits also argued that France had discovered and "taken actual possession of all the country" years before the English arrived and thus legally owned the area because "no Christian had ever been [here] … [and] this hitherto unknown region [was] brought … under [French] jurisdiction." France and England were unable to settle these differing Discovery claims short of war. Ultimately they fought a "world war" in 1754–1763, which is known in the United States as the French and Indian War, over conflicting rights in North America and elsewhere. At the termination of the war, in 1763, France transferred its Discovery claims in Canada and east of the Mississippi River to England and its Discovery claims to lands west of the Mississippi to Spain.[20]

In addition to their Discovery disputes in the New World, France and England faced a common problem from the beginning regarding their exploration and colonization interests. Both England and France were Catholic countries in 1493. Their kings were very concerned with infringing Spain's rights by exploring in the New World and possibly violating Alexander VI's papal bull and running the risk of excommunication. Yet they were also hungry to get their share of the new territories and spoils. Therefore, the legal scholars of England and France analyzed canon law, the papal bulls, and history and devised a slightly new theory of Discovery that allowed their countries to explore and colonize in the New World. Not surprisingly, Europeans were very creative at interpreting Discovery in new ways to benefit their own specific situations.

The new legal theory, primarily developed by English legal scholars, argued that the Catholic king of England, Henry VII, would not be violating the 1493 papal bull, which had divided the world for the Spanish and Portuguese, if English explorers restrained themselves to only claiming lands not yet discovered by any other Christian prince. This expanded definition of Discovery was further refined by Elizabeth I and her advisers in the mid-1500s. They added a crucial new element to the Discovery test. They argued that the Doctrine required a European country to actually occupy and have current possession of non-Christian lands to perfect a Discovery title to newly found lands. This seemed logical because any country could falsely claim first discovery, as European countries did from time to time. This type of problem, and the problems created for France and England from the papal bulls, were solved by the requirement of actual occupation and current possession. Then there should be no argument about who held the rights of Discovery; it only came down to whether a European country was in actual possession of the non-Christian, non-European territory at the time French and English explorers arrived. Possession is, after all, nine-tenths of the law.

Consequently, Henry VII, his granddaughter Elizabeth I, James I, and other English monarchs repeatedly instructed their explorers to discover and colonize lands "unknown to all Christians" and "not actually possessed of any Christian prince." More specifically, in the 1606 First Charter to Virginia and the 1620 Charter to the Council of New England, James I granted the colonies property rights in America because the lands were "not now actually possessed by any *Christian* Prince or People" and "there is noe other the Subjects of any Christian King or State … actually in Possession … whereby any Right, Claim, Interest, or Title, may … by that Meanes accrue." English monarchs also invoked other elements of Discovery when they granted colonial charters because they ordered their colonists to take Christianity and civilization to American Indians for the purpose of "propagating *Christian* Religion to those [who] as yet live in Darkness and miserable Ignorance of the true Knowledge and Worship of God, and [to] bring the Infidels and Savages, living in those Parts, to human civility, and to a settled and quiet Government." King James also granted the Virginia colonists the Discovery right of contiguity ownership to the lands, woods, marshes, and rivers within one hundred English miles around the sites where they actually built their settlements.[21]

Even a Spanish King, in 1523, used the argument of the necessity of current possession when he denied that Portugal could had gained Discovery rights in Mallucco just by finding the lands: "to 'find' required possession, and that which was not taken or possessed could not be said to be found, although seen or discovered." The Dutch also rationalized when they came to North America that the English king could not prevent "trade in countries whereof his people have not taken, nor obtained actual possession from the right owners."[22]

England and France thus added to the Doctrine the element of actual occupancy and current possession as a requirement to establish European claims to title by Discovery, and they applied this new element in their dealings with Spain and Portugal. For example, Elizabeth I wrote to the Spanish minister in 1553 and stated that first discovery alone "cannot confer property." England repeatedly argued in 1580, 1587, 1600, and 1604 that it could colonize anywhere other Europeans were not already in possession. In addition, in the 1550s both England and France tried to negotiate separate treaties with Spain and Portugal to settle issues regarding discoveries in the New World. France insisted on a general right to trade in the West Indies while Spain relied on its papal title to argue for monopoly rights to the entire region. The Spanish negotiators wrote their king that they could not convince the French to stay away from "such places which are discovered by us, but are not actually subject to the King of Spain or Portugal. They are willing only to consent not to go to the territories actually possessed by your majesty or the King of Portugal." Spain and Portugal refused to agree to treaties that allowed England and France to colonize where Spain and Portugal were not currently in possession but where they had been granted authority under papal bulls.[23]

This debate over the exact definition of Discovery demonstrates that European countries often argued for the application of Discovery that best fit their own situations and interests. In contrast to their usual arguments, on a few occasions even England, France, and Holland claimed new lands based only on first discovery and "symbolic possession" established by performing the rituals of Discovery. For instance, in 1642 Holland ordered an explorer to take possession of new lands by hanging posts and plates to "declare an intention … to establish a colony." In 1758 a French explorer claimed Tahiti on the grounds of first discovery and took symbolic possession by performing Discovery rituals and formalities on the island. In 1770, England's King George III instructed Captain Cook to find uninhabited lands and "take possession of it for His Majesty by setting up proper marks and inscriptions as first discoverers and possessors." In 1774, Cook even erased Spanish marks of possession in Tahiti and put up his own marks to prove English possession and "ownership" of the island. Upon hearing of this act, Spain immediately dispatched explorers to reestablish Spain's claim by restoring its marks of symbolic possession.[24]

In 1776–1778, Captain Cook also engaged in symbolic possession activities in what is today British Columbia, Canada. He claimed to take possession of lands by performing Discovery rituals such as leaving English coins in buried bottles. Another interesting example of this Discovery conduct and ritual is that at least three times France claimed symbolic possession of territory in America by burying inscribed lead plates. In 1742–1743, French explorers buried a lead plate at the mouth of the Bad River, and sometime before 1763, a combined Spanish and French mission ran a boundary line up the Sabine River where they built a small fort and "buried some leaden plates." Also, in 1749 France sent a military force 3,000 miles through the Ohio country in America to renew its 1643 Discovery claim to the territory. The French forces "buried small lead plates … 'as a monument' … 'of the renewal of possession.'" An Englishman reported on these French Discovery items: "It appears by a leaden plate found by the Indians upon the River Ohio, in the year 1749, that the Crown of France assumes a Right to all the Territories lying upon that River." The United States also utilized these identical kinds of Discovery rituals in making its claim to the Pacific Northwest.[25]

The fact that European countries would claim property by such acts as hanging or burying plates, coins, and signs and engaging in Discovery rituals such as planting the cross and their country's flag in the soil is not a surprise. It was really the only option they had to claim ownership in situations where they were just passing through a new land. Moreover, this type of conduct is a direct descendant from accepted feudal formalities of passing land ownership in the days before written deeds and title insurance offices. In fact, up to the middle of the seventeenth century, to demonstrate the sale of land in England, the buyer and seller engaged in a ritual called "livery of seisin." This was the process of transferring and delivering the possession and ownership of land to a new owner. It was accomplished by a formal ritual performed on the land itself and in the presence of neighbors and witnesses. The delivery of ownership was demonstrated by the old owner turning over some dirt with a shovel and handing a clod of dirt or a twig from the property to the new owner. Europeans and Americans utilized analogous rituals in making Discovery claims to new lands.[26]

England and France also developed another element of Discovery to justify their alleged right to the lands of native peoples. This was the principle called *terra nullius* (literally a land or earth that is null or void), or less often called *vacuum domicilium* (literally an empty, vacant, or unoccupied house or domicile). This element stated that lands that were not occupied by any person or nation, or which were occupied but not being used in a fashion that European legal systems approved, were considered to be empty and waste and available for Discovery. One author defined *terra nullius* as having two meanings: "a country without a sovereign recognized by European authorities and a territory where nobody owns any land at all." Another author stated that *terra nullius* defined an area that was populated by inhabitants who were not members of the family of nations and subject to international law. Europeans did not recognize the sovereignty of such "noncivilized" peoples to the land they occupied. Needless to say, "Europeans regarded North America as a vacant land that could be claimed by right of discovery."[27]

England and France no doubt developed these additional Discovery elements because they could not rely on papal grants to trump the rights of the native inhabitants to lands in the New World. They had to develop alternate "legal" principles to justify their actions. Consequently, England and France developed and relied on two new Discovery factors: first, land was available for their Discovery claim if other European countries were not in actual occupancy and current possession when the English or French explorers arrived on the scene, and second, land was available for taking from indigenous people even if it was occupied and being used by natives if it was considered legally "vacant," "empty," or *terra nullius*. France, England, and later the American colonies and the United States often used this argument against American Indians when claiming that Indians were using the land only as hunting grounds and leaving it as wilderness and "empty" or "vacant." The development of these additional elements of Discovery demonstrated the creativity and adaptability that Europeans used to make the Doctrine work in favor of their particular situations.

HOLLAND AND SWEDEN

Sweden and Holland both established colonies in America for brief times long after England, France, and Spain had claimed first discoveries on this continent. Sweden and Holland also operated under the international legal principles of Discovery. Because they could not rely on claims of first discovery, they adopted the principles best suited to their interests and relied on the English and French arguments that actual occupation and current possession of land was the crucial factor for the application of Discovery rights.[28]

The Swedish colonies only lasted about 17 years in present-day southeastern Pennsylvania and southern New Jersey. Yet during that time, Sweden entered politically based treaty relationships with Indian Nations and purchased from the tribes, one sovereign to another, the land its colonies utilized. In 1654 the Queen granted her citizens the right to purchase land "from the savages" in New Sweden. This conduct demonstrated Sweden's recognition of preemption, that only the discovering country could buy lands or authorize land purchases from Indians, the right of tribal occupancy and use in their lands, and the international sovereign status of the Indian Nations.[29]

The Dutch colonies, during their 40 years of existence in parts of present-day New York, New Jersey, and Pennsylvania, also entered treaties with Indian Nations, purchased land from tribes, and relied on the Doctrine of Discovery. In a 1651 document demonstrating the elements of first discovery and actual occupancy, the Dutch claimed that they were "the earliest comers and discoverers of the river [in New York], who also, first of all settled thereon." Furthermore, Holland objected to Sweden establishing a colony in the same area because Holland claimed its alleged rights as the discovering government. Yet Sweden ironically turned the same Discovery-based argument of actual occupancy against the Dutch—an argument that the Dutch had used against England, and that England had used against Spain. Sweden justified its colonization rights in the New World by arguing that the Dutch were not actually occupying and possessing the area where the Swedish colony was established when the Swedish arrived to settle those lands.[30]

In turn, England strongly protested Holland's colonies. England was annoyed because it claimed first discovery of North America from Newfoundland to at least Virginia and claimed that it was permanently occupying and in possession of the areas where the Dutch settled because of the Discovery principle of contiguity. Remember that contiguity allowed a European nation to claim a large extent of land around its settlements even though it did not physically occupy all the territory. Thus, England claimed under the Discovery principles of preemption and contiguity that the Dutch had no right to buy land from Indians or to engage in trade with them anywhere within the areas contiguous to those areas discovered and settled by England. The Dutch countered with the standard English argument that because the English colonies were located nowhere near the Dutch settlements, England was not actually occupying or currently in possession of the areas where the Dutch settled and purchased land from the natives. The Dutch used the very same arguments England and France had made to Portugal and Spain in 1555 and 1559 regarding Discovery rights and commercial activity in lands that were not actually occupied or possessed by Portugal or Spain. The Dutch claimed the lands they colonized had been open for settlement under Discovery principles.[31]

In addition, Holland understood and relied on other elements of Discovery in its activities in the New World. In a charter granted in 1621 to the Dutch West India Company, Holland granted privileges in the New World that demonstrated its use of the principle of contiguity because its colonists were directed not to settle any nearer than seven leagues to lands which the "first occupiers," apparently the English, had already occupied. The charter also adopted the idea of *terra nullius* because the Dutch settlers were granted the right to "take possession of as much land as they shall be able properly to improve," implying that they could settle lands that were unimproved or vacant. Furthermore, if colonists settled outside the designated Dutch colony, they were required to buy the land from the Indians. This provision plainly recognized that the native people had a property right, an Indian title, that they could sell to the colonists with the approval of the Dutch government. This provision also protected Holland's Discovery right of preemption because it authorized colonists to buy land from natives. Moreover, the charter expressly recognized the Discovery elements of first discovery of new lands and current possession when it stated that any person who "shall discover any shores [or] bays … may take possession thereof, and begin to work on them as their own absolute property, to the exclusion of others." Clearly, Holland understood and followed the Doctrine of Discovery.[32]

In conclusion, it is obvious that all the European countries that operated in the New World utilized the international law Doctrine of Discovery and its elements. The Doctrine was widely accepted and applied by Europeans as the legal authority for colonizing and settling America and for the domination of its native inhabitants. Europeans may have occasionally disagreed over the exact meaning of Discovery and even sometimes violently disputed each other's claims; but one principle about which they never disagreed was that the indigenous people and the Indian Nations lost sovereign, commercial, and real property rights immediately upon their "discovery" by Europeans.

MODERN DAY

The Doctrine of Discovery is not a relic of ancient history in either American law or international law. It continues to have relevance and application today. Here we briefly review a few examples of the use of Discovery by Europeans in more modern times.

In addition to the New World, European monarchs used Discovery when they carved up Africa. Portugal began this process in the 1450s under the authority of the papal bulls. More recently, European powers explicitly legitimized colonial rule in Africa on the basis of the principles of Discovery. At the Berlin Conference in 1885, called to settle issues of African colonization, several European countries agreed to partition the continent on "the principle of acquisition by occupation: a state could validly hold a colony as long as it occupied and governed it." In addition to the elements of gaining property and sovereign rights by occupation and depriving natives of their commercial and governmental rights, Europeans also promised to pursue the Discovery element of civilizing and caring for native people because they agreed to the "preservation of the native tribes, and to care for the improvement of their moral and material well-being."[33]

As recently as the 1970s, Namibia and South Africa argued over the ownership of a coastal bay under Discovery principles. South Africa traced its ownership claim from Great Britain's earlier annexation of the bay under the Discovery element of *terra nullius*. Furthermore, in 1974 the International Court of Justice was asked by the United Nations General Assembly to decide whether lands in the Western Sahara had "belong[ed] to no one (*terra nullius*)" when they became a protectorate of Spain in 1884. The court had to examine the acquisition of "legal title by a sovereign over remote and sparsely inhabited territory" and what kind of a legal system was necessary to establish the sovereign rights of an indigenous people. The court accepted Spain's argument that the legal system had to be operational to such an extent as to be evidence of an effective application of sovereignty by the indigenous people over their territory and that they had sufficiently developed social and political organizations. The court decided that the people in the Western Sahara had such organizations in 1884 and their land had not been *terra nullius* and subject to annexation by Europeans.[34]

Other international tribunals in 1928, 1931, 1933, and 1953 addressed similar questions about the ownership of remote and sparsely inhabited lands. The United States lost such an arbitration in 1928 in a dispute with the Netherlands over ownership of the island of Palmas in the Philippine island chain. The arbitrator expressly relied on elements of international law, contiguity, first discovery, incomplete titles based on first discovery, European titles derived from discovery, actual occupation and conquest, and "symbolical ... possession ... completed eventually by an actual and durable taking of possession within a reasonable time," in reaching his decision.[35]

In sum, it is obvious that the European powers developed and used the international law Doctrine of Discovery to colonize and settle North America and other parts of the world. Did the American colonies adopt the Doctrine of Discovery? Did Discovery become part of American law and government, and did it prompt the march of Manifest Destiny across the continent?

CHAPTER 2

⁓

The Doctrine of Discovery in America

T he European countries that colonized North America imported the international law Doctrine of Discovery to this continent and utilized the elements of Discovery to justify their actions and relationships with the indigenous nations. It is no surprise that the North American colonists and colonial governments, considering their European ancestry and legal history, also adopted and applied Discovery in their interactions with American Indians and their governments. We will see that the colonies, the newly formed American states, and then the various forms of American federal governments all adopted and used Discovery and its elements in dealing politically and commercially with the Indian Nations.

AMERICAN COLONIAL LAW OF DISCOVERY

The Doctrine of Discovery was the international law under which America was explored and was the legal authority the English Crown used to establish its colonies in America. Discovery passed to the Crown the "title" to Indian lands, preempted sales of these lands to any other European country or any individual, and granted sovereign and commercial rights over Indian Nations to the Crown and its colonies. For example, a 1622 letter to the Virginia Company of London recounted that the colony was the king's property because it was "first discouered" at the charge of Henry VII in 1497 by John Cabot, who "tooke possession thereof to the Kings vse [use]." A Virginia legislative committee repeated this Discovery principle in a 1699 report. Additionally, a history of New Jersey in 1765 defined the English claims as being based on Cabot's voyage and discovery, subsequent English possession, and "from the well known *Jus Gentium,* LAW OF NATIONS, that whatever waste or uncultivated country is discovered, it is the right of that prince who had been at the charge of the discovery." This author also stated that discovery of such lands "gives at least a right of preemption, and undoubtedly must be good against all but the Indian proprietors." Moreover, Benjamin Franklin stated at the Albany Congress in 1754 that "his Majesty's title [in] America appears founded on the discovery thereof first made, and the possession thereof first taken, in 1497." Consequently, American colonists in the 1600s, Benjamin Franklin in 1754, and an American historian in 1765 all plainly relied on the elements of the Doctrine of Discovery to prove the English king's title to the lands in the thirteen colonies. The elements of Discovery, such as first discovery, *terra nullius,* possession, and the power of preemption, were well known and applied by the colonists.[1]

COLONIAL STATUTORY LAWS

The English colonists in America and their governments established political and diplomatic relationships with tribal governments and dealt with them as sovereign entities from the earliest colonial times. The colonists assumed that the Crown legally held the Discovery power over tribes and that the colonies were authorized to conduct political affairs and property transactions with the Indian Nations under the Discovery authority granted to the colonies in their royal charters. All thirteen colonies enacted numerous laws exercising this delegated authority from the king to purchase Indian lands, to protect their exclusive right of preemption to buy Indian lands, to exercise limited sovereignty over tribes, and to grant titles in Indian lands to others even while Indians still occupied and used their lands. The colonies assumed that their charters from the king granted this Discovery authority. A Pennsylvania state court demonstrated this thinking: "The royal charter did indeed convey to *William Penn* an immediate and absolute estate in fee [over Indian lands]."[2]

In their more than 150 years of existence, the English colonies spent an enormous amount of time dealing with Indian affairs and enacted a staggering number of laws concerning Indians, their governments, and Discovery issues. It is impossible to even cite them all, not to mention trying to discuss them all. Here we will examine only a sufficient number of colonial era laws to observe the general Discovery themes and elements that the colonial governments utilized. These laws are worth examining because they help to trace the evolution of Discovery into American law, and they are legal evidence of the historical application of the Discovery elements to the Indian Nations and their lands in America.

The colonial laws regarding Discovery, Indians, and tribal governments fell into four general categories. First, each individual colony enacted multiple statutes exercising their preemptive right to control and regulate sales of Indian lands. Second, the colonies tried to control all trade and commercial activities between Indians and the colonists. Third, several colonies even created trust relationships to allegedly benefit tribal nations, apparently demonstrating a responsibility they felt to protect and help Indians while they were progressing to a "civilized" state. Finally, several colonies passed laws striving to exercise the sovereign authority that they assumed Discovery had granted them over Indians Nations.

In addition to the 1622 Virginia Company letter mentioned previously, one of the earliest examples of a colonial legal claim of Discovery powers, which was based expressly on Discovery principles, was demonstrated by Maryland in 1638 when the colony enacted a law to control trade with Indians. This act stated that its specific legal authority was based on the Crown's "right of first discovery" in which the king had "became lord and possessor" of Maryland and had gained outright ownership of the real property or real estate in Maryland. This was an accurate statement of the legal and sovereign rights that the Doctrine purportedly passed to a discovering European country. It also shows how expansively the Doctrine of Discovery was read.[3]

The first category of Discovery-related colonial laws concerned governmental attempts to exercise the preemption power to regulate Indian land sales. James Madison, for example, recognized the importance of preemption over Indian lands. He wrote about "pre-emption" in 1783 and in 1784 when he stated to James Monroe that preemption "was the principal right formerly exerted by the Colonies with regard to the Indians [and] that it was a right asserted by the laws as well as the proceedings of all of them." The thirteen colonies agreed with that statement because they repeatedly enacted laws declaring preemption a governmental prerogative that had passed to the colonies from the Crown. The colonies exercised the power of preemption by requiring individuals to get licenses or the permission of the colonial legislative assembly or governor to buy, lease, or occupy Indian lands; the colonies declared all sales or leases of Indian lands without prior governmental approval to be null and void. Sometimes colonial governments retroactively ratified previously unapproved purchases, and most colonies imposed forfeitures and heavy fines on unapproved land purchases. These laws were required because all the colonies experienced frequent problems resulting from colonists buying land directly from Indians. "Land fever" was a common problem for all the colonies and later for the American states and the United States. Consequently, every one of the thirteen English colonies in America enacted numerous laws that applied the Doctrine of Discovery and the element of preemption to sales of Indian lands so that only the colonial governments could buy or regulate the purchase of such lands. The colonial governments had several interests at stake. They were interested in creating a managed and orderly advance of their borders, maintaining a profitable and beneficial trade with Indians, keeping the peace with powerful tribes, and enforcing the power of Discovery and preemption that had been granted them by the king against their own citizens, against other colonies and countries, and against the Indian Nations.[4]

The colonies also utilized the *terra nullius,* or vacant-lands, principle of Discovery. They did this even though it was obvious that much of this allegedly "vacant land" was owned and utilized by the thousands of Indian people who lived near the colonists and far outnumbered the colonists. One chaplain for the Virginia Company even asked, "By what right or warrant can we enter into the land of these Savages [and] take away their rightful inheritance?" The stock answer was *terra nullius.* "In order to justify the expropriation of indigenous populations, the British colonists came up with a distinctive rationalization, the convenient idea of '*terra nullius*', nobody's land." The colonists helped themselves to as much land as they could because, as one early governor of Virginia stated, their first work was the "expulsion of the Savage." Similarly, the famous philosopher John Locke said that if Indians resisted the expropriation of their lands, they should "be destroyed as a *Lyon* or a *Tyger,* one of those wild Savage Beasts, with whom Men can have no Society or Security." This sentiment was repeated in George Washington's infamous analogy of Indian people as "the Savage as Wolf." Thus, while relying on the Discovery legal principle of *terra nullius,* several colonies, such as Virginia in 1676, 1688, and 1699, defined lands that they considered vacant to be available for colonial disposal while ignoring Indian rights to these same lands.[5]

The second general category of colonial laws regarding Indians demonstrated the colonies' assumption of sovereign and superior positions over tribal governments in order to control all commercial relationships between colonists and Indians. The colonies enacted dozens of statutes requiring licenses for traders who wanted to engage in trade with Indians (a legal requirement which is still federal law to this day) and other commercial aspects. The colonies, for example, hoped to control the trade of weapons and alcohol to Indians and to prevent fraudulent trade practices perpetrated on Indians because these activities often caused friction and conflicts for European and American colonial governments. There was a long tradition of these governments trying to control the Indian trade.[6]

Interestingly, in the third category of laws there are many examples of colonies establishing trust or fiduciary-like relationships with tribes, ostensibly to protect tribal interests. This idea probably arose from English and French monarchs' charging their colonists with responsibilities to civilize and Christianize American Indians. Colonies might also have been attempting to keep the peace and prevent wars by treating Indian Nations fairly. One suspects, however, that the real motivation was not a concern for Indian rights but rather an attempt to serve the Discovery idea that the colonial governments had ultimate control over all dispositions of tribal lands, control over tribal–colonial relationships, and a role in "civilizing" and converting "heathen" Indians. It is also possible that many of these trust situations were actually shams and nothing more than another attempt to confiscate tribal assets easily and cheaply. Many of these statutes, for example, stated that certain individual colonial citizens had an oversight role for tribal property.[7]

In the fourth category, many colonies read the Discovery Doctrine and the Crown's power in the New World very expansively to include Crown and colonial sovereignty over Indian tribes and individual Indians. In an extreme application of ethnocentrism, or just plain wishful thinking, some colonies assumed that Indians had become subjects of the King of England and that Indian Nations had become the king's tributaries due to Discovery. In several instances, in a perverse twist on the preemptive element of Discovery, colonial laws even required tribes to apply for a deed or title for their own lands from the Crown or colony. Also, in an apparent attempt at conciliation, several colonies granted land to Indians because it was "most Just that the Indians the auncient Inhabitants of this Province should have a Convenient dwelling place in this their native Countrey." Other colonies maintained that they had the authority to grant tribes titles to land, to restrict the movements of individual Indians, and to expect tribal chiefs to pledge loyalty to the colonial governments.[8]

The breadth of the subject matter and the sheer number of the hundreds of laws relating to Discovery issues that were enacted by the thirteen colonies demonstrate the express and unanimous acceptance of the elements of Discovery such as first discovery, preemption and European title, Indian title, limited tribal sovereignty, *terra nullius,* and the superior position of European civilizations and religions. The English colonies all adopted the idea that they held and could exercise the power of Discovery over the Indian Nations. Discovery and its elements were such widespread and accepted ideas in colonial times that Indian individuals and tribal nations were often aware of how their property rights were defined by the colonists and by Discovery principles like preemption and conquest. Tribes often argued against these Eurocentric principles. Some tribes claimed the Discovery right of conquest themselves over the lands of other Indian Nations, some Indian leaders argued that Europeans could not trade tribal property rights back and forth, and the Mohegan Nation sued in colonial and royal courts for decades to stop the application of the elements of Discovery against its lands. Notwithstanding the tribal views on property rights and their rights to lands they had occupied for centuries, the colonial governments and legislative bodies enacted hundreds of laws adopting the elements of Discovery to benefit the colonies.[9]

COLONIAL COURTS

We have only a small number of colonial court cases readily available today. Of those cases, we have a very limited number that address Discovery issues directly. One commentator reports, however, that the second most important group of cases the colonial courts heard concerned the laws governing interactions with Indians just discussed in the previous section. Clearly, then, the colonial courts were actively involved in issues of Discovery. The few cases for which information is available demonstrate the understanding and use of the Doctrine by the colonial judicial systems in cases that involved tribal lands.[10]

The most relevant English case of the era was *Calvin's Case* in 1608. Calvin was a Scotsman who petitioned an English court to restore his ownership in land that he claimed had been unjustly taken from him by an Englishman named Smith. Smith argued that Calvin was an alien, not an Englishman, and because Calvin owed no allegiance to the king, he did not even deserve an answer to the lawsuit he brought in an English court. The court reasoned that friendly aliens from other Christian European countries could access English courts, but because infidels were the perpetual enemies of the king and all Christians, they were unfriendly aliens and could not use the king's courts. The court also inferred, while discussing the rights of infidels, that military conquest of infidel lands gave a Christian king outright title to the infidels' lands whereas, in contrast, a similar conquest by one Christian king of another Christian king's domain did not alter the real-property rights of the conquered people. Thus, this court defined the conquest element of Discovery the same way we defined it in this book's introduction. This definition of "conquest" of infidels and the infidels' resulting loss of the title to their lands became an element of Discovery as defined in English law in *Calvin's Case*. This element was imported to America and also adopted by the U.S. Supreme Court in *Johnson v. M'Intosh* in 1823.[11]

The Discovery element of conquest became an important issue in colonial courts, such as in a Connecticut case that lasted from the 1640s to 1773. In this case, the Mohegan Indian Nation litigated its land rights against the colony of Connecticut for over 130 years, even winning a judgment in 1705, before finally losing the appeal in the King's Privy Council in 1773. The parties litigated issues concerning the ownership of Mohegan lands, the significance of the military conquest of the neighboring Pequot Tribe and its lands by Connecticut, the validity and meaning of Connecticut laws that prohibited purchases of tribal lands, and the significance of land conveyances by tribal chiefs to Connecticut and to individuals. Over many decades, the parties argued in various courts about the meaning of Discovery elements such as conquest, preemption, and the right to purchase Indian lands and about the Connecticut laws that declared void the individual purchase of Indian lands. This case was called by one attorney of the time "the greatest cause that ever was heard at the Council Board." Therefore, issues regarding the ownership of Indian lands and various elements of Discovery were made well known and were well publicized in the colonies by just this one case alone. The case was so famous that the Supreme Court discussed it in 1823 in *Johnson v. M'Intosh*.[12]

Many other colonies also litigated issues about the ownership of Indian lands and the impact of Discovery. Some colonies litigated boundary disputes with each other on the basis of the validity of Indian titles and tribal land sales. Some Indians even used the colonial courts to try to protect their property rights. Individual colonists also used Indian titles and land purchases from Indians to make claims against each other and against their colonial governments. In *Barkham's Case*, for example, in 1622, a colonist tried to affirm in London a title for lands in Virginia that had been granted to him by the colonial governor George Yeardley and affirmed by the Indian chief Opechancanough. The directors of the Virginia Company in London, sitting as a court with jurisdiction granted by the king, were troubled by the involvement of the Indian chief and the question of the power of a tribe to grant land titles. The court reasoned that because Discovery was considered to have terminated tribal powers over their own lands and limited their ability to sell their land, only the king's power could be used to grant titles in America. The Virginia Company's right to grant titles to Virginia lands came only from the king and could not be contingent on the approval of an Indian Nation or a chief. Accordingly, the Virginia Company held Barkham's title invalid because it had not been issued by the king through the Company in London and because it recognized "a Soveraignity in that heathen Infidell ... and the Companies Title thereby much infringed."[13]

The few reported colonial-era cases available demonstrate that the elements of Discovery and the Crown's preemption power to grant titles to the soil in America were well understood by the colonial court systems.

ROYAL ATTEMPTS TO ENFORCE DISCOVERY

The English Crown could not afford or did not want to pay to colonize America. Elizabeth I in the late 1500s and James I in the early 1600s relied on private companies to enlist settlers, pay for the voyages, and take the risks. Sir Walter Raleigh, for example, was granted a charter in 1587 to explore and colonize America, to seek profits, and to obtain lands in fee-simple ownership for himself and his heirs while at the same time he was also making claims of jurisdiction and sovereignty for Queen Elizabeth and paying her a percentage of the profits. Under James I, the Crown granted far-ranging powers to individuals, named them the proprietors or owners of various colonies, and granted them vast tracts of land in America in fee-simple ownership. Later, the Stuart line of English kings rescinded most of the colonial charters and made them into royal or crown colonies, which turned them into the king's property. Even so, the Crown still exercised very loose control over the colonies, and the American colonists became very independent. For example, the Crown appointed governors for the royal colonies, but the individual colonists elected their own legislative assemblies. The king and Parliament did not begin taxing and regulating the colonies by statutes until the 1760s. Prior to that, Parliament had taken almost no steps to interfere with the king's right to manage what was in essence the Crown's private property in the New World.

The Seven Years War (started in North America in 1754 and ended with a treaty signed in Europe in 1763), called the French and Indian War in America, was in reality a world war that was largely caused by conflicting claims between England and France in the New World. The war cost the English Crown dearly and left it deeply in debt. Consequently, the Crown decided to get more involved in colonial governance to hopefully prevent such problems in the future. The English king, George III, tried to impose his authority in America to control the main issues that led to conflicts: trade and land purchases with the Indian Nations.[14]

The Crown primarily took three steps that were all extremely unpopular in America. First, it imposed taxation on the colonists in the form of several acts, including the 1764 Stamp Act, to pay for the debts incurred in protecting the colonies in the French and Indian War and to finance the costs of keeping troops in America to maintain the peace and to control the colonists' actions against the Indian Nations. Second, the Crown centralized the control of Indian affairs in itself by establishing two districts in America with sole jurisdiction over Indian affairs and all interactions with the Indian Nations. The king then appointed the superintendents who were to manage the two Indian districts. Finally, and most significantly, the king tried to assert his authority over Indian affairs and exercise his Discovery power by taking control of all the trade with Indians and all purchases of tribal lands. George III did this by issuing the Royal Proclamation of 1763. The

Proclamation shows clearly that his government understood its Discovery powers, including preemption and other elements. The Crown plainly intended to exercise those powers to the exclusion of the colonies. The royal actions undertaken to control the commercial and political relationships with the tribal nations were very unpopular with American colonists and were even cited in the Declaration of Independence as part of the justifications for the American Revolution.[15]

The Proclamation, issued in October of 1763, established a boundary line along the crest of the Appalachia and Allegheny mountains over which British citizens were not to cross. The English colonists were to stay east of that line. In essence, the king defined Indian country, Indian lands, as all territory west of the line to the Mississippi River, where England's claim ended. England had gained a recognized Discovery claim to the Mississippi River in February 1763 when France ceded by treaty all its Discovery claims in Canada and east of the Mississippi to England to settle the French and Indian War. King George now exercised his new Discovery authority over this area and stated in the Proclamation that the tribes in this territory "live under *our protection*" [emphasis added] and that it was essential to colonial security that the Indian Nations not be "disturbed in the possession of such parts of *our dominions and territories* [emphasis added] as, not having been ceded to or purchased by us, are reserved to them." This statement is nothing less than George III expressly claiming his Discovery title to tribal lands, his right of preemption over these lands, and his duty to protect and civilize Indian people. Notice that he called Indian country "our dominions" even though the lands had not "been ceded to or purchased by" England.[16]

The statement is worth closer examination. George III claimed that the Indian governments between the Allegheny and Appalachia Mountains and the Mississippi River lived under his "protection" and that the tribes were currently in "possession" of his "dominions and territories" even though these Indian Nations had not yet "ceded" the lands to the king, nor had the king yet "purchased" them. This is an express allegation of several of the elements of the international law of Discovery. The king very accurately stated the rights defined by first discovery, the power of preemption and of European title, the limited Indian title to possess and use their lands, and the limited tribal sovereign and commercial rights to deal only with the discovering European country.

The king then exercised even more of his Discovery powers. He ordered in the Proclamation that none of his colonial governors or military commanders could allow surveys or grant titles in any lands in this area and that none of his subjects could purchase or settle on Indian lands without royal permission. In fact, any British subject who had already settled in these areas had to return east of the boundary line. Further defining his power, the king said that these Indian lands were "reserve[d] under our sovereignty, protection, and dominion, for the use of the said Indians." The king also took control of all trade with Indians by requiring traders to post monetary bonds as guarantees of good conduct and to be licensed by royal governors. The Proclamation and the king's conduct demonstrated clearly that the Crown understood its Discovery powers over the Indian Nations and the lands in North

America. The Proclamation also foreshadowed the definition of Discovery accepted by the U.S. Supreme Court that Discovery granted the European discovering country a title in tribal lands subject to the later transfer to the European government of the tribal right of use and occupancy. This, of course, defines the Discovery elements of European title, Indian title, and limited tribal sovereign and commercial rights.

The Crown's Royal Proclamation and Parliament's taxation efforts led to intense dissatisfaction among the colonists and then to rebellion and the war for independence. The attitude of the colonists toward the Proclamation was well demonstrated by George Washington, who had always been active in buying Indian land as a speculator, and by Benjamin Franklin and other Founding Fathers. Notwithstanding the king's new Proclamation, which Washington thought was just "a temporary expedient to quiet the Minds of the Indians," Washington made secret arrangements to continue buying Indian lands west of the Allegheny and Appalachia Mountains. The colonists also deeply resented being taxed by Parliament because they did not have an elected representative in Parliament. Further problems developed between the Crown and the colonies from the Crown's exercise of its Discovery authority to control the Indian trade and to stop individual colonists from buying Indian lands. All of these actions demonstrated clearly that the Crown understood its Discovery powers and worked vigorously to bring Indian affairs exclusively within the control of the central royal government.[17]

AMERICAN STATE LAW OF DISCOVERY

After the Revolutionary War, the new American state governments and courts continued exercising Discovery and the power of preemption to control all sales of Indian lands and interactions with Indian Nations because they thought these were powers that now belonged to their central governments after winning their independence from the English Crown. It is interesting, and more than a little ironic, to study how the new state and federal governments consolidated the Discovery authority and total control over Indian affairs into their central governments in the identical fashion that King George III had done.

The new American states actively struggled against the federal government for preeminence in Indian affairs because they claimed that Discovery and preemption powers had devolved from England to the states after they declared their independence and had not passed to the national Congress. The solution to this issue required an important compromise that was one of the major factors leading to the adoption and ratification of the 1787 United States Constitution and the formation of our present-day federal government. We now track the evolution of Discovery into the law of the new American states, noting that there was widespread acceptance of Discovery long before the *Johnson* case in 1823.

STATE LAWS

The thirteen new American states began adopting constitutions and enacting state statutes after declaring their independence from England. They continued, not surprisingly, to assert the same Discovery power and sovereignty over tribal lands as they had during colonial times as English colonies. In fact, several states immediately enshrined in their new constitutions their alleged Discovery authority and various elements of the Doctrine. In Virginia's May 1776 constitution, for example, the people and the state claimed the right of preemption over Indian lands because they mandated that "no purchase of lands shall be made of the *Indian* natives but on behalf of the public, by authority of the General Assembly." The state was plainly attempting to exercise the Discovery authority of preemption and bring that power to its central government.[18]

New York's 1777 Constitution also claimed the preemption power over Indian lands and even applied the power retroactively. Section 37 provided that "no purchases or contracts for the sale of lands, made since the fourteenth day of October ... one thousand seven hundred and seventy-five, or which may hereafter be made with or of the said Indians ... shall be binding on the said Indians, or deemed valid, unless made under the authority and with the consent of the legislature of this State." New York took steps to enforce this constitutional provision by enacting a law in 1788, also retroactive to 1775, which imposed criminal sanctions on violations of the constitutional ban on private purchases of Indian lands.[19]

North Carolina and Tennessee also placed Discovery principles into their constitutions in 1776 and 1796, respectively. North Carolina enacted a retroactive provision and even went far beyond Discovery powers by claiming that Indian Nations in North Carolina only possessed real property rights if their rights had been recognized by the colonial legislature or were recognized by the state legislature in the future: "this Declaration of Rights shall not prejudice any nation or nations of Indians, from enjoying such hunting-grounds as may have been, or hereafter shall be, secured to them by any former or future Legislature of this State." In 1796, Tennessee claimed in its constitution the same Discovery sovereign and land rights that had existed under the royal charter granted to North Carolina because the state of Tennessee was carved out of lands originally granted by the Crown to North Carolina.[20]

Georgia also made an express Discovery claim in its constitution. Georgia alleged that its new status as a state and its constitution did not prevent its legislature from exercising authority to "procure an extension of settlement and extinguishment of Indian claims in and to the vacant territory of this State [and that] no sale of territory ... shall take place ... unless ... the Indian rights shall have been extinguished thereto." This provision is nothing less than Georgia claiming the sovereign and real-property aspects of Discovery and asserting that it was the only government that could deal with tribes and extinguish Indian title within its territory. Georgia also recognized in this provision the vacant-country, or *terra nullius*, element of Discovery and tribal rights in land. These constitutional provisions demonstrate that many states assumed from their beginning that they possessed the power of Discovery over Indians and their lands.[21]

Furthermore, the laws that the new states enacted regarding Indian affairs also demonstrated their belief that England's Discovery power had transferred to the state governments. Virginia, for example, immediately took control of Indian land sales and as early as June 24, 1776 insisted on its legislature's right to decide the validity of titles held by private individuals from sales by Indians. In May 1779, Virginia responded to two years of petitions from such individuals and from land-speculation companies who objected to Virginia's constitutional prohibition on Indian land sales to individuals. These parties tried to get the state legislature to ratify the titles to the lands that individuals and companies had purchased directly from tribes pre-1776. The state ultimately said no and enacted the 1779 law declaring all such purchases void because they had been conducted within Virginia's territory and without the permission of the colonial or state governments. This law expressly reaffirmed that only Virginia possessed the "exclusive right of preemption" to extinguish Indian titles to lands within its borders.[22]

Numerous other states enacted similar laws, which demonstrated the widespread acceptance of Discovery, its elements, and the assumption that the states held the preemption power over sales of tribal lands. Connecticut took control of such sales within its borders in 1776 and banned them unless they were allowed by the state assembly. In 1783, 1789, and 1802, North Carolina also statutorily declared purchases of Indian lands within its borders to be void unless they had been or were approved by the colonial or state governments, and it took steps to control other activities on tribal lands. In 1780, 1783, 1784, and 1787, Georgia passed laws that declared null and void any attempts by private parties to purchase Indian lands. Even as late as 1798, Rhode Island tried to take total control of Indian affairs within its state, including the purchases of Indian lands. Pennsylvania exercised its governmental Discovery right of preemption and otherwise controlled Indian land purchases. All of the states also relied on the *terra nullius* element of Discovery and "simply continued the old British practice of treating traditional native hunting grounds as *terra nullius,* free, ownerless land."[23]

Several states vigorously contended with the federal government for authority over Indian affairs even long after the federal government was granted by the Constitution, and had asserted by federal laws, all the Discovery and political authority that any American government could exercise over tribes. These states signed treaties with tribes and bought tribal lands even after a 1790 federal law forbade such state actions. In fact, when the U.S. secretary of war warned New York Governors Clinton and Jay that a 1795 treaty between New York and an Indian Nation would violate federal law, the state ignored the warnings and went ahead and concluded the treaty. New York also continued to legislate regarding Indian affairs and to authorize treaties with New York tribes well into the 1820s. Other actions by New York with tribes in the 1830s led to Discovery Doctrine cases that the federal courts had to decide and in which the courts held such state–tribal treaties enacted after 1790 to be invalid. From the foregoing evidence, it is obvious that state governments well understood the Doctrine of Discovery and wanted to exercise that power over the Indian Nations and their lands and citizens.[24]

STATE COURT CASES

There are relatively few reported state court cases about Discovery issues from the earliest days of the American states. There are, however, some intriguing cases that demonstrate state judicial views on Discovery and its elements and that evidence the battle some states waged with the federal government over the control of Indian affairs and tribal land sales.

In 1835, long after the federal government had taken complete control over Indian affairs and Discovery issues, the Tennessee Supreme Court was still supporting state activities in this field. In *Tennessee v. Forman,* the state court upheld the authority of the state legislature to extend the state's criminal jurisdiction into Indian country. The state court approved of this action even though it had to expressly repudiate a U.S. Supreme Court case that had reached the exact opposite decision just three years before. The Tennessee court instead reached back to 1823 and the Supreme Court's *Johnson v. M'Intosh* decision and expressly relied on Discovery and its elements of first discovery, European title, limited tribal sovereignty, religion, and conquest to hold that the state government possessed sovereign power over Indian Nations and could impose state laws in tribal territory. "The principle declared in the fifteenth century as the law of Christendom, that discovery gave title to assume sovereignty over, and to govern the unconverted natives of Africa, Asia, and North and South America, has been recognized as a part of the national law, for nearly four centuries." The court also noted the Spanish principle of "just war" and held that Americans could fight to "defend" themselves if Indians resisted Americans moving in and taking over tribal lands. Just like Franciscus de Victoria stated in the 1530s, the court stated that if Indians opposed American rights to occupy tribal lands, Americans could "use force to repel such resistance."[25]

Moreover, many other state courts demonstrated their agreement with Discovery and upheld state assertions of sovereignty and jurisdiction over tribes, the imposition of state laws in Indian territory, and even the idea of royal, colonial, and state ownership of tribal lands in fee simple. In *Arnold v. Mundy,* in 1821, the New Jersey Supreme Court had to decide who owned oysters planted in a river by the plaintiff. The case was primarily about the control of the fisheries by the English king in the exercise of his sovereign power. But in analyzing that issue, the court stated that "when Charles II took possession of the country, by his right of discovery, he took possession of it in his sovereign capacity." The court also stated that the people of New Jersey had "both the legal title and the usufruct [use rights in land] ... exercised by them in their sovereign capacity." According to this court, the king and later the people of New Jersey owned tribal lands because of first discovery and possession and as part of their inherent sovereignty. The court also relied on the Discovery idea of *terra nullius,* or vacant land, because this court claimed New Jersey was "an uninhabited country found out by British subjects." The court totally ignored the fact that Indian Nations were living on and using this real estate when the English arrived.[26]

In 1807 the North Carolina Supreme Court defined the tribal real-property right to be just a possessory right, just a right of occupancy and use. This describes exactly the definition of the Discovery element of Indian title. The Pennsylvania Supreme Court agreed with this idea in 1813 and noted that even though the royal charter had conveyed to William Penn the "immediate and absolute estate in fee in the province of Pennsylvania" he had, out of good policy and justice, "obtained the consent of the natives" by purchasing his lands from the tribes. This court expressly relied on the well-known elements of Discovery of the limited Indian title and preemption. The court also stated that "the king's right was ... founded ... on the right of discovery." Another judge on this same case relied on the Discovery elements of first discovery, preemption, limited Indian title, religion, and civilization when he stated that Indians could not own real property because "not being Christians, but mere heathens [they were] unworthy of the earth" and that the "right of discovery" had given the colony an interest that was "exclusive to a certain extent [and brought] ... the *Indian* to his own market, where, if he sells at all, the *Indian* must take what he could get from this his only customer." This statement clearly demonstrates the court's knowledge of the impact that the exclusive right of preemption and European title had on the prices Indian tribes could receive for their lands when there was only one possible buyer. The judge also demonstrated the religious and cultural bias that lurked and still lurks today behind the Doctrine of Discovery and the discounting of the human, governmental, and commercial rights of Indian Nations.[27]

State courts understood Discovery well enough that they sometimes accurately foretold the application and definition of its principles in advance of later more famous U.S. Supreme Court cases. Several state courts, for example, had already ruled on and foretold the statement in *Fletcher v. Peck* (1810) that states could grant away the Discovery titles they held in Indian lands and give to non-Indians a limited future title in Indian lands without the consent or knowledge of the Indian Nation and even while Indians were still occupying and using the land. In 1808, in a lawsuit between non-Indians, the New York Supreme Court considered the effect of the Mohawk Nation's preexisting possession of land that the colonial government had granted to a white citizen in 1761. The court refused to address the issue of land ownership by the Nation because it considered the issue "of granting lands in the possession of the native *Indians*, without their previous consent ... a political question.... The competency of government to grant cannot be called in question."[28]

Also foretelling the *Fletcher* Court's decision was the Virginia Supreme Court in 1791 in a suit over Indian lands between Chief Justice John Marshall's father and George Rogers Clark, the brother of William Clark of Lewis and Clark fame. In *Marshall v. Clark*, the Virginia court used several elements of Discovery to consider the issue of how Indian land titles were extinguished: "The dormant title of the Indian tribes remained to be extinguished by government, either by purchase or conquest; and when that was done, it enured to the benefit of the citizen, who had previously acquired a title from the crown, and did not authorize a new grant of the lands." Consequently, the grant of a land title by the colonial government, even though at the time the land was still legally occupied and being used by Indians, was valid, and the grantee just had to wait until the government extinguished the Indian title by purchase or conquest. The court added that "the Indian title did not impede either the power of the legislature to grant the land ... [because] the grantee, in either case, must risque the event of the Indian claims, and yield to it, if finally established, or have the benefit of a former or future extinction thereof." That 1791 court statement agreed exactly with how Secretary of State Thomas Jefferson defined states' Discovery rights in Indian lands in 1790, as is discussed in chapter 3, and also accurately foretold the *Fletcher* Court's statement in 1810.[29]

This discussion clearly demonstrates that the colonial and state governments understood and applied the Doctrine of Discovery to exercise sovereign, commercial, and real-property rights over the Indian Nations. These governments, from their very beginnings, enshrined Discovery in their constitutions, laws, and court cases.

AMERICAN FEDERAL LAW OF DISCOVERY

The newly created national government of the thirteen states immediately adopted the Doctrine of Discovery. This is not surprising in light of the widespread use of the Doctrine by the European, colonial, and state governments in North America before there was a national United States government. It is also not surprising because the exercise of Discovery powers by a national government for the thirteen colonies had already been proposed by Benjamin Franklin in 1754 when he presented his Albany Plan for unifying the colonies. Franklin's plan placed all matters of Indian affairs, including "Treaties," "peace or ... War," "Laws as they judge necessary for the regulating all Indian Trade [and] all purchases from Indians ... of lands [or] mak[ing] new settlements" in the hands of the national President-General and Grand Council.[30]

In September 1774, the thirteen colonies created their first national, federal governmental entity, the loosely organized Continental Congress, to manage their national affairs and the struggle for independence from England. Indian affairs were a very important aspect of political events at this time but this Congress was primarily preoccupied with the monumental task of fighting the Revolutionary War. The Continental Congress did, however, deal with Indian Nations on a diplomatic and political basis, tried to control the trade with tribes, and spent significant time and money trying to gain their support or keep them neutral in the War. This Congress signed one treaty with the Delaware Nation and perhaps several others.[31]

The Continental Congress quickly realized its own weakness resulting from operating without a written constitution and without delineated powers. One of the primary powers this Congress lacked was the sole authority to deal with the Indian Nations. Just as Benjamin Franklin had foreseen decades before, the central, national government, had to have the sole authority in Indian affairs. Accordingly, in 1777 the Continental Congress drafted the Articles of Confederation, which were designed to give more governing authority, taxation power, and especially the power of Discovery and the sole voice over Indian affairs to the central federal government. The Articles were ratified in 1781, and a new, more structured, and more authoritative federal government began operation.

ARTICLES OF CONFEDERATION CONGRESS 1781–1789

The thirteen American states convened a new Congress in 1781 under the written constitution called the Articles of Confederation. This Congress undertook radical steps to incorporate the Doctrine of Discovery into federal law and to take Discovery powers under the control of the central federal government. Of course, it took considerable negotiating, compromise, and time to pry these powers from the states.

The Articles of Confederation were designed to place the power over Indian affairs and Discovery into the hands of the federal government. Section IX of the Articles provided that the Congress "shall also have the sole and exclusive right and power of … regulating the trade and managing all affairs with the Indians." This language repeated the same claims of sovereign control over Indian affairs that had been previously made by the Crown, the colonies, and the states. Regrettably, the states insisted on two caveats in this section that ultimately doomed the attempt of the Articles of Confederation Congress to acquire sole control of Indian affairs and to be the only sovereign to exercise Discovery powers. The caveats protected state authority because Article IX did not allow Congress to manage Indian affairs if the Indians involved were "members of any of the states," and Congress could only manage affairs "provided that the legislative right of any state within its own limits be not infringed or violated." This ambiguous wording, James Madison wrote, left the exact meaning of Article IX in "great uncertainty" as to the full extent of federal power over Indian affairs and in effect "annul[led] the power itself." These caveats gave states legitimate and nonlegitimate legal arguments to meddle in Indian affairs and to frustrate the attempts of Congress to formulate and conduct unified Indian policies. Ultimately, this impasse led to a call for an even stronger national government and to the creation of the U.S. Constitution of 1787 and the present-day United States federal government.[32]

Notwithstanding the problems that developed later, the Articles of Confederation Congress exercised its Discovery powers. In 1783, a committee of Congress solicited the views of General George Washington and others on how best to begin exercising its Article IX authority to control Indian affairs. Washington answered the committee and Congress in September 1783 with a very influential letter in which he proposed that the United States not fight tribes for land but instead deal with them under a policy that Washington described as "the Savage as Wolf." Washington said that Indian lands would fall to the United States soon enough, without bloodshed and without wasting tax dollars on military forces, as the borders of white settlement and population naturally increased and as Indians naturally retreated like the wild beasts and died off. Washington was also, oddly enough, in favor of the Congress controlling all the Indian trade and drawing a boundary line between American settlements and Indian country. Washington's proposals seemed out of character because he had abhorred these same ideas when King George III had used them in the Royal Proclamation of 1763. Now that the United States was in charge of Discovery and dealing with the Indian Nations, Washington thought the ideas behind the Royal Proclamation were good policies and that the United States should control Indian affairs.[33]

In another letter to Congress in June 1783, Washington demonstrated his understanding and approval of using Discovery elements as part of his proposed Indian strategies. He suggested that to "combat the Savages, and check their incursions," the United States should increase its trade with Indians because that "would be the most likely means to enable us to purchase upon equitable terms of the Aborigines *their right of preoccupancy;* and to induce them to *relinquish our Territories,* and to remove into the illimitable regions of the West" [emphasis added]. Washington was suggesting that Congress enforce the United States' Discovery rights by controlling tribal commercial activities, taking advantage of the limited Indian title of occupancy, "preoccupancy" as he called it, and exercising its preemption and European title rights to buy the lands when tribes were ready to sell. He wanted the United States to exercise sovereign authority over tribes by removing them westward at its pleasure. Washington was well aware that the United States had just gained these Discovery powers from England for all the lands west of the Allegheny and Appalachia Mountains to the Mississippi River by winning the Revolutionary War. Notice that Washington called tribal lands "our Territories." This is the exact same Discovery principle that King George III used in the Royal Proclamation of 1763 to describe Indian country as "our dominions and territories."[34]

The Articles of Confederation Congress readily accepted Washington's advice, and his proposals formed the basis for the federal Indian policy of the era. The Congress adopted the Doctrine of Discovery with gusto as soon as it officially ended the Revolutionary War by signing the Treaty of Paris in 1783. In this treaty, England ceded to the United States all its property, sovereignty, and Discovery claims to lands between the Mississippi River and the Appalachia and Allegheny mountains. The moment Congress acquired these powers it adopted Washington's suggestions and even the precedent of the Royal Proclamation of 1763. On September 22, 1783, Congress issued a resolution stating that no one could settle on or purchase Indian lands "without the express authority and directions of the United States in Congress assembled" and "that every such purchase or settlement, gift or cession, not having the authority aforesaid, is null and void." This was nothing less than a dramatic statement by the Articles of Confederation Congress that it, and only it, possessed and could exert the Discovery powers and preemption rights over Indian lands and peoples. Thereafter, Congress tried to enforce its preemption power and its exclusive sovereign power to control the trade, Indian land sales, and all political and commercial interactions with Indians against American citizens, states, and the Indian Nations.[35]

Congress also tried to take a hard line with the Indian Nations and enforce other elements of Discovery. In 1783–1784, federal officials tried to convince various tribes that they had lost the ownership of their lands according to the element of conquest since they had fought for the British in the Revolution. The military defeat suffered by the English was not an actual military defeat of the tribes, but the United States argued that it was a "conquest" under Discovery. Under the definition of conquest that the U.S. Supreme Court adopted in 1823, the Indian Nations should have lost all title and property rights to their lands. Indians refused to accept this argument, and the United States gave it up for the time being. England had also unsuccessfully tried this same argument in 1751 against tribes that had fought for the French. Indians argued vigorously to both England and the United States that affairs between those countries could not impact tribal land ownership rights.[36]

The Articles of Confederation Congress also tried to settle with the thirteen states the issue of which government possessed the Discovery and preemption power over the western lands that England had ceded to the United States in 1783. The treaty with England clearly stated that England passed all of its property rights to the United States, but at least seven states still claimed ownership of the lands to the Mississippi River and even to the Pacific Ocean under their royal charters. These states aggressively contested their ownership claims. In fact, Massachusetts and New York sued each other over their land claims in a suit that clearly reflected Discovery claims by these states because they were arguing over "sovereignty and jurisdiction" and "the right of preemption of the soil." Finally, though, all thirteen states came to realize that a winner-take-all attitude would not prevail and that it was in the best interests of all the states to allow Congress to govern the western lands and to settle them and make them federal territories and later full-fledged states. The states began offering their western lands claims to Congress. Compromise and negotiation were of course an important part of these transactions. The states agreed to transfer their land claims if Congress assumed all the states' Revolutionary War debts and if the proceeds from sales of the western lands would benefit all the states. It seems obvious why ultimately all thirteen states accepted this compromise: it served the economic interests of the federal and state governments and came at the expense of the Indian Nations.[37]

In 1781, for example, Virginia offered to cede its western land claim to Congress, but it took until March 1, 1784, for all the issues to be worked out before Congress would accept the cession. Thomas Jefferson was one of the architects of this effort. He signed the Virginia deed ceding the western lands to Congress, and on the same day he offered a draft bill establishing federal control over the western lands. Consequently, the question of which government would hold and exercise the Discovery powers over Indian lands in the west was authoritatively settled. The U.S. Congress became the governmental body with the undisputed power of Discovery to control the western Indian lands, with the authority to buy the lands from the Indian Nations, sell the lands to settlers, and organize new territories and states, all in exchange for paying the state and national Revolutionary War debts. The thirteen states agreed to transfer whatever residual Discovery power they possessed over the western lands to Congress.[38]

The Articles of Confederation Congress began exercising that power immediately. The proposed bill to govern the western lands that Jefferson submitted with Virginia's cession of its western land claim became the federal Land Ordinance of 1784 and was followed by the Land Ordinance of 1785. These acts provided for the orderly expansion of American settlements, the creation of federal territories and territorial governments, the establishment of new American states, and the sales of Indian lands with the profits to go to the federal government to pay the Revolutionary War debts. Everyone's interests were considered and accommodated, except for Indian property and commercial rights, which were already largely ignored by the Doctrine of Discovery.[39]

The final and most extensive law enacted by the Articles of Confederation Congress for opening the western Indian lands for settlement and incorporation into the union was the Northwest Ordinance of 1787. This law was designed to organize the settlement of the old Northwest Territory and to create new states. This territory covered the modern-day states of Ohio, Illinois, Indiana, Wisconsin, and Minnesota. The Northwest Ordinance expressly adopted several elements of Discovery: "The utmost good faith shall always be observed towards the Indians, their lands and property shall never be taken from them without their consent; and in their property, rights and liberty, they shall never be invaded or disturbed, unless in just and lawful wars." This new law expressly recognized the elements of Indian title and the necessity of tribal consent to sales of real property, it implicitly exercised the federal government's exclusive preemption power, and it also raised the specter of conquest by "just war," which was an aspect of Spain's and Franciscus de Victoria's interpretation of Discovery. It is noteworthy that this law was also applied to the Oregon Territory by Congress in the Organic Act of 1848, and these Discovery elements were thus applied to the Pacific Northwest.[40]

Throughout this time period, the newly formed United States desperately needed to keep the peace with the potentially hostile Indian Nations on its borders. Therefore, the Articles of Confederation Congress dealt with tribes in a diplomatic and political relationship. This Congress ultimately signed at least eight treaties with Indian tribes between 1781 and 1789—and probably many more than eight. These treaties vividly demonstrated the adoption of Discovery by the Congress. The elements of Discovery are well represented in the eight treaties that we know for certain that the Congress enacted with various Indian Nations. The clearest example is demonstrated in a 1789 treaty in which Congress agreed with six tribes that they "shall not be at liberty to sell or dispose of [land] or any part thereof, to any sovereign power, except the United States; nor to the subjects or citizens of any other sovereign power, nor to the subjects or citizens of the United States." This is the exact definition of the Discovery real-property right of preemption.[41]

In addition, Congress exercised its preemption power to buy land from several tribes in these treaties, to buy even more land in later treaties, and to define the borders of lands that the United States would recognize as tribally owned. The United States also ceded its claim to various lands it gave to some tribes.

Moreover, the United States exercised the sovereign and commercial element of its Discovery authority when it took "the sole and exclusive right of regulating the trade with the Indians, and managing all their affairs in such manner as [the United States] think proper." Furthermore, the United States promised to take the tribes under its protection, and the tribes acknowledged themselves "to be under the protection of the United States and of no other sovereign whatsoever." These treaties mirrored exactly the colonial-era understanding of the Discovery powers possessed by the Crown and the colonies, and they defined exactly the Discovery elements of Indian title, preemption and European title, and limited tribal sovereign and commercial rights.[42]

The historical and legal evidence demonstrates that the Articles of Confederation Congress exercised the powers of Discovery against its own citizens and state governments and over the American Indian people and their nations. It is also certain, however, that this Congress could have exercised even more Discovery authority in Indian affairs if the Articles had clearly granted Congress the sole and exclusive power to deal with all tribes and all tribal lands and had prevented the states from playing any role in these activities. Because of the limitations on the federal power in Article IX, various states meddled in Indian affairs and caused armed conflicts with some tribes because the states entered treaties with tribes to buy land and to manage Indian affairs. These problems led many people, primarily James Madison, to call for the formation of a new and stronger U.S. government wherein the exclusive power over all Indian affairs and all Indian land purchases would be placed only in the hands of the national government and would be taken completely away from the states.[43]

UNITED STATES CONSTITUTIONAL ERA

The call for a stronger federal government due to the weaknesses of the Articles of Confederation, primarily in taxation and Indian affairs, led to a constitutional convention that convened at Philadelphia in May of 1787. Our "Founding Fathers" finished drafting a new constitution on September 17, 1787. It was ratified by a sufficient number of states by June 1788 to become effective as the national governing document. George Washington and John Adams were then sworn in as the first president and vice-president on April 30, 1789, and the first Congress under the new Constitution met in New York on March 4, 1789. This new and stronger national government wasted no time in appropriating to itself the full Discovery power over the Indian Nations and in attempting to completely exclude the states from Indian affairs.

Constitution

The drafters of the Constitution solved the problem of states meddling in Indian affairs and interfering with the exercise of federal Discovery powers by placing the sole authority to interact and deal with the Indian Nations in the hands of the new Congress. In Article I, the Constitution expressly excludes states and individuals from Indian commercial affairs by stating that only Congress has the power "to regulate Commerce with foreign Nations, and among the several States, and with the Indian Tribes." The U.S. Supreme Court has interpreted this language to mean that Congress was granted the exclusive right and power to regulate trade and intercourse with Indian Nations and that it has plenary, or absolute, power in Indian affairs.[44]

This constitutional authority to be the only entity to control commercial affairs with the Indian Nations, which obviously included the sole power of buying Indian lands and trading with tribes, unambiguously granted the Doctrine of Discovery powers to Congress. The president and the Senate were also granted the sole constitutional authority to control treaty making in Article VI. Those entities had the power to continue making treaties with the Indian Nations as the United States had already been doing since 1778. The Constitution, then, incorporated and enshrined the Discovery power into our federal system and placed that power solely into the hands of the national government, as James Madison and the Founding Fathers desired.

Legislative Branch

The very first Congress under the new Constitution immediately began exercising the Discovery powers it had been granted. In the first five weeks of its existence, it enacted four laws concerning Indian affairs out of just thirteen laws that it enacted in that time. In 1789 the new Congress established a War Department with responsibility over Indian affairs and appropriated money and named federal commissioners to negotiate treaties with tribes. Most significantly, on July 22, 1790, the first Congress enacted a statute that is a perfect and express example of its Discovery power and of preemption. On that date, Congress passed the first of a series of temporary Indian Trade and Intercourse Acts that forbade states and individuals from dealing politically or commercially with Indians Nations and from buying Indian lands.

> No sale of lands made by an Indian, or any nation or tribe of Indians within the United States, shall be valid to any person or persons, or to any state, *whether having the right of pre-emption to such lands or not,* unless the same shall be made and duly executed at some public treaty, held under the authority of the United States. (emphasis added)

This act was plainly an exercise of Congress's preemption authority and prevented states and individuals from dealing with tribes and buying Indian lands without federal approval even if the state claimed it still held "the right of preemption." Congress could not have more expressly and clearly taken the Discovery right of purchasing Indian lands for itself. There was no confusion in 1790 about what this act meant. President George Washington clearly understood it because he told Seneca Chief Corn Planter that under the 1790 act "the General Government only has the Power to treat with the Indian Nations.... No State, nor Person, can purchase your Lands." This act avoided the problems the Articles of Confederation Congress had suffered because it erased any doubt about whether states had a right of preemption even for tribal lands within a state's borders. This act used the Discovery power the Constitution had granted Congress, and Congress placed the preemption power solely into the hands of the federal government.[45]

The 1790 act was only authorized for three years. It was amended slightly several times and was reenacted as a temporary law in 1793, 1796, and 1799. In 1802 it was enacted as a permanent law. Thus, Discovery and preemption are still enshrined in federal statutory law today.[46]

The 1790 Trade and Intercourse Act also exercised Congress's constitutional Discovery authority to regulate all commerce by American citizens and states with Indians. The act and its later versions required persons desiring to trade with Indians and tribes to secure a federal license, to provide a bond, and to not trade alcohol in Indian country. In 1796, in 1799, and in 1802, Congress even required federal passports for non-Indians to enter Indian territory. The central federal government was now firmly in charge of Indian affairs, the sovereign and commercial Discovery powers, interactions between Americans and Indians, and the power of preemption, just as King George III had tried to do in the Royal Proclamation of 1763 and just as the Articles of Confederation Congress had tried to do with its Proclamation of 1783.

In 1795, Congress continued exercising its Discovery power over the sovereignty of the tribal nations by completely monopolizing all trade and commercial interactions with tribes. At President Washington's urging, Congress established federal trading posts across the Indian frontier to conduct all the trade with tribes. Washington's rationale was that fairly priced goods and shopping at federal trading posts would bind Indians to the United States and avoid the friction, fraud, and problems that private traders had so often caused in the past. Congress repeatedly renewed this bill at the suggestion of Washington and later presidents. Ultimately, the federal government operated up to 28 federal trading posts across the frontier from 1795 to 1822 until objections, primarily from private commercial interests, led to the demise of the federal program.[47]

Executive Branch

The Constitution created the new position of president to exercise the executive powers of the federal government with the assistance of various executive departments and officers. President Washington formed an executive branch of four departments with four cabinet members. The president and his cabinet were very well acquainted with the Discovery powers that the U.S. government possessed, and they did not hesitate to use them.

As already discussed, President Washington was well aware of the power of preemption, was the creator of the "Savage as Wolf" federal policy that assumed that Indian tribes would slowly disappear as American settlements expanded and the United States purchased tribal lands, and was involved in the Articles of

Confederation government and the drafting of the Constitution. Washington was a key figure during the decades that the colonies became organized, won their independence, created a national governing body, and worked to take the Discovery powers solely into the hands of the central federal government. Washington had perceived that the meddling of individual frontiersmen, traders, land speculators, and the states in Indian affairs created problems with Indian Nations and actual wars. He ultimately came to adopt the very tactics of the English Crown and worked to exclude these entities from Indian affairs once he was in charge of national policy.

Washington and the federal government were heavily involved in Indian affairs in the early decades of the American republic. Dealing with tribes was the major United States foreign policy issue at that time, and the legislative and executive branches spent a considerable amount of time and effort on these issues. The principles of Discovery played a large role in the daily conduct of the federal government. As already mentioned, Washington devised the idea for the federal trading posts to help placate Indians and keep the peace. When Thomas Jefferson was president, he was also a strong advocate of expanding the federal trading program to exclude the private traders and to help control and befriend the Indian Nations through trade and commerce.

The executive branch was cognizant from the start of its preemption power over tribes and the states. President Washington and his officers readily exercised that power and utilized Discovery in developing Indian policies and in using treaties to buy Indian lands whenever possible and to limit foreign nations, American states, and individuals from dealing with American Indian tribes. John Adams, the first Vice-President and second President of the United States, was also well aware of the Discovery powers of the United States, the claim of federal dominion over Indians, and the exclusive right to purchase Indian lands. He was cognizant of the rights Discovery recognized in the tribal nations, including Indian titles and a right of possession and limited ownership of their lands. These are clear examples of the sovereign and real-property aspects of the Doctrine of Discovery at work in the U.S. government.[48]

Washington's cabinet was well aware of Discovery. Secretary of War Henry Knox, for example, demonstrated his clear understanding of Discovery in his congressional reports and statements on the federal power of preemption and other elements. In June of 1789, Knox stated,

> The Indians being the prior occupants, possess the right to the soil. It cannot be taken from them unless by their free consent, or by the right of conquest in case of a just war. To dispossess them on any other principle, would be a gross violation of the fundamental laws of nature, and of that distributive justice which is the glory of a nation.

This statement is an accurate definition of the Discovery elements of possession, preemption and European title, Indian title, conquest, and just war.[49]

The first secretary of the treasury, Alexander Hamilton, also showed his working knowledge of Discovery. In discussions on the role of federal treaty commissioners,

Hamilton wrote that they should "do nothing which should in the least impair the right of pre-emption or general sovereignty of the United States over the Country [and should] impress upon the Indians that the right of pre-emption in no degree affects their right to the soil … excepting that when sold it must be to the United States." Earlier in his legal career, Hamilton even litigated Discovery issues. In 1785–1786, he represented the state of New York in its land claim case versus Massachusetts. The case depended entirely on which state held the preemption power to buy Indian lands during colonial times. In preparing his case, Hamilton created an extensive chart that documented the first discoveries and settlements in America of the English, Spanish, and Dutch, and analyzed the English colonial charters and the 1493 papal bull of Alexander VI. Hamilton obviously understood the Discovery elements of first discovery, preemption and European title, Indian title, and tribal limited sovereign and commercial rights.[50]

In 1790 to 1793, the first secretary of state, Thomas Jefferson, demonstrated clearly that he also operated under the principles of Discovery and understood fully their ramifications and the limitations they created on tribal sovereignty and property rights. Jefferson continued these efforts during his eight years as president. We consider in depth Jefferson's views on Discovery in chapter 3.

The executive branch was very busy in its early years in negotiating, and the Senate in ratifying, at least one hundred treaties with the Indian Nations between 1789 and 1823. These treaties reflected the contours of Discovery and preemption, just as did the already-discussed Indian treaties with the Continental and Articles of Confederation Congresses in 1778–1789. The most obvious examples of the exercise of Discovery by the Executive Branch in its first decades were demonstrated in five treaties from 1791–1808.

Specifically, in 1791 the United States limited the sovereignty of the Cherokee Nation by extracting a promise that the Cherokee would not engage in diplomatic relations with any countries, states, or individuals other than the United States. The Cherokee agreed not to enter treaties with "any foreign power, individual state, or with individuals of any state." Moreover, in 1794, the United States promised the Seneca Nation "the free use and enjoyment" of its reservation and that "it shall remain theirs, until they choose to sell the same to the people of the United States, who have the right to purchase." Then in 1795 the United States secured a promise from the Wyandot and eleven other tribes that when any of them desired to sell their lands, they would do so "only to the United States." In 1804 the United States promised the Sauk and Fox Nations that it would "never interrupt" the tribes' "possession of the lands" and would protect the "quiet enjoyment" of their lands against any intruders, and the United States secured a promise in return from the tribes that they would "never sell their lands or any part thereof to any sovereign power but the United States, nor to the citizens or subjects of any other sovereign power, nor to the citizens of the United States." In 1808 the United States also secured a promise from the Osage Nation "disclaiming all right to cede, sell or in any manner transfer their lands to any foreign power, or to citizens of the United States … unless duly authorized by the President." In addition, the United States also repeatedly exercised its preemption power to buy land from the Indian Nations. Clearly, these federal actions mirrored the specific Discovery elements of Indian title and occupancy of land and the sovereign and preemption rights the United States acquired under the Doctrine.[51]

The Indian treaties from 1789 to 1823 also demonstrate other aspects of the United States' Discovery power. The United States exercised a limited sovereignty over tribal governments by controlling all trade and commerce with them. The United States included a provision in almost every one of these treaties in which the tribes agreed that "the United States shall have the sole and exclusive right of regulating their trade." Pursuant to this authority, the executive branch occasionally agreed to build federal trading posts in a tribe's territory and often secured promises from tribes to prevent traders without federal trading licenses from entering their territory. The United States also requested and sometimes forced tribes to allow the United States to build roads and postal routes across tribal lands and to allow free passage to persons using the roads. And the United States continued to promise to protect tribes, and the tribes acknowledged themselves "to be under the protection of the United States of America, and of no other sovereign whosoever." All of these actions were implicit and explicit acknowledgments and exercises of the United States' alleged sovereign, diplomatic, and commercial Discovery powers over the tribes.[52]

Moreover, as we will examine in chapter 6, the executive branch explicitly used the Doctrine of Discovery for decades to argue its territorial claims against England, Spain, and Russia to first discovery and ownership of the Pacific Northwest. All of these countries relied on the elements of Discovery in these diplomatic disputes. Spain and Russia relinquished their claims to the United States through treaties in the 1820s, and only England and the United States continued to contest their rights. The United States and England never really settled the legal question of who held the superior claim to the Pacific Northwest under Discovery. The two countries argued the subject for decades, signed two treaties to jointly occupy the territory in 1818 and 1827, and finally in 1846 drew the dividing line between the United States and Canada where it is today.

The foregoing facts illustrate clearly that the U.S. Constitution, the Congress, and the executive branch utilized the Doctrine of Discovery and its elements long before the U.S. Supreme Court adopted it as federal case law in 1823 in *Johnson v. M'Intosh*. These federal entities understood the meaning of Discovery and its elements and the legal property and governmental rights that Discovery granted the United States over the Indian Nations and their lands and over any state, individual, or foreign nation that tried to deal with American Indians.

THE UNITED STATES SUPREME COURT

In the early 1800s, issues regarding tribal lands, and thus Discovery and preemption, slowly began to make their way onto the Supreme Court's docket. A troubling aspect of almost all these cases was that they involved non-Indians suing over real estate issues wherein one party had allegedly acquired its title from a tribe. These important cases that determined Indian land-rights issues rarely had a tribal or Indian litigant and rarely heard any legal arguments advocating the tribal position. The Court's Indian law jurisprudence assumed from the start that the Doctrine of Discovery was the controlling legal principle, and in 1823 the Court expressly embraced the Doctrine. In the nearly two hundred years since *Johnson,* the federal courts have consistently applied Discovery to the Indian Nations and the states, even up to 2005.

Pre–Johnson v. M'Intosh Supreme Court Cases

In 1810, the Supreme Court relied on the Doctrine of Discovery the very first time it addressed Indian property rights. In *Fletcher v. Peck,* the Court considered whether Georgia could enact a law granting Indian lands to private companies and then change its mind the following year and enact another law nullifying the first statute. The Court held that under the U.S. Constitution Georgia could not enact the second statute and destroy the contract it had created in the first law. In addition, the Court was briefly faced with an Indian law question whether Georgia was "legally seised [in possession] in fee of the soil thereof subject only to the extinguishment of part of the Indian title thereon." That is a complicated way of asking whether Georgia currently owned a legal interest, or a fee title, in the tribal lands within Georgia such that it could transfer its title to others, even while the Indian Nation was still occupying and using the land. You might guess already that Georgia could do that under the Doctrine of Discovery, and you would be right. That is so because the right of preemption and the other elements of Discovery had been passed by the English Crown to Georgia in its colonial charter.[53]

In answering the question, the Supreme Court reviewed the jury verdict that had traced the transfer of title to the disputed lands from the charter granted by Charles II, through the Royal Proclamation of 1763 and the American Revolutionary War, and decided that the land lay "within the state of Georgia, and that the state of Georgia had power to grant it." The Court implicitly and explicitly relied on the elements of Discovery such as the rights the Crown had gained by first discovery and that Indian lands were "vacant lands" or *terra nullius.* In addition, even the dissenting judge and the arguments of the attorneys, including future president John Quincy Adams and future Supreme Court Justice Joseph Story, all expressly relied on Discovery.[54]

Chief Justice John Marshall recognized that there were doubts about whether Georgia could be "seised" in fee simple (considered to own and possess a title) of lands still subject to the Indian title of occupancy and use and whether Georgia could transfer this title while the Indian Nation was still in possession and the Indian title was not yet extinguished. The Court, however, answered that question clearly: "the particular land ... lie within the state of Georgia, and ... the state of Georgia had the power to grant it.... The majority of the court is of opinion that the nature of the Indian title, which is certainly to be respected by all courts, until it be legitimately extinguished, is not such as to be absolutely repugnant to seisin in fee on the part of the state." Thus, the Court held both that Georgia possessed a limited kind of fee-simple title to the Indian lands, even while the lands were still in the possession and use of the tribe, and that Georgia could transfer its title to its grantees; the people Georgia transferred its title to took the title subject only to the future extinguishment of the Indian title of occupancy. Georgia could grant a sort of limited-fee title while the lands were still in tribal hands.[55]

Five years later, in *Meigs v. M'Clung's Lessee,* the Supreme Court reaffirmed *Fletcher* that states possessed a limited fee-simple title to Indian lands even while tribes occupied and used their lands and that states could grant their interest in Indian lands to individuals who then had to await possession of the land subject to the future extinguishment of the Indian right of occupancy and use. Such a grant of Indian land would only become effective, of course, after the Indian title was extinguished.[56]

Fletcher and *Meigs* demonstrate the Court's implied acceptance in its early years of Discovery and preemption to decide ownership rights in Indian lands. It remained for 1823 and *Johnson v. M'Intosh* for the Court to expressly adopt Discovery as the binding legal doctrine of American Indian law and to define the elements of the Doctrine.

Johnson v. M'Intosh (1823)

In 1823 the Court was presented with long-anticipated questions regarding the nature of Indian land titles, how Indian titles were extinguished, and whether individuals could buy Indian lands. *Johnson v. M'Intosh* is an extremely important case because it was the first major Indian law case to reach the Supreme Court. It was also vitally important because it tested the ownership of all the real estate in the United States. In fact, it is still a crucial case for modern-day American life because an Indian title is the original link in almost all land titles in the United States. As we will see, the decision of the Court was not a surprise after the long history of the adoption of the Doctrine of Discovery by the colonial, state, and federal governments we have already examined.

In June 1773, William Murray, a partner in a land-speculation company, purchased land from Indians in what is now Illinois. Despite the warnings of local British officials that he was violating the Royal Proclamation of 1763, Murray purchased two large tracts of land from the decimated Kaskaskia, Peoria, and Cahokia Nations. In October 1775, Murray, working for another company, bought two more large tracts of land from the Piankeshaw Nation, land that straddled what is now the Illinois and Indiana border. When all political attempts to get these private land purchases ratified by the Crown and the colonial, state, and federal governments failed, the companies turned to the federal courts in the 1820s.[57]

In the meantime, the United States was carrying out its own strategy of expansion and was creating new states out of the old Northwest Territory pursuant to the Land Ordinances of 1784 and 1785 and the Northwest Ordinance of 1787. The Northwest Ordinance was part of the compromise of the 1780s, when the original thirteen states ceded all their western land claims to the United States. According to the compromise, the federal government was authorized to manage settlement of the old Northwest, govern the new territories, and earn the profits off the western land sales in order to benefit all the states. Pursuant to that policy, in 1803 and 1809, the federal government negotiated treaties with the same Indian Nations that William Murray had dealt with in 1773 and 1775. The United States purchased enormous tracts of land from these tribes in what is now Illinois and Indiana. These purchases included the lands Murray had allegedly purchased for his companies three decades before. The United States immediately began surveying the area, opening land offices, and making land sales to prospective settlers. The defendant William McIntosh purchased his land from the United States in 1815 and received his patent, or governmental land title, in 1818.

The plaintiffs in *Johnson* were Joshua Johnson and Thomas Graham. They had inherited the disputed property in 1819. They then brought an ejectment lawsuit in federal court to remove William McIntosh from the property they claimed as their own. McIntosh won the case in the trial court. On appeal in the Supreme Court, Johnson's attorneys argued in favor of the Indians' natural-law rights to sell the real estate they had owned and occupied since time immemorial. Even these attorneys, however, did not think that the "savage tribes" possessed full title to their lands. Instead, they called it a "title by occupancy" and one that was held in common by all the tribal citizens. These attorneys argued that because England and various treaties recognized a tribal right in the soil, and because Indians were not English subjects, the Royal Proclamation of 1763 could not have limited the tribes' natural rights to sell their own lands. In contrast, McIntosh's attorneys argued that Indians had been uniformly treated "as an inferior race" and were not recognized as having a permanent property interest in land or the right to sell land to private individuals: "Discovery is the foundation of title, in European nations, and this overlooks all proprietary rights in the natives."[58]

Chief Justice John Marshall stated the issue in the case to be "the power of Indians to give, and of private individuals to receive, a title which can be sustained in the courts of this country." Marshall then determined the legal rule to apply to answer this issue. He stated that a nation or society where land is located has to make the rules of how property can be acquired, and a court cannot just look to "principles of abstract justice" or natural law. Instead, a court must look to the principles of its own government. Marshall then methodically investigated the rules of property that had been adopted in North America to see what rule applied in *Johnson*. The Court examined much of the history we have already discussed as well as the law that had developed to control the European exploration and settlement of North America. The Court noted that the legal rule for real-property acquisitions and transfers applied by Holland, Spain, Portugal, France, and England in North America was the Doctrine of Discovery. All these countries "relied on the title given by discovery to lands remaining in the possession of Indians." The Court repeated for emphasis that "all the nations of Europe, who have acquired territory on this continent, have asserted in themselves, and have recognised in others, the exclusive right of the discoverer to appropriate the lands occupied by the Indians." Marshall then traced the English Crown's title in American lands from first discovery, through grants in royal charters to the colonies, and finally to the American states and the United States.[59]

From the foregoing, Marshall reasoned that the Crown had "absolute title" in Indian lands "subject only to [the] Indian right of occupancy" and that this situation was "incompatible with an absolute and complete title in the Indians." Since the American states and then the United States had inherited this title, "it has never been doubted, that either the United States, or the several States, had a clear title to all the lands ... subject only to the Indian right of occupancy, and that the exclusive power to extinguish that right, was vested in that government which might constitutionally exercise it."[60]

Marshall then arrived at a succinct statement of the Doctrine of Discovery, which he alleged that all European and American governments had accepted for acquiring land in North America: the "principle... that *discovery gave title* to the government by whose subjects, or by whose authority, it was made, against all other European governments, which title might be consummated by possession" [emphasis added]. He also stated that "the original fundamental principle" governing American land titles and transfers of title was "that discovery gave *exclusive title* to those who made it" [emphasis added].[61]

It appears that the case would have been easy to decide once the Court had agreed on this legal rule because it follows naturally from these statements that if the discovering European government owned the exclusive title to Indian real property, how then could tribal chiefs transfer land titles to private individuals? In fact, Marshall stated that the case was an easy one. In light of the Discovery rule, the Court's answer to the issue was obvious: the purchase of land directly from Indian Nations by private individuals did not transfer a title "which can be sustained in the Courts of the United States." Consequently, the private land speculators lost out in their decades-long battle for the right to buy Indian lands directly from the Indian Nations. The Doctrine of Discovery had triumphed over any claim of exclusive real property rights or natural rights for Native Americans and their tribal governments.[62]

The Court clearly recognized this fact and understood that under the Doctrine Indians had lost two very important rights, without their knowledge or consent, upon first discovery of their territory by Europeans. This was true even while the Indian people continued to have the right to use and occupy their lands. First, tribes lost the valuable governmental and property right of free alienability; that is the right to sell their real estate to whomever they wished for whatever amount they could negotiate. In addition, Indian Nations lost significant sovereign and commercial powers because of Discovery. They lost the political right to deal commercially and diplomatically in the international arena with any country other than their "discoverer." These "legal principles" would not have been enforceable against tribes in the long run, of course, unless the Europeans and Americans were militarily strong enough to force these provisions upon tribal governments. In fact, the Court recognized that the United States' Discovery powers had been "maintained and established as far west as the river Mississippi, by the sword."[63]

It is unnecessary to quote line after line from the opinion as the Court reemphasized and reiterated its definition of Discovery, the rights Europeans and Americans had gained by first discovery, and the rights the tribal nations had lost. The following statement, though, is worth quoting as the holding of the case:

> The United States, then, have unequivocally acceded to that great and broad rule [Discovery] by which its civilized inhabitants now hold this country. They hold, and assert in themselves, the title by which it was acquired. They maintain, as all others have maintained, that discovery gave an exclusive right to extinguish the Indian title of occupancy, either by purchase or by conquest; and gave also a right to such a degree of sovereignty, as the circumstances of the people would allow them to exercise.

Here in a nutshell the Court explicated many of the elements of Discovery: first discovery, occupancy and possession, preemption and European title, Indian title, tribal limited sovereign rights, uncivilized Indians, and conquest and just war. The European countries and later the United States claimed through Discovery that they had gained "the ultimate dominion" over tribal lands and the "power to grant the soil, while yet in possession of the natives" and to have a power to convey "a title to the grantees, subject only to the Indian right of occupancy." Consequently, the United States possessed the Discovery authority it acquired from England by the Treaty of Paris of 1783 to exercise its exclusive preemption power to buy land from the Indian Nations in the old Northwest territory. William Murray's private land purchases from tribes were null and void, and thus Johnson's claim to own the land in dispute was rejected. McIntosh was instead the legal owner of the property because he received his title from the United States, which had acquired the land through the exercise of its Discovery right of preemption.[64]

It bears repeating that this 1823 Supreme Court decision determined the validity of purchases of Indian lands by private British citizens in 1773 and 1775. This was when the thirteen colonies were still English possessions. Thus, when the U.S. Supreme Court invalidated those private purchases, it did so because the Doctrine of Discovery was the controlling law in the colonial era for buying Indian lands under international law, under the colonial common law and statutory laws, and under the Royal Proclamation of 1763. The Supreme Court did not just make up in *Johnson v. M'Intosh* a new legal rule that only applied from 1823 forward. No, the Supreme Court adopted Discovery as federal judicial authority and thus ratified all the prior actions of the American colonial, state, and federal governments in using Discovery and its elements to control the purchases of tribal lands and the political and commercial interactions between the United States and its citizens and the Indian Nations and their citizens.

CASES SUBSEQUENT TO JOHNSON

The federal courts have continued to follow the precedent of *Johnson v. M'Intosh*, and have enforced the Doctrine of Discovery against the Indian Nations and the states, and have continued to recognize the federal Discovery power in hundreds of cases since 1823. In many cases, the courts followed the *Johnson* holding that Discovery gave the United States sovereign and real-property rights over tribes and tribal lands. In other cases, the courts invalidated state actions that interfered with the federal government's exclusive Discovery sovereign and preemption powers to be the only government allowed to buy Indian lands and to deal politically with tribes.

In two very important Indian law cases in 1831 and 1832, the Supreme Court touched on issues of Discovery and demonstrated its continued adherence to the Doctrine. In *Cherokee Nation v. Georgia*, the Court had to decide whether the Cherokee Nation was a "foreign state" for constitutional purposes when the Cherokee brought a lawsuit in the Supreme Court to prevent Georgia from imposing state laws in Cherokee territory. In a fractured decision, in which six justices wrote three opinions, all three opinions relied on the Doctrine of Discovery in their analysis. Chief Justice Marshall clearly pointed out that under Discovery the Cherokee had limited tribal sovereignty and real-property rights and that this played a significant part in his determination that Indian Nations were not "foreign" states and could not sue Georgia directly in the Supreme Court.

> In any attempt at intercourse between Indians and foreign nations, they are considered as within the jurisdictional limits of the United States.... They occupy a territory to which we assert a title independent of their will, which must take effect in point of possession when their right of possession ceases. Meanwhile they are in a state of pupilage. Their relation to the United States resembles that of a ward to his guardian.

Marshall also demonstrated that tribal nations had lost some of their international sovereign and commercial rights under Discovery because the United States and foreign nations considered tribes to be "so completely under the sovereignty and dominion of the United States, that any attempt to acquire their lands, or to form a political connexion with them, would be considered by all as an invasion of our territory, and an act of hostility." Marshall directly relied on several of the elements of Discovery in making these statements.[65]

In even less charitable opinions, Justice Johnson relied on "the right of discovery" and the sovereignty, dominion, and exclusive right of preemption granted by international law to the first European discoverers and then to the United States as evidence that tribes were never even considered political states. And Justice Baldwin agreed that the case should be dismissed because tribes had signed treaties placing themselves under the protection and commercial control of the United States and had never been treated, Baldwin claimed, as foreign states by any Congress of the United States because the "ultimate absolute fee, jurisdiction and sovereignty" in their lands had always been held, under the Doctrine of Discovery, by the Crown, colonies, states, and later the United States. The principles of Discovery played a significant part in the analysis of these three opinions.[66]

The very next year, in 1832, the Court had to decide in *Worcester v. Georgia* whether Georgia's laws could apply in Indian country to criminalize activity by a New England missionary who was living in Cherokee territory with the permission of the Nation. The Court held that the laws of Georgia could have no effect in Indian country and were void because they conflicted with the federal Constitution, treaties, and laws that established that all relations between Americans and Indians were the exclusive business of the federal government. In reaching this decision, Chief Justice Marshall discussed some of the history of Discovery in the New World and utilized its elements.

In looking back at Discovery, Chief Justice Marshall seemed to disparage the Doctrine because he said it was "difficult to comprehend" how inhabitants of one part of the globe could claim property rights or dominion over the inhabitants of other places or how "the discovery of either [could give] the discoverer rights ... which annulled the pre-existing rights of ancient possessors." Marshall also stated that it was "extravagant and absurd" for England to claim that its "feeble settlements made on the sea coast ... acquired legitimate power by them to govern the people, or occupy the lands from sea to sea." He even asked, but did not address, the rhetorical question of why explorers sailing along a coast could acquire for European governments property and dominion rights over the native people. Notwithstanding these concerns, Marshall and the Court clearly relied on the elements of Discovery and preemption in deciding this 1832 case. In fact, Marshall stated five times that the Court had to face "the actual state of things" and that the reality was that "power, war, conquest, give rights, which, after possession, are conceded by the world." In discussing these rights, he meant that Europeans and then the United States held preemptive rights over tribal lands and held Discovery rights vis-à-vis other countries to be the only power allowed to deal politically and commercially with the "discovered tribal nations." The Court even quoted approvingly the 1823 *Johnson* opinion and its statement that "'discovery gave title to the government by whose subjects or by whose authority it was made, against all other European governments, which title might be consummated by possession.'" Thus, the *Worcester* Court in 1832 relied on *Johnson v. M'Intosh* and perpetuated the Doctrine of Discovery.[67]

Another Supreme Court case worth examining, out of the dozens that have utilized Discovery, concerned William Clark of Lewis and Clark fame. In 1839, in *Meriwether L. Clark v. Smith,* the heirs of the recently deceased William Clark appealed a case that William had originally filed to protect a deed transferred to him by his brother George Rogers Clark. One of the defendant's defenses was that George Rogers Clark's original grant was for land in Indian territory and was thus void. The Court answered this question by looking to the colonial, state, and royal practices of granting lands even while they were still in Indian possession, cited its own cases of *Fletcher* and *Meigs,* discussed previously in this chapter, and held that the grant to George Rogers Clark was valid. "The ultimate fee (encumbered with the Indian right of occupancy) was in the crown previous to the Revolution, and in the states of the Union afterwards, and subject to grant. This [Indian] right of occupancy was protected by the political power, and respected by the Courts until extinguished; when the patentee took the unencumbered fee." Consequently, Clark had been properly granted title even though the land was then in Indian possession and use. He would gain the "unencumbered fee" once the Indian title, the right of occupancy, was properly extinguished by the government with the power to do so. This power in the state and federal governments to grant Indian lands and only later extinguish Indian titles by preemption came straight from the elements of the Doctrine of Discovery.[68]

Finally, we must note the Supreme Court's use of the Discovery elements of *terra nullius* and contiguity. In 1842 the Court stated that the "English possessions in America were not claimed by right of [military] conquest, but by right of discovery. For, according to the principles of international law ... the absolute rights of property and dominion were held to belong to the European nation by which any particular portion of the country was first discovered.... the territory occupied was disposed of by the governments of Europe, at their pleasure, as if it had been found without inhabitants." In 1846 the Court again noted the use of *terra nullius* when it stated that "the whole continent was divided and parceled out, and granted by the governments of Europe as if it had been *vacant and unoccupied land*" [emphasis added].[69]

Modern-Day Discovery

The most striking example of the Court applying the Discovery power in the modern era is the 1955 case of *Tee-Hit-Ton Indians v. United States.* In *Tee-Hit-Ton,* a clan of Tlingit Indians brought a claim against the United States for timber the United States had cut and sold off of lands the Tee-Hit-Tons claimed. The Federal Court of Claims held that the clan possessed original Indian title or the Indian right of occupancy to the lands, but because Congress had never specifically recognized the Tee-Hit-Ton's title to the lands, they did not possess legally recognizable rights in the land or its timber.

The Supreme Court considered the nature of the tribe's interest in the land. The tribe argued that it had full ownership of the land, that it had continuously occupied and used it since time immemorial with no interference from Russia or the United States, and that Congress had enacted federal laws that recognized and confirmed its right to occupy the land. The United States claimed that if the tribe possessed any property interest, it was only "the right to the use of the land at the Government's will." The Court, in turn, stated that there was no evidence that Congress had ever recognized or granted the tribe ownership or permanent rights in the disputed land. Thus, the Court had to address the meaning of "Indian title" under the principles of Discovery.[70]

The Court then turned the Doctrine of Discovery and *Johnson* inside out. Questions regarding Indian title were "far from novel," and it was well settled, the Court stated, that "after the coming of the white man," tribes held their lands "under what is sometimes termed original Indian title or permission from the whites to occupy. That description means mere possession not specifically recognized as ownership by Congress." That statement is false. In contrast, *Johnson* and numerous other Supreme Court cases had called the Indian real-property right a legal right of use, occupancy, and possession and said that it was a protectable property right, a title that was "as sacred as the fee of the whites." Furthermore, Congress had expressly and continually recognized in the Northwest Ordinance of 1787, in the July 1790 Trade and Intercourse Act, and in numerous treaties that Indian lands could only be purchased by the United States when tribes consented. The Indian Nations possessed original property rights in their lands that did not rely on "permission from the whites" as the *Tee-Hit-Ton* Court incorrectly stated.[71]

The Court went even further and stated, "After conquest they were permitted to occupy portions of territory.... This is not a property right but amounts to a right of occupancy which the sovereign grants and protects against intrusion by third parties but which right of occupancy may be terminated and such lands fully disposed of by the sovereign itself without any legally enforceable obligation to compensate the Indians." This statement is also false. First, the United States obtained virtually all Indian lands in America by treaty purchases with tribal consent and not by military conquest (it is a different question whether the treaties were fair and legitimate transactions), and the Supreme Court had always recognized tribal legal property rights because it was a title "as sacred as the fee of the whites" and had authorized tribal legal actions to protect their rights in land.[72]

Six members of the *Tee-Hit-Ton* Court, however, obviously accepted the idea that Indian lands had been acquired by physical military conquests that had terminated the Indian title. The Court said that "every American schoolboy knows that the savage tribes of this continent were deprived of their ancestral ranges by force" and that even the land sales that took place were "not a sale but the conquerors' will that deprived [Indians] of their land." This statement is also false and flies in the face of the proven fact that the vast majority of Indian lands in America were purchased with tribal consent at treaty sessions and were not taken by military conquests.[73]

The Court ended its opinion with yet another false statement. The Court did not choose, it said, "harshness" over "tenderness" toward Indians but left to Congress "the policy of Indian gratuities for the termination of Indian occupancy of Government-owned land rather than making compensation for its value a rigid constitutional principle." This Court ignored that it was already the law and policy of the United States, as established in the Northwest Ordinance of 1787 and the 1790 Trade and Intercourse Act and in the United States' entire treaty-based land-purchasing policy with the Indian Nations, to always buy Indian lands and only with tribal consent. Consequently, the *Tee-Hit-Ton* Court went far beyond the meaning of Discovery and the holding of *Johnson v. M'Intosh* when it allowed the federal government to take the Tee-Hit-Ton's property without consent and without paying compensation.[74]

In 2005 the Supreme Court was faced with another case that potentially raised issues of Discovery and its impact on tribal legal rights in the twenty-first century. In that case, the Oneida Indian Nation of New York alleged that a New York county and cities were interfering with federal Discovery powers in Indian law. The Oneida argued that the Supreme Court was required to decide under issues of Discovery and preemption whether modern-day land purchases made by the Oneida Nation within its original territory brought the parcels of land back into "Indian country" status and thus exempted them from state taxes. The federal trial court had agreed with the Oneida Nation, reviewed the history of federal Indian policy, including the federal Discovery power of preemption under the 1790 Trade and Intercourse Act, and held that the lands were Indian country and were now exempt from state taxation. The Second Circuit U.S. Court of Appeals also reviewed the history of land purchases from the Oneida Nation and state and federal treaties and agreed that the lands the Nation had repurchased were now Indian country.[75]

The U.S. Supreme Court heard the appeal. It could have decided the case based on *Johnson v. M'Intosh* and Discovery, given that the Oneida Nation alleged that its title had been improperly transferred in the 1800s when the state and federal governments negotiated treaties with the nation in violation of the 1790 Trade and Intercourse Act and the U.S. Constitution. Consequently, many commentators expected the Supreme Court to consider and apply the Doctrine of Discovery to this dispute. The Court, however, surprised many people and decided the case in favor of the New York county and cities without addressing Discovery principles. Notwithstanding that result, the case demonstrates that Discovery issues continue to arise in federal Indian law today.[76]

The Doctrine of Discovery obviously played a major role in the legal history of the American colonies, states, and federal governments. Discovery and its elements were adopted and applied by European and American governments to claim rights on this continent and to define and limit tribal natural-law rights to their own real estate and their legal, political, and commercial rights. There is no question that England and the other European countries that explored and settled North America applied the international legal Doctrine of Discovery here. There is also no question that Discovery was then incorporated into American law, that it became a predominant feature in the law of the colonial era and in American state and federal law, and that it has been a crucial factor in the territorial expansion of the United States.

CHAPTER 3

❧

Thomas Jefferson and The Doctrine of Discovery

T his book focuses specifically on Thomas Jefferson for several reasons. First, he was one of America's primary Founding Fathers and early political leaders and demonstrated an understanding and avid use of Discovery throughout his legal and political careers. Second, Jefferson was the architect of the removal policy of Indian affairs and exercised the government's sovereign Discovery authority over the Indian Nations. He created the idea of moving all the eastern Indian tribes west of the Mississippi River and developed other strategies to apply Discovery policies to the eastern and western tribes. Third, he was the motivation for the Louisiana Purchase, an enormous expansion of U.S. territory. The Louisiana Territory was an area that was occupied and owned by Indian Nations in which the Doctrine would become the controlling legal principle. Fourth, Jefferson was thinking of a continental American empire early on and used the Doctrine of Discovery and other legal and political tools to assist in this national expansion. He was well aware of the role the Indian Nations would play in his plans. Fifth, Jefferson expressly applied the elements of Discovery in the Louisiana and Pacific Northwest territories when he developed and launched the Lewis and Clark expedition and set American Manifest Destiny in motion. Finally, Jefferson's use of all the elements of Discovery and his words and actions help us to understand how the Doctrine and Indian land titles and sovereign and commercial rights were legally interpreted early in our nation's history.[1]

Thomas Jefferson was often immersed in Indian affairs throughout his legal and political careers and always utilized Discovery principles. The historical record and, most importantly, Jefferson's own words demonstrate clearly that he understood the exact definition of Discovery and agreed with and operated under its elements in his dealings with American Indians and their tribal governments. He did so at least three decades before the Supreme Court adopted the Doctrine as federal judicial law in *Johnson v. M'Intosh* in 1823. He did so, as we have already seen, because Discovery was the accepted law in North America for dealing with the Indian Nations and for defining Indian sovereign, commercial, and property rights long before 1823.

ATTORNEY THOMAS JEFFERSON

Thomas Jefferson was an attorney before he began his state and national political careers. He practiced law full-time from 1767 to 1774 and kept very detailed records on his cases. Authors who have analyzed these records estimate that nearly half of his law practice consisted of disputes over Virginia land titles and land ownership. Out of the 941 cases Jefferson handled during his legal career, 429 of them were land-claim disputes. Indian title, tribal ownership, the sale of Indian lands, and Discovery issues would have been intimately involved in almost all of these cases because England and the Virginia colony recognized and protected Indian titles at the time Jefferson was litigating these issues. He would have known Indian rights as they were defined by Discovery. In addition, John Adams said even as late as 1818, "There is scarcely a litigation at law concerning a title to land that may not be traced to an Indian deed." Lawsuits about land ownership in Jefferson's time would have always raised issues of Indian title and tribal ownership. Jefferson would have been intimately aware of Indian titles and how those rights were defined and extinguished under the principles of Discovery.[2]

The land cases Jefferson handled were of two types. All of these cases involved issues of whether the Indian title had been legally extinguished by the government that possessed the Discovery power of preemption. His first class of cases were called caveats. Jefferson was hired to handle 283 caveat lawsuits. Caveats were objections or challenges to the validity of another person's land title. His second class of cases were called petitions, and Jefferson handled 146 of them. In these cases, the plaintiff filed a lawsuit to request a land grant from the government. Jefferson described the petition as a "mode of acquiring lands, in the earliest times." To be granted a petition for land, the colonial government must have "cleared [the land] of the Indian title ... from the Indian proprietors." Jefferson wrote that only the colony and later the state of Virginia held the "sole and exclusive power of taking conveyances of the Indian right of soil." He knew that under Discovery "there resulted to the State a sole and exclusive power of taking conveyances of the Indian right of soil" and that "an Indian conveyance alone could give no right to an individual, which the laws would acknowledge." These statements by Jefferson demonstrate his knowledge of the elements of Discovery. It is clear that he understood the preemption power and that he worked with Discovery issues nearly every day because the caveat and petition lawsuits "constituted the predominant feature of Jefferson's law practice."[3]

These cases were very popular in Jefferson's day because much of the frontier land was held by persons who had not yet perfected their land titles by making improvements on the land or by paying rents to the Crown. There were many titles that were vulnerable to caveat lawsuits. Sometimes landholders even arranged for what is called a collusive suit, a sham lawsuit, in which they asked a friend to challenge their deed but to purposely lose the case. This was beneficial for the original landholder because once his deed was determined to be valid in a caveat lawsuit, no one else could ever challenge his deed again. Jefferson handled several of these collusive or sham suits during his legal career and he even arranged for some collusive suits to be brought against him in 1767 to protect his ownership of lands in Bedford, Virginia.[4]

Jefferson's extensive legal experience with land claims also made him well acquainted with the process Virginia governments had historically used to extinguish Indian titles. Jefferson wrote about the Virginia procedures of marking and protecting tribal claims to lands and the process for the colonial government to grant land petitions to settlers when the land had been cleared of its "Indian title." Jefferson agreed with the element of Discovery that considered the unappropriated lands in the Virginia colony to be under the control of the Commonwealth's pre-emption power and that held that the lands could only be sold on the authority of the Commonwealth and were "subject to the extinguishment of Indian titles." He had researched this process in colonial history and land records, probably while handling his many cases, and he had found "repeated proofs of purchase" of Indian lands. He believed that most of the land in Virginia had been purchased from Indians with their willing consent and not taken by force.[5]

Jefferson would also have been very familiar with buying Indian lands and Discovery issues because he was part of a culture that lusted for land and the subject of buying Indian lands was a general topic of his day. He had an active interest in extinguishing Indian titles so that land could be opened for Virginia settlers. Jefferson even inherited shares in a land-speculation company that had purchased Indian land in the west. Consequently, he understood Indian title, he worked with the subject on a daily basis, and he knew how Indian title could be legally extinguished in colonial Virginia and how Indian lands could be legally purchased under the Doctrine of Discovery.[6]

VIRGINIA STATE LEGISLATOR AND GOVERNOR

Jefferson became involved in Virginia colonial politics when he was elected to the House of Burgesses from 1769 to 1776. He attended the 1775 Virginia state convention and wrote at least two drafts of the new state constitution. In 1775 and 1776, he attended the Continental Congresses in Philadelphia. He was then elected to the Virginia House of Delegates for one-year terms from 1776 to 1779 and was elected for two one-year terms as the governor of Virginia in 1779 and 1780.

Jefferson entered these offices with the extensive knowledge of Discovery and Indian land titles and the process for extinguishing those titles that he had already acquired while he was a law student and a lawyer. In 1776 he helped draft the new Virginia State Constitution, in which Virginia claimed and then exercised the Discovery power of preemption over all lands in Virginia. He was in the House of Delegates in May 1779 when Virginia enacted the law that declared all past and future private purchases of Indian lands in Virginia to be null and void and in which the state claimed the "exclusive right of preemption" over such sales. Jefferson biographer Merrill Peterson notes that in these actions Jefferson made his intentions about Virginia's preemption power "abundantly clear by providing that no purchases should be made of the Indians except by the authority of the General Assembly and 'on behalf of the public.'" Jefferson also favored a policy of disposing of tribal lands only "after they were cleared of the Indian titles" and "after Indian titles were extinguished."[7]

In addition, in the two years Jefferson was governor, he granted about 3,000 land titles in Virginia. That is an average of more than four titles every day for two years. The vast majority of these would have involved official questions of Indian land ownership and the extinguishment of the Indian title. Jefferson obviously worked regularly with Discovery issues while he was a Virginia elected official, and he used the elements of Discovery in his everyday work. It is apparent, then, that Jefferson's legal and early political careers were heavily involved with Indian land-ownership issues and that he was intimately aware of the Doctrine of Discovery and the claims of England and Virginia to the right of preemption and other Discovery powers over Indian lands and tribal governments.[8]

CONGRESSMAN

Jefferson represented Virginia in national offices several different times. He was appointed in 1775 by the Virginia legislature to the Continental Congress, where he took the leading role in drafting the Declaration of Independence, in which he included several provisions that expressed American outrage at King George III over Discovery issues.

Jefferson was elected to the Articles of Confederation Congress in 1783–1784 and was involved in the negotiations for Virginia to cede her claim to the western lands to Congress. Virginia first offered to cede its claim in 1781, but the negotiations were only concluded in 1784. Jefferson signed the deed that ceded Virginia's claim to Congress and immediately offered a draft bill on how the western lands would be managed by the federal government. He was appointed to chair the committee that worked on the bill. The issue being considered in this bill was nothing less than the exercise by the Congress of the Discovery power over the western lands and the sale of these lands to future settlers. The bill that he and the committee produced became the federal Land Ordinance of 1784. This was not his first experience, however, with managing the Discovery power over the lands north and west of the Ohio River. In 1777–1778, he and George Mason had drafted resolutions for the western lands to be sold to pay the public debt, and then they drafted bills for the Articles of Confederation Congress to manage those "waste and unappropriated lands." As Professor Merrill Peterson noted, while Jefferson was a Congressman, he worked on the question of title to Indian lands and whether the western lands "still belonged to the Indian tribes or had fallen to the

Americans by right of conquest." We can see, then, that while he served in the Congress, Jefferson was often occupied with issues of Discovery.[9]

FIRST U.S. SECRETARY OF STATE

Jefferson served as American ambassador to France from 1785 to 1789 and played a very small part in national politics and the 1787 Constitutional Convention during that time. George Washington appointed Jefferson to be the first U.S. secretary of state in 1789, and he served in that office until the end of 1793. He was now in charge of all U.S. domestic and foreign affairs and was heavily involved with Indian policies and Discovery issues. His work and his words continued to demonstrate graphically that he understood and used the elements of Discovery. Jefferson utilized the United States real-property right of preemption, the exclusive option to buy Indian lands, and the sovereign and commercial aspects of the United States Discovery authority over tribes. In fact, while secretary of state, Jefferson defined the Discovery powers over tribal real property, commercial, and sovereign rights exactly as the Supreme Court would later in *Johnson v. M'Intosh* (1823) and *Fletcher v. Peck* (1810).

Jefferson apparently never used the phrase "Doctrine of Discovery," nor did he use the word "discovery" as a term of art. The title "Doctrine of Discovery" came into use only after *Johnson v. M'Intosh* in 1823. But this does not mean that Jefferson did not know or use the legal principles that came to be called Discovery. In contrast, Jefferson repeatedly discussed and utilized the elements of Discovery to define European and Indian property, diplomatic, and commercial rights in North America. He often wrote about the rights that first discovery granted to European countries in North America, the power of preemption, Indian title and rights of occupancy and use, contiguity, *terra nullius,* the need to civilize Indian people, and the limits on tribal property, sovereignty, and commercial rights.

In his official opinions, Secretary Jefferson manifested his knowledge and use of the elements of Discovery. In May 1790, for example, he was asked three questions:

1. Did the state of Georgia possess title to Indian lands within its borders?
2. Did Georgia have the right to grant this title to non-Indians even when the Indian title had not been extinguished and while Indians were still occupying and using the land?
3. Could Georgia extinguish Indian title, the tribal right to occupy and use its lands?

In analyzing these questions, Jefferson started by reciting the following rule that he said controlled the discovery of America and Georgia's alleged rights:

If the country, instead of being altogether vacant, is thinly occupied by another nation, the right of the native forms an exception to that of the new comers; that is to say, these will only have a right against all other nations except the natives.

Consequently, they have the exclusive privilege of acquiring the native right by purchase or other just means. This is called the right of preemption, and has become a principle of the law of nations, fundamental with respect to America. There are but two means of acquiring the native title. First, war; for even war may, sometimes, give a just title. Second, contracts or treaty.

This statement graphically demonstrates Jefferson's familiarity with most of the Discovery elements. He plainly understood European Discovery claims to ownership over "vacant" lands or *terra nullius*. He stated that this was not the case, though, in America because the lands had not been vacant but were instead "thinly occupied" when Europeans arrived. Therefore, the Indian Nations retained a legal title to their lands, or, as he put it, "the right of the native" formed "an exception to [that] of the new comers." Europeans still gained a Discovery right in the lands, Jefferson claimed, but it was not an absolute right. Instead, the discovering Europeans gained "a right against all other nations except the natives." This right was "the exclusive privilege of acquiring the native right by purchase or other just means." Jefferson called this power or privilege "the right of preemption." He knew that it was "a principle of the law of nations, fundamental with respect to America." He also knew that this European Discovery right of preemption could only be used to acquire native rights of occupancy by two methods: "war; for even war may, sometimes, give a just title. Second, contracts or treaty."[10]

This remarkable statement says just about everything a person needs to know to understand the Doctrine of Discovery. Jefferson defined most of the elements of the Doctrine that we have been discussing: its international law origination; that first discovery of new lands by Europeans granted property rights to the discoverer; that native people retained property rights to occupy and use their lands; the power of preemption and European title allegedly gained by first discovery; Discovery claims to vacant lands; and that voluntary sales and conquest by "just wars" were the only methods for Europeans to acquire the Indian title to land.

After analyzing the issues in light of this legal rule of Discovery, Secretary of State Jefferson answered yes to question one; Georgia did possess a legal title to the lands the Indian Nations occupied within the borders of Georgia. He described this legal title as a future right to possess and use the lands whenever the tribal right of occupancy and use ended. Jefferson also answered yes to question two regarding whether a state could pass its title, this future right in Indian lands, to other people. In answering these two questions, he accurately foretold Supreme Court statements in 1810 and 1815 in *Fletcher v. Peck* and *Meigs,* which we have already looked at and which defined the nature of Indian title and the state title in this exact same manner.[11]

Finally, Jefferson addressed question three: could a state extinguish the Indian title, the tribal right to occupy, and use its lands? Georgia claimed that the colonies and now currently the new American states possessed the power to extinguish Indian titles. Jefferson disagreed with the second part of this argument. He said that as part of the constitutional agreement of 1787–1789, the states had surrendered part of their Discovery preemption right, the power to extinguish Indian titles, to the exclusive control of the new federal government. "The States of America before their present union possessed completely, each within its own limits, the exclusive right to use these two means [just war or consent] of acquiring the native title ... [but] they have as completely ceded both to the general government."[12]

Consequently, Jefferson answered the questions posed to the State Department by using the Doctrine of Discovery and the U.S. Constitution. He said that states still possessed part of the Discovery power of preemption over Indian lands within a states' borders. They held the legal right to receive the occupancy and use of the Indian lands whenever and if ever the Indian title was extinguished in the future. States also had the right to grant that restricted and future title to Indian lands within their borders to other persons. These people then held a future right to receive the occupancy and use of the particular Indian land whenever and if ever the Indian title was extinguished in the future. The exclusive power and means to extinguish Indian titles of occupancy and use by just wars or voluntary sales, however, had been ceded by the states to the U.S. government when the states ratified the U.S. Constitution. The states still possessed part of the "European title" to Indian lands within their borders, and they could make grants of that future title in Indian lands to non-Indians. Their grantees received only what the state owned: a limited fee title to the Indian lands, subject to the Indian right of occupancy and use, which might last forever. States no longer possessed and could not grant their grantees the means to extinguish Indian title by purchases or just wars. Jefferson's answer exactly foretold the Supreme Court's approval in 1810 of Georgia granting a limited and future fee simple title to its non-Indian grantees subject to Indian occupancy and use in their lands and the determination that such an act did not violate the rights of the Indian title.[13]

Jefferson reaffirmed this opinion of the Discovery elements of preemption and Indian titles in other official State Department rulings in August 1790 regarding claims by North Carolina and in answer to a question posed to him by the U.S. House of Representatives in February 1793. In 1790, Jefferson repeated that the Cherokee Indians "were entitled to the sole occupation of the lands within the limits guaranteed to them" and that under international law "North Carolina, according to the *jus gentium* [international law] established for America by universal usage, had only a right of pre-emption of these lands against all other nations: It could convey, then, to its citizens only this right of pre-emption, and the right of occupation could not be united to it till obtained by the United States from the Cherokees." The Cherokee Nation, Jefferson wrote, "possess the right of occupation, and [North Carolina has] the right of preemption." Thus, North Carolina held the incomplete "European title," and it would not become a complete fee title until the United States extinguished the "Indian title" of use and occupancy and joined those possessory rights with the state's future fee title.[14]

In 1793, Jefferson issued an official opinion to the U.S. House regarding a Revolutionary War veteran's claim that Virginia had granted him Indian land

and he now demanded occupancy. Jefferson stated that Virginia could only allot actual possession of Indian lands after "a purchase of the Indian right … which purchase, however, has never been made." The tribal "right of occupation" was still valid since it had "never been obtained by the United States."[15]

In addressing other issues, Jefferson continued to rely on the elements of Discovery. In 1791 he issued a report on what rights Spain had gained by the Discovery element of conquest in relation to Indian lands and Indian titles in Georgia. This discussion also foreshadowed the Supreme Court's statement in *Johnson v. M'Intosh* that European and American governments could gain title to Indian lands by conquest, both by military conquests in just wars and under the element of "conquest" that was part of the general definition of Discovery. In his opinion, Jefferson discounted Spain's claim to lands in Georgia and Florida because he doubted that "the possession of half a dozen posts scattered through a country of seven or eight hundred miles extent, could be considered as the possession and conquest of that country." He thought these few Spanish posts did not establish the kind of military conquest or the Discovery element of "conquest by possession" that acquired the Indian title of occupancy and use. He also wrote in 1791 to the secretary of war that Indians held the right to occupy their lands independent of the states' rights of Discovery.[16]

In June 1792, Jefferson had a very illuminating conversation and exchange of letters about Discovery with Sir George Hammond, an English diplomat. Hammond asked Jefferson what the United States' rights were "in the Indian soil" in the lands east of the Mississippi River and west of the Appalachia and Allegheny Mountains. This was of interest to the British minister because England had ceded this territory to the United States in 1783 and because English traders and forts were still operating in the area. Jefferson explained to Hammond the United States' rights and invoked many elements of Discovery including preemption, Indian title, U.S. sovereignty over the Indian Nations in trade and other matters, the exclusion of other governments from diplomatic dealings with tribes, and its international law pedigree. Jefferson told him that the United States had

> 1st. A right to preemption of their [Indian] lands; that is to say, the sole and exclusive right of purchasing from them whenever they should be willing to sell. 2d. A right of regulating the commerce between them and the whites. Did I suppose that the right of preemption prohibited any individual of another nation from purchasing lands which the Indians should be willing to sell? Certainly. We consider it as established by the usage of different nations into a kind of *Jus gentium* [international law] for America, that a white nation settling down and declaring that such and such are their limits, makes an invasion of those limits by any other white nation an act of war, but gives no right of soil against the native possessors. [Hammond asked if the English traders had to stay out. Jefferson said yes].… He said they apprehended our intention was to

exterminate the Indians and take the lands. I assured him that, on the contrary, our system was to protect them, even against our own citizens: that we wish to get [borders] established with all of them.[17]

Jefferson also demonstrated his understanding of how Discovery limited tribal sovereign rights when he told Hammond that it was "an established principle of public law among the white nations of America, that while the Indians included within their limits retain all other national rights, no other white nations can become their patrons, protectors, or mediators, nor in any shape intermeddle between them and those within whose limits they are."[18]

Jefferson repeated his understanding of this Discovery element several times in 1793 when Spain undertook "to espouse the concerns of Indians within our limits; to be mediators of boundary between them and us; to guarantee that boundary to them; to support them with their whole power." Jefferson stated emphatically that these "are pretensions so totally inconsistent with the usages established among the white nations, with respect to Indians living within their several limits, that it is believed no example of them can be produced."[19]

In May 1792, the American Robert Gray sailed his ship *Columbia Rediviva* into the mouth of an unknown river in the Pacific Northwest. He named this river the Columbia, after his ship. A Spanish sea captain, Bruno Hezeta, had probably already discovered the Columbia in 1775 on one of several expeditions Spain sent to the Pacific Northwest in the 1770s. Spain chose to keep silent about these discoveries. It assumed, perhaps, that it could better exploit the discoveries by keeping them secret from the world. Because of Spanish secrecy, however, it was Robert Gray's name that was attached to the discovery of the Columbia, it was the name Columbia that he gave the river that was placed on the world's maps, and it was the United States who announced to the world its Discovery claim to the river.[20]

Thomas Jefferson was obviously aware of Gray's discovery. He knew that the discovery of the Columbia "gave the United States a claim recognized by the polity of nations ... over the valley and watershed of the river and over the adjacent coast." Jefferson also knew exactly what this Discovery claim meant for the native people who lived in this area. In 1792, for example, he instructed American diplomats on rights that Discovery recognized in the Indian Nations: "You know that the frontiers of [Spain's] provinces, as well as of our States, are inhabited by Indians holding justly the right of occupation, and leaving to Spain and to us only the claim of excluding other nations from among them, and of becoming ourselves the purchasers of such portions of land, from time to time, as they may choose to sell."[21]

During Jefferson's tenure as secretary of state, the Indian Nations grew tired of American and European claims to their lands and rebelled against the continuous pressure to sell lands to the United States. In February 1793, President Washington even asked his Cabinet whether the government could legally relinquish back to the Indian Nations some lands that they had already sold to the United States.

In Jefferson's notes on the meeting, he opined on the nature of the United States' Discovery sovereign and preemption rights:

> Our right of pre-emption of the Indian lands, not as amounting to any dominion, or jurisdiction, or paramountship whatever, but merely in the nature of a remainder after the extinguishment of a present right, which gave us no present right whatever, but of preventing other nations from taking possession, and so defeating our expectancy; that the Indians had the full, undivided and independent sovereignty as long as they choose to keep it, and that this might be forever.[22]

As Jefferson explained to President Washington, the Doctrine of Discovery granted the United States a future right of preemption if Indians ever consented to sell their lands and allowed the United States to prevent other countries from dealing with Indian tribes within U.S. borders. According to Jefferson, the United States held valuable property rights in Indian lands and a limited form of sovereignty over tribal international relationships.

The foregoing evidence that Secretary of State Thomas Jefferson understood exactly Discovery and its elements is overwhelming.

PRESIDENT OF THE UNITED STATES

As the third president of the United States from 1801 to 1809, Thomas Jefferson continued to expressly rely on the Doctrine of Discovery and applied its elements in his interactions with Indian Nations and the European countries as he worked to expand America's borders. The Doctrine is also plainly visible in the plans Jefferson had for the Lewis and Clark expedition. Jefferson used Lewis and Clark to begin to exercise America's political and commercial control of the Louisiana Territory and to dominate the fur trade and political interactions with the tribal nations in the territory. By 1803, he had also set his sights on the unclaimed Pacific Northwest, the Oregon country, and on his goal for the United States to possess that region if it could perfect its first discovery claim. Discovery and the Lewis and Clark expedition are discussed in chapter 5.[23]

In November 1801, President Jefferson wrote his friend Virginia Governor James Madison and applied issues of Discovery to a very controversial resolution then pending in the U.S. House to move ex-slaves to areas outside the borders of the United States. Jefferson suggested that if the proponents of this idea were looking toward Canada, that would be a problem because that "is the property of Indian nations whose title would have to be extinguished." Further raising the Discovery element of preemption, Jefferson added that the idea would also require the "consent of Great Britain." Jefferson also called the Canadian tribes "the Indian proprietors" of those lands. In addition, Jefferson discussed the idea of placing ex-slaves in the Louisiana Territory. He told Madison that while "Spain holds [that] immense country, the occupancy … is in the Indian natives," and he did not think "the Indians would sell" the land and thought that Spain "would not alienate [sell] the sovereignty." In this one brief passage, Jefferson again raised issues of Indian title, European title, land ownership, occupancy rights, the extinguishment of Indian title, and Spain's sovereign and preemption rights in the areas it claimed by Discovery.[24]

In 1803 the United States purchased the Louisiana Territory and bought the very sovereign and preemption rights of Discovery that Jefferson had written about to Madison. The Louisiana Territory had been originally claimed under Discovery principles by France because French explorers had traveled north and south on the Mississippi River in the 1680s. France transferred its Discovery rights in the drainage system of the Mississippi River to Spain and England in 1763. England received France's Discovery claim to the lands east of the Mississippi, and Spain received it to the lands on the west. Spain transferred its Discovery claim back to France in a secret treaty in 1800. Jefferson did not learn of this event for certain until 1802. It worried him greatly. As is examined more closely in chapter 4, Jefferson was content while Spain possessed the Discovery claim to Louisiana because he thought the United States could obtain the territory from Spain whenever it wanted. In his mind, though, it was a very different situation if France and the aggressive Napoleon possessed it. Consequently, as soon as Jefferson learned of the 1800 treaty passing the Discovery claim from Spain back to France, he immediately began making plans to oppose France's possession of the territory. He also opened negotiations to buy the city of New Orleans from France to ensure American use of the Mississippi River. After protracted negotiations, France suddenly offered to sell all of Louisiana. The American negotiators quickly agreed, Jefferson was delighted, and the Congress ultimately approved the treaty to buy Louisiana.

The Louisiana Purchase and Jefferson's comments and actions about the transaction are perfect examples of Discovery principles at work. Jefferson was not the only American politician who linked the purchase to Discovery. One congressman, during the debate on ratifying the Louisiana Purchase treaty, raised the Discovery elements of contiguity and civilization when he stated that Louisiana's boundary lines should be drawn "equi-distant" between other European settlements "on the principle generally admitted by European nations forming establishments in savage countries."[25]

Jefferson was of course very interested in the actual borders of the Louisiana Territory because he wanted to know the extent of the area where the United States now owned Discovery rights. In 1804 he personally researched this question and drafted a 40-plus page paper called "The Limits and Bounds of Louisiana." This document is filled with Jefferson's reliance on the elements of Discovery as legal evidence to establish the borders of the territory. He cited the international law precedent of the rights Europeans gained in North America due to first discovery, and he considered other Discovery elements such as symbolic possession, actual occupancy, contiguity, and the discovery of rivers. For example, he relied on France's 1685 Discovery claim on the Gulf Coast and up the Mississippi River, which he said was established by explorers "tak[ing] possession

... [and] building and garrisoning forts." Jefferson claimed that "from these facts ... France had formal & actual possession of the coast from Mobile to the bay of St. Bernard, & from the mouth of the Misipi up into the country as far as the river Illinois." Jefferson also wrote that France had complied with "the practice of nations, on making discoveries in America," and this included a "principle that 'when a nation takes possession of any extent of sea-coast, that possession is understood as extending into the interior country to the sources of the rivers emptying within that coast, to all their branches, & the country they cover.'" As a result of these actual and symbolic acts of occupancy and possession, France had "a virtual and declared possession ... [which] Great Britain ... opposed ... not on a denial of this principle, but on a prior possession taken & declared by repeated charters, thro' the space of an hundred years preceding, as extending from sea to sea." Thus, Jefferson noted, England did not dispute that France's actions were valid under the elements of Discovery. England only disputed that it had already established its Discovery claim to these areas by Cabot's 1496 voyages, contiguity, and the grant of charters in America from the Atlantic to the Pacific Oceans.[26]

Jefferson also relied, as Spain and France had, on contiguity arguments in deciding where the boundary of the Louisiana Territory should be marked between the ancient Spanish and French settlements. He drew the line "midway between the adversary possessions of Mobile [France] & Pensacola [Spain]" because Discovery principles required the boundary to be "midway between the actual possession of the two nations...." Jefferson also thought it important that Louis XIV claimed ownership of the area and had granted letters of authority to explorers to discover and colonize the entire region. In conclusion, Jefferson wrote that all the waters and country "are held and acted on by France" and that France's "titles derived, 1. from the actual settlements on the [Mississippi] river and it's waters, 2. from the possession of the coast, & 3. from the principle which annexes to it all the depending waters."[27]

The intriguing part of Jefferson's research paper is a discussion on the northwest boundary of the Louisiana Territory. This is contained in a "P.S." called "The Northern boundary of *Louisiana*." Jefferson seems to have thought or hoped that the Pacific Northwest might be part of the Louisiana Territory. In considering what Jefferson wrote on this subject, one should keep in mind Jefferson's goal for a continent-wide American empire and his inclusion of the Northwest in his objectives, which is further discussed in chapters 4 through 6. Admittedly, though, it is unclear from his paper whether he thought in 1804 that the Oregon country was part of the Louisiana Territory.

In the postscript, Jefferson argued that the country drained by the Missouri River and its tributaries would determine the northernmost reaches of Louisiana. He seems to argue that if there were no Spanish land claims westward of Louisiana north of the 49th parallel (the modern-day boundary line between the United States and Canada), the 49th parallel line would run indefinitely to the west. Was he arguing to run the 49th parallel boundary line between Canada and the United States as far west as the Pacific Ocean if Spain did not have any intervening claims? Jefferson was working with imperfect geographical knowledge and a lack of knowledge about the existence of Spanish claims for the area he was discussing. But he was aggressive and ambitious to expand the United States borders and to broadly interpret the boundaries of Louisiana. I read his description of the boundaries of Louisiana with the same wide-ranging vision that I think he was employing. It appears that Jefferson was hoping in 1804 that the Pacific North-west was within the borders of the Louisiana Territory.[28]

Notwithstanding the intriguing question about the northwest boundary of Louisiana, we can see that President Jefferson was fully aware of the impact of Discovery in the territory and the rights the United States had acquired through the Purchase. A similar understanding on our part of the legal significance and impact Discovery played in the Louisiana Purchase points out a common myth that most Americans believe today and that most historians and writers repeat with regularity. You have no doubt read that the Louisiana Purchase was the "greatest real estate deal in history" because the United States paid only "three cents an acre." That statement is false. This is a common mistake that many, many historians and authors have made because they do not understand the Doctrine of Discovery. Thomas Jefferson would have known that these statements are false, and this discussion proves that point with his own words and with the facts.[29]

First, the Louisiana Purchase was not a real estate deal. The United States did not buy land in the Louisiana Territory because France did not own land in the territory. (France and Spain may have owned a few parcels of land where their forts, trading posts, and official buildings were located, but there were very few such sites in the territory.) Instead of real estate, the United States purchased what France and Spain did own in the region: their Discovery claims to a limited form of sovereign, political, and commercial power over the Indian Nations and the real-property right of preemption. These are the very rights that Jefferson explained European countries held in the territory under Discovery in his 1801 letter to James Madison that was examined earlier in the chapter. Do not forget that Jefferson told Madison that the Indian nations were the "proprietors" of the lands in Canada and the Louisiana Territory, owned the "occupancy" property right, and had to consent to any sales of land. Jefferson wrote at least five times that Indian tribes were the "proprietors" of their lands in the Louisiana Territory and elsewhere.

Second, the commonly accepted myth is wrong because the United States paid far more for the complete fee-simple title to the lands in the Louisiana Territory than just the $15 million the United States paid France. You already know the facts that prove this point. For roughly one hundred years after the 1803 treaty with France, the United States struggled with the Indian Nations in the Louisiana Territory, fought wars with some of them, negotiated treaties with most of them, and purchased the actual land, the fee titles, and the Indian right of occupancy and use from the "native proprietors." The possessory fee-simple titles to the lands in the territory cost the United States far more than $15 million. In fact, calculations show that the United States paid about $300 million to Indian tribes in the

Louisiana Territory in treaty payments to buy the actual lands the tribes agreed to sell. In addition, many tribes still own large portions of land today in what was the Louisiana Territory.[30]

If Jefferson were alive, he would tell us that it is a mistake to assume that the Louisiana Purchase was a real estate transaction or that the United States bought the land in the territory for $15 million. He plainly understood what he purchased from France. In addition to what he wrote to James Madison in 1801 about tribal property rights in Canada and Louisiana, he demonstrated several times his knowledge that the United States had not purchased the lands or the fee-simple titles in the Louisiana Territory in 1803. Jefferson showed his understanding of preemption and Discovery when he wrote Congress on February 13, 1805 about a treaty with the Sac and Fox Nations to buy "a portion of country on both sides of the river Mississippi." He also sent messages to the Senate on January 15, 1808, and to the House on January 30, 1808, that "the United States should obtain from the native proprietors the whole left bank of the Mississippi." It is apparent that Jefferson knew the United States had bought France's Discovery powers, which included the right of preemption, a future right to buy the lands west of the Mississippi, on its "left bank." Jefferson knew that the United States had not purchased any real estate in the territory from France. Instead, the United States bought the Discovery right to a limited sovereignty over the territory, the right to be the only government the Indian Nations could deal with politically and commercially, and the preemption right, the exclusive option to purchase the real estate whenever the owners, the Indian Nations, chose to sell. In addition, Jefferson told Congress the Sac and Fox treaty strengthened "our means of retaining exclusive commerce with the Indians on the western side of the Mississippi." Jefferson well understood the Discovery powers he had purchased from France. As he wrote in 1803, Jefferson hoped that the United States would "endeavor to procure the Indian right of soil, as soon as they can be prevailed on to part with it, to the whole left bank of the Mississippi," and, as he stated in his Annual Message on November 8, 1804, to buy Indian lands, the United States had to gain the "relinquishment of native title." The Louisiana treaty was not a purchase of land. It was not the greatest real estate deal in history.[31]

In one particularly illuminating statement, Jefferson demonstrated his clear understanding of Discovery and the type of land title the first discoverer gained under the concept of "European title." We have not yet emphasized this aspect of Discovery very much, but the discovering Euro-American country gained only an incomplete title to new lands that it spied, and it took symbolic possession of land via Discovery rituals. It was not a complete fee title of ownership and possession until the Euro-Americans extinguished the Indian title of occupancy and use and actually occupied the land. Jefferson showed his complete understanding of this principle when he commented to the Senate in January 1808 on the activities of Lieutenant Zebulon Pike who had acquired Indian land on both sides of the Mississippi River. The Senate's ratification of the treaty purchasing the Indian title, Jefferson wrote, would "give to our title a full validity."[32]

President Jefferson also demonstrated his use of Discovery on other occasions. He often accurately explained preemption to tribal leaders who visited him in Washington, DC, and in his speeches and letters to them. He repeated to chiefs that the Indian Nations owned their lands and possessed the legal rights of use and occupancy and that the United States could only buy their lands with their consent and when they were willing to sell. He referred to the July 22, 1790, Trade and Intercourse Act and explained to tribes that American law did not allow individual Americans or states to buy tribal lands. He even gave tribal leaders copies of the Trade and Intercourse Act. Of course, he never neglected to tell tribal chiefs that whenever they wished to sell land, the United States was always ready to buy.[33]

Jefferson also fully understood the limited sovereignty aspect that Discovery granted the United States and its corresponding limitation on tribal sovereignty. Jefferson knew that the tribes in the Louisiana Territory were still sovereign governments but that they had lost some of their governmental powers to France and then to the United States because of the Doctrine. Five brief examples are sufficient to support that statement. First, before the United States purchased the Louisiana Territory, Jefferson wrote that France was "the present sovereign of [Louisiana]." Second, after the United States purchased the territory, Jefferson initially thought that the acquisition required a constitutional amendment, and so he drafted a proposed amendment to authorize the Purchase. In his draft, Jefferson would have had the U.S. Constitution expressly guarantee to the Indian Nations in the Louisiana Territory their "rights of occupancy in the soil, and of self-government" and guarantee that the principle of preemption would apply to the lands they actually possessed while the United States' rights of sovereignty and full possession of land would apply to any non-Indian lands in Louisiana.[34]

In the third example of Jefferson's understanding of the sovereign Discovery power, he wrote privately in July 1803, very soon after learning of the Louisiana Purchase, that the United States would occupy New Orleans and attempt to introduce American law there but that the "rest of the territory will probably be locked up from American settlement, and under the self-government of the native occupants." Fourth, in October 1803, in his Third Annual Message to Congress, Jefferson recommended that Congress prepare to occupy and provide a temporary government for the Louisiana Territory and "for confirming to the Indian inhabitants their occupancy and self-government, [and] establishing friendly and commercial relations with them."[35]

Finally, in January 1804, after the United States had purchased the territory, Jefferson amended his instructions to Meriwether Lewis in a way that demonstrated that Jefferson clearly understood that the United States had purchased France's sovereign Discovery power and preemption rights in Louisiana. In this new instruction, Jefferson explained that Lewis's mission had changed significantly because the United States had now gained a form of sovereignty over the Louisiana Territory tribal governments. He now instructed Lewis to proclaim American sovereignty in the territory.

> When your instructions were penned, this new position [the Louisiana Pur-
> chase] was not so authentically known as to effect the completion of your
> instructions. *Being now become sovereigns of the country, without however any dimi-
> nution of the Indian rights of occupancy* we are authorised to propose to them in
> direct terms the institution of commerce with them. It will now be proper you
> should inform *those through whose country you will pass,* or whom you may meet,
> that their late fathers the Spaniards have agreed to withdraw … that they have
> surrendered to us all their subjects … *that henceforward we become their fathers
> and friends.* [emphasis added][36]

Jefferson correctly understood that the Indian Nations remained the occupants
of their lands and sovereign governments. But he realized that through the
Louisiana Purchase and the Doctrine of Discovery, the United States had acquired
a limited or partial sovereignty over the tribes in the territory but that this power
did not abrogate the existence of tribal governments or tribal laws.[37]

Jefferson's knowledge of another element of Discovery and his interest in
acquiring the Pacific Northwest were demonstrated in the absolute importance
he placed on Americans permanently occupying the Northwest. We know that
Discovery required a first discovering country to occupy and possess its new
discoveries within a reasonable amount of time after a first discovery to complete
or perfect the incomplete title it had gained by first discovery and symbolic
possession alone. Jefferson knew that this element would become a significant
aspect of any American claim and legal argument to the Pacific Northwest based
on Robert Gray's first discovery of the Columbia River in 1792. Actual occupancy
would also be significant in the realpolitik sense of establishing American control
in the Northwest. Thomas Jefferson was very eager for Americans to return to the
mouth of the Columbia River and perfect the American title to the region.

In December 1806, Senator William Plumer reported in his diary that President
Jefferson had expressed this very concern to him and stated his desire for an
American merchant to commence operations in the Pacific Northwest. Senator
Plumer wrote, "The President … said, That he was anxious to have some
enterprizing merchantile Americans go on to the river Columbia & near the Pacific
ocean, & settle the land there. That they might easily engross the fur & peltry
trade with the Indians—which he conceived would soon be very lucrative—That
he believed no European nation claimed either the soil or jurisdiction." This statement shows that Jefferson was very interested in 1806 in American merchants
building permanent establishments on the Columbia River and that he tied this
possession and occupancy of the region to Discovery claims. Note that Jefferson
thought that no European country had yet claimed the soil or jurisdiction of the
region.[38]

Soon thereafter, John Jacob Astor, the American fur magnate, proposed to build
a fur trading post at the mouth of the Columbia. He sought federal approval and
assistance. Jefferson was very interested in this development. He had already
been working to spread the American fur trade into the Louisiana Territory. This

was one of the benefits Jefferson had promised Congress would result from the Lewis and Clark expedition. Jefferson also understood the significance under Discovery if America could establish a permanent occupation of the Northwest before any other European government. He was of course aware of Robert Gray's discovery of the mouth of the Columbia in 1792, and he had personally aimed Lewis and Clark's expedition at that identical spot. Obviously, Jefferson was now excited by Astor's proposal because of the necessity that the United States permanently occupy the Northwest within a reasonable time after claiming first discovery. Jefferson was very eager to see an American company build the first permanent settlement at the mouth of the Columbia. Therefore, he wrote Astor in April 1808, "I consider it as highly desirable to have that trade centered in the hands of our own citizens.... All beyond the Mississippi is ours exclusively." Note Jefferson's claim that the United States owned the west clear to the Pacific Ocean! He promised Astor all the help the executive branch could give him in establishing a fur post on the Columbia.[39]

Ultimately, Astor sent expeditions by land and sea to the mouth of the Columbia River and built the Astoria trading post in April 1811, at the site of today's Astoria, Oregon. The occupation of Astoria was a significant factor in America's Discovery claim and in geopolitical terms. We examine later, in chapter 6, just how significant the permanent American post on the Columbia became in diplomatic arguments between England and the United States over who held the Discovery claim to this area. President Jefferson was delighted with Astoria. He came to believe that the entire American claim to the lands west of the Rockies rested on "Astor's settlement near the mouth of the Columbia." Astor's efforts fit perfectly into the President's Doctrine of Discovery goal to acquire the Pacific Northwest for the United States.[40]

EX-PRESIDENT JEFFERSON

Thomas Jefferson retired to his Monticello home in 1809. He continued to comment on the American political scene for the 17 years after he left the presidency until his death in 1826. He also continued to rely on the elements of Discovery and to be very interested in Astoria and its importance in the expansion of the United States and American Discovery claims to the Pacific Northwest.

In May 1812, Jefferson clearly stated that the Pacific Northwest was already United States territory in a letter to John Jacob Astor about Astoria. Jefferson stated that Astoria was "a great public acquisition [and] the commencement of a settlement on that point of the Western coast of America." In fact, he "looked forward with gratification to the time when [America's] descendants should have spread themselves through the whole length of that coast, covering it with free and independent Americans." Jefferson was concerned that Congress had not passed legislation to tax British goods being sold to Indians in the Northwest, an area that Jefferson called "our country." He also wanted Congress to support "so interesting an object as that of planting the germ of an American population on the shores of the Pacific."[41]

By 1813, Jefferson was getting even more excited about Astoria: "I view it as the germ of a great, free, and independent empire on that side of our continent, and that liberty and self-government, spreading from that as well as this side, will insure their complete establishment over the whole." Jefferson thus saw the Discovery element of contiguity as demanding, and the magnet of Astoria as pulling, American expansion toward the Pacific Northwest.[42]

By 1816, Jefferson was positively ecstatic about Astoria and its significance to an American Discovery claim to the Northwest. He wrote, "If we claim [the Pacific Northwest], it must be on Astor's settlement near the mouth of the Columbia, and the principle of the *jus gentium* [international law] of America that when a civilized nation takes possession of the mouth of a river in new country, that possession is considered as including all its waters." Here we see Jefferson again using the Discovery elements of international law, first discovery, actual occupancy and current possession, the contiguity principle of finding new rivers, and the rights of "civilized countries" over the lands of indigenous people.[43]

Thomas Jefferson's own words and actions over a 60-year time span demonstrate beyond doubt that he understood and operated by the legal principles and elements of Discovery and preemption in dealing with Indian Nations and in working to expand the territory and power of first Virginia and then the United States. It is clear from the foregoing evidence that Jefferson knew and utilized this international law Doctrine throughout his entire legal and political careers.

CHAPTER 4

~

Thomas Jefferson, Manifest Destiny, and the Indian Nations

Thomas Jefferson looks to us today to have been a kind and gentle man of books and letters, a man of the Enlightenment Era primarily interested in science, politics, history, and literature. He also appears to have had enlightened and progressive views on Indian people, tribal governments, and Indian property rights. Yet he was also one of the most aggressive and strategically expansionist presidents who ever held the office. Jefferson was eager to expand America's borders, power, and influence, and he utilized every strategy he could devise to promote those aims. He knew, as did almost every other American of his time, that American territorial expansion could only come at the expense of Indian Nations and tribal property rights. The apparent contradiction or dichotomy between his stated views on Indians and his actual conduct undermines the viewpoint of Jefferson as a man of peace and benevolence and as the author of that famous line from the Declaration of Independence, "All men are created equal." His actual conduct informs our understanding today of his real views of Indians, their governments, and their legal and natural rights.

There is no confusion about the fact that Thomas Jefferson was an ardent expansionist. His words and conduct during his entire political career demonstrated a strong desire to expand the borders of the United States. Although Jefferson never used the words "Manifest Destiny," there is no question that he fully supported the idea that it was America's destiny to overspread and control the North American continent from coast to coast and even beyond. We see in his own words and actions that he worked diligently and often in a Machiavellian way to promote American expansion.

On a personal level, Jefferson held an almost idealized or romantic view of Indians and their governments. He spent a significant amount of time studying Indians during his lifetime and planned on spending a major part of his retirement studying Indian languages and the question of the origination of Indians. Here we examine this work and his views that Indians were the equal of white Americans and that they possessed the best forms of government in the world. Jefferson said that he wanted this race of people to be assimilated and incorporated into American society and life, and he even wrote that Indian and white blood would mix together. That was surely an enlightened view in the early 1800s.

Jefferson's actual plans, though, for Indians, the Indian Nations, and their property rights and his real life actions in carrying out these strategies stand in stark contrast to his idealistic words. There is such a chasm between what he said about Indians and what he did to them that we can hardly fathom this contradiction today. The ultimate problem was that the Indian Nations stood squarely in the way of his expansionist dreams for America. Jefferson knew this, and he did not hesitate to do something about it. We will see that as early as 1802–1803, he was developing and planning a policy for Indian removal. Removal was the idea that all the eastern Indian Nations had to move west of the Mississippi River to make room for the inevitable expansion of the United States and the American people. The federal policy of removal is most often blamed on President Andrew Jackson in the 1830s. We have already seen that George Washington first visualized this idea—that Indians would just disappear as an obstacle to American expansion—and called it the "Savage as Wolf." We see in this chapter that Jefferson was actually the first person to formulate an official federal policy of removal, the first to set it in motion, and the first to start removing tribes west of the Mississippi. We will also see that Jefferson called for the extermination of any Indians or tribes that dared to oppose his expansionist policies and dared to defend their homelands and cultures from being overrun by the United States. So much for the kind and gentle man of the Enlightenment!

Finally, in this discussion we briefly dabble in amateur psychoanalysis and consider Jefferson's motivations and objectives in light of the extreme contradiction between his idealistic views of Indians and his dictatorial, strong armed tactics in destroying their cultures and lives and moving them out of the way of American expansion. Was he a hypocrite or a liar, or was he just being a "politician" in the worst meaning of the word (saying one thing to satisfy or fool certain groups while really planning to do another)? Was he just appeasing American consciences in claiming to work toward assimilation and the best interests of Indians, or did he perhaps really delude himself that he was acting consistently with his stated views?

JEFFERSON'S VISION OF AMERICAN MANIFEST DESTINY

Thomas Jefferson was an aggressive expansionist and worked to increase the limits of American territory throughout his entire political career. Although the phrase "Manifest Destiny" was apparently unknown to Jefferson, he worked for and believed in the idea that the future expansion of American territory was guaranteed. For example, he stated in his first inaugural address in 1801 that America was a "rising nation ... advancing rapidly to destinies beyond the reach of mortal eye." He became so identified by his work to create an American empire that various historians have said that his "imperial aspirations ... were ambitious" and that he "was determined to make the United States an imperial contender." Jefferson has also been called "perhaps the greatest expansionist" of all the Founding Fathers and "a fervent advocate of American expansion." Joseph Ellis stated, "For Jefferson more than any other major figure in the revolutionary generation, the West was America's future."[1]

Some historians, however, have read Jefferson's words on expansion to mean that he was not interested in the United States getting larger but that he really just desired the growth of American-style democracy into other countries and regions. Jefferson did express sentiments that can be interpreted this way. He said that he wanted to see an "Empire of Liberty" expand across the North and South American continents. That of course does not mean the "empire of liberty" had to be just within the U.S. borders or extended by the U.S. government. In 1801, for example, Jefferson wrote James Madison that he expected the United States or at least the descendants and governmental structures of the original thirteen states to spread over the entire North and South American continents. "However our present interests may restrain us within our own limits, it is impossible not to look forward to distant times, when our rapid multiplication will expand itself beyond those limits, and cover the whole northern, if not the southern continent, with a people speaking the same language, governed in similar forms, and by similar laws." Furthermore, in 1804, in discussing the Louisiana Purchase, Jefferson wrote about America's expansion across the Mississippi River and whether the east and the west sides could remain one nation in this great expanse of territory. "Whether we remain in one confederacy, or form into Atlantic and Mississippi confederacies, I believe not very important to the happiness of either part. Those of the western confederacy will be as much our children and descendants as those of the eastern, and I feel myself as much identified with that country, in future time, as with this." Finally, in 1813, Jefferson wrote John Jacob Astor about Astoria, the American outpost on the Pacific Ocean, "I view it as the germ of a great, free, and independent empire on that side of our continent, and that liberty and self-government, spreading from that as well as this side, will insure their complete establishment over the whole."[2]

I agree that a conservative interpretation of these statements can make it sound like Jefferson was not so interested in the expansion of the United States per se but just in an altruistic objective of seeing human freedom and liberty and the benefits of American democracy spread far and wide. But I do not read Jefferson as being either that meek or that altruistic. We address the subject of his actual motivations and objectives more closely in the concluding part of this chapter, but I think the facts show that Jefferson was aggressively planning and acting to dramatically increase the landmass of the United States. I think his moderate statements that America's sons and daughters would people these new democracies in North and South America, if they spun off from the original thirteen states, were either smoke screens to hide his real intentions—political "spin" if you will—or just fall-back positions, an example of Jefferson being careful in expressing out loud his actual agenda. In reality, Jefferson's other statements and his actual conduct demonstrate that he wanted America's territorial borders to be enlarged and that he worked aggressively to reach that goal.

In contrast with the meek and unambitious Jefferson, there is an enormous amount of evidence of an aggressive, expansionist Jefferson. In 1809 he wrote President James Madison about the U.S. Constitution: "no constitution was ever before so well calculated as ours for extensive empire." Even as early as 1786, Jefferson saw the thirteen states as the seed for populating North and South America. "Our confederacy must be viewed as the nest, from which all America, North and South, is to be peopled." That was a very aggressive opinion given that indigenous peoples and various Spanish colonies already inhabited much of the area Jefferson was talking about.[3]

Jefferson continued his theme of U.S. expansion in his first inaugural address on March 4, 1801, because, as already quoted, he saw proof of god's will and the inevitability of America's growth in this "rising nation" that was "advancing rapidly to destinies beyond the reach of mortal eye." He also raised the idea of divine inspiration because he was already looking beyond the frontier settlements toward the west as America's future because he thought that America "possess[ed] a chosen country, with room enough for our descendants to the thousandth and thousandth generation ... [and] an overruling Providence [that] ... delights in the happiness of man." And, by 1812, Jefferson "looked forward with gratification to the time when" the entire Pacific Coast would be populated "with free and independent Americans."[4]

Jefferson did more than just talk about American expansion. He worked vigorously to acquire the territory of North America for the United States. For example, in 1802, his administration signed a compact with Georgia to remove the Cherokee Nation from the state as soon as possible. This agreement was reached despite federal treaties with the Cherokee guaranteeing them their lands. Jefferson obviously planned on terminating the Indian title and handing Cherokee lands to Georgia as soon as he could.

Moreover, in 1803, President Jefferson dispatched the Lewis and Clark expedition. The expedition is an excellent example of the president's Manifest Destiny goal to extend America's borders across the continent. In fact, Jefferson had attempted three other times to send expeditions to the Pacific Northwest. He well understood the geopolitical and commercial value of the land and assets in the Northwest. But he was also anxious to explore this area to establish an American presence for Discovery purposes as well. He was, after all, the Secretary of State in 1792 when Robert Gray found the mouth of the Columbia River. Jefferson understood the commercial and political potential of a route across the continent and the value of controlling the very lucrative fur trade. The Lewis and Clark expedition demonstrated Jefferson's desire to have the United States cross the continent and gain control of the Louisiana Territory and dominate the trade and political interactions with the Indian Nations in the territory. The expedition was also targeted at the mouth of the Columbia River—the very spot that Gray had discovered in 1792. This demonstrated that Jefferson also had his sights set on the unclaimed Pacific Northwest and the goal that the United States could possess that region if it could perfect its 1792 first discovery claim. The Lewis and Clark expedition was a crucial part of those Jeffersonian goals and was the physical manifestation of Jefferson's ambitions for a continental American empire.[5]

If it is incorrect to say that Jefferson was thinking of America expanding across the continent, what was his motivation in sending Meriwether Lewis to the mouth of the Columbia River on the Pacific Ocean? Is it not too much of a coincidence that Jefferson sent Lewis and Clark to the identical spot where Robert Gray first discovered the Columbia River? We will discuss the expedition and Discovery in detail in the next chapter. For now, suffice it to say that Jefferson had the ambition to gain more territory for the United States when he aimed Lewis and Clark at the Northwest.

Just after Meriwether Lewis headed for the Pacific Northwest in June 1803, the news arrived in Washington, DC, that France had agreed to sell the Louisiana Territory to the United States. This act doubled the size of the United States. Jefferson gained congressional approval for the Louisiana Purchase even though he thought he had violated the Constitution because he did not believe it provided authority for the federal government to increase American territory. He personally drafted and proposed to his Cabinet a constitutional amendment to give the government the authority to buy the Louisiana Territory. His Cabinet prevailed on him to keep his amendment and his doubts about federal authority quiet. Ultimately, he abandoned his constitutional scruples and his usual strict construction of the Constitution and pushed the Louisiana Purchase Treaty through the Congress even though he wrote that he had "done an act beyond the Constitution."[6]

Long before the Louisiana Purchase, Jefferson demonstrated his intent that it was the destiny of the United States to possess the Louisiana Territory and to expand westward to the Oregon country. He was happy in fact to allow the territory to stay in the possession and control of Spain until the United States was ready to take the area. As early as 1786, he wrote about the territory and its future American ownership: "We should ... not ... press too soon on the Spaniards. [The Louisiana Territory] cannot be in better hands. My fear is that [the Spanish] are too feeble to hold them till our population can be sufficiently advanced to gain it from them piece by piece. The navigation of the Mississippi we must have." Jefferson historian Joseph Ellis wrote that this strategy "conveniently bided time for the inevitable American sweep across the continent."[7]

Just as Jefferson feared, Spain did not hold onto Louisiana until the United States was ready to take it. In a secret treaty in 1800, Spain ceded Louisiana to France and Napoleon. Jefferson did not hear of that agreement until probably May of 1801 and did not know of it for certain until well into 1802. The sale to France was a disaster for the United States. Jefferson was furious. He feared, correctly, that Napoleon would send troops to occupy the territory and block U.S. expansion westward. In fact, Napoleon did send a 10,000-man contingent to Louisiana, but they were sent first to Santo Domingo to quell a slave revolt.

None of the French troops survived that island. In the interim, Jefferson was so worried by the French possession of Louisiana that he talked of an alliance with England, and some historians allege he even purposely leaked a private letter to French officials that French possession of Louisiana would lead to war between the United States and France. Jefferson wrote in 1803 that Louisiana was the one spot on the globe that whatever country possessed it was the enemy of the United States This had been tolerable while feeble Spain held Louisiana, but it was not acceptable when aggressive and strong France held it. So much for the image of a meek, antiexpansionist Jefferson.[8]

Once these potential problems disappeared with the American purchase of the territory, Jefferson began vigorously arguing about the boundaries of Louisiana with Spain. He argued for a broad reading of the limits of the territory in his 1804 paper called "The Limits and Bounds of Louisiana." In the last chapter we considered this pamphlet and its extensive use of Discovery elements. Here, we are only interested in the document's evidence of Jefferson's views on American Manifest Destiny and territorial claims. In this paper, Jefferson put forward the factual evidence that supported his claim that Louisiana included parts of present-day Texas and Florida. We also observed in the last chapter how Jefferson vaguely claimed that Louisiana even included part of the Pacific Northwest. Some members of the House of Representatives agreed with this idea. In an 1804 House Report, which several historians think Jefferson had a hand in, the Committee of Commerce and Manufactures reported that it believed the Louisiana Territory "to include all the country which lies to the westward between that river [the Mississippi] and the great chain of mountains [the Rockies] … and beyond that chain between the territories claimed by Great Britain on the one side, and by Spain on the other, quite to the South Sea." Consequently, besides parts of Texas and Florida, many persons, perhaps Jefferson included, believed as early as 1804 that the Louisiana Territory included part of the Pacific Northwest. Several historians allege that certainly no later than 1808, Jefferson believed that was so. Donald Jackson, a Lewis and Clark and Jeffersonian historian, also argues that negotiations the Jefferson administration held in 1808 with England on the Canadian–U.S. border in the Midwest demonstrated an American claim that the Louisiana Purchase included land on the Pacific coast.[9]

Notwithstanding President Jefferson's views on the boundaries of Louisiana, there is ample evidence that he was actively working to expand America's western border to the Pacific Ocean. In 1806, Jefferson told a senator at a White House dinner that he hoped an American merchant would go to the Columbia River and engage in the fur trade. Plainly, he was thinking of solidifying America's first discovery claim to the Columbia region by permanently occupying it and thereby making the area part of the United States. Jefferson was also no doubt thinking of Meriwether Lewis's recent September 1806 letter in which Lewis wrote the president that the United States would "derive the benefits of a most lucrative trade" if it could build a fur trading post on the Columbia. Lewis also told a congressman in 1806 that the establishment of a trading post at the mouth of the Columbia would be the most important result of his expedition. Jefferson must have agreed with Lewis. He more than anyone realized the significance of such a venture to Discovery, Manifest Destiny, and American expansion. Therefore, Jefferson encouraged John Jacob Astor in 1808 to build a trading post on the Columbia and told Astor, "All beyond the Mississippi is ours exclusively." In 1812 he wrote Astor that the Pacific Northwest was "the Western coast of America" and "our country." By 1816, Jefferson sounded convinced that the trading post Astor had built on the Columbia in 1811 had established the United States' Discovery claim and ownership of the Pacific Northwest because he wrote that the U.S. "claim [to the Northwest] must be on Astor's settlement near the mouth of the Columbia."[10]

Jefferson no doubt dreamed of an American Empire of Liberty that would spread due to the persuasive appeal of democracy. But he was also interested in expanding American territory by military force. During the War of 1812, the ex-president made even more widely known his aggressive expansionist views. He wrote several times that he hoped the United States could gain Cuba and East Florida in the war. He also wrote Secretary of State James Monroe in 1813, encouraging a U.S. invasion of Canada. Moreover, by 1817, he wanted Texas. Jefferson was not alone in these dreams of expansion. Many other politicians and citizens were just as ambitious. The War of 1812 was partially motivated in fact by American dreams of territorial expansions in the west, north, and south. One historian has stated that the War of 1812 was "the first general appearance of the idea which later received the name of 'Manifest Destiny.' Although enthusiasts like Jefferson had dreamed years before of a nation destined to embrace the continent."[11]

Thomas Jefferson and American Manifest Destiny. It is certainly correct to link that person with that idea. Jefferson's vision for America was as large as the North American continent, and he took active and aggressive steps to make his vision come true. Some readers, however, might remember vague statements Jefferson made about the need to keep the American republic small to succeed as a unified nation. But that grandiose dreamer, the expansionist Jefferson, certainly thought differently about that subject by 1817, if he ever really thought that the United States had to remain small. In that year he wrote, "we shall proceed successfully for ages to come; and that, contrary to the principles of Montesquieu [who believed republics had to stay small to succeed], it will be seen that the larger the content of country, the more from it's republican structure, if founded, not on conquest, but [on] principles of compact & equality, my hope of it's duration is built much on the enlargement of these resources of life going hand in hand with the enlargement of territory." Some historians think that Jefferson never believed in a need to keep the United States small but that he made those statements to placate his opponents and to justify the Louisiana Purchase. By 1817, Jefferson was publicly arguing that the larger the country was, the safer the democratic republic would be. Bigger was better. A larger country and a large population would reduce, he said, regional differences and the risk that such squabbles could fracture the country. This exact argument was used to support Manifest Destiny in later years.[12]

Historians have recognized Jefferson's ambitions for an American empire. Reginald Horsman connected Jefferson's aggressive actions with the later-named policy of Manifest Destiny. "The sense of 'Manifest Destiny,' of moralistic expansion, is plainly evident in Jefferson's Indian policy." Jefferson biographer Merrill Peterson agreed and stated that Jefferson had a vision of an "expanding continental empire … as the Americans took possession of a nearly vacant continent. There were, in fact, almost no limits to his dreams of expansion." And, finally, Professor James Ronda stated that Jefferson's vision "made empire not only possible but somehow almost predetermined."[13]

Who would have thought it: scholarly, educated, man of the Enlightenment, President Thomas Jefferson—an aggressive empire builder, the first emperor of the American Empire? This leaves us with a question, however: where did Jefferson think American Indians and their governments and their political, human, and property rights would fit into this continental wide American empire?

JEFFERSON'S IDEALISTIC VISION OF INDIANS

Jefferson had a significant amount of experience with Indian people, cultures, and governments. Most of his public writings on these topics sound very enlightened for his time, and they seem positive and hopeful for the future of Indians in America. We will try to understand his enlightened viewpoint in comparison with his aggressive stance on American expansion. We also look closely in the next section at his actions and his private words in regard to Indians and the Indian Nations.

Jefferson grew up in an era when Indian Nations were feared opponents. He was very aware of the French and Indian War in 1754–1763 when he was 11 to 20 years of age. He was also exposed to other armed conflicts between colonists and Indians during his life. Yet he was able to maintain what looks like a very admirable interest in and opinion of Indians and the tribal nations despite the often-adversarial relationship of the Indian Nations and the thirteen colonies/states.

In 1762 Jefferson heard a speech by an Indian chief who was on his way to London. Jefferson was quite taken with his eloquence and message. He also wrote about groups of Indians who returned to his local area to visit the graves of their ancestors, as Jefferson surmised. Perhaps these events started his lifelong academic interest in Indians. For example, he very methodically excavated an Indian burial mound near his home. He was also very interested his entire life in the question of where Indians had come from. He and John Adams exchanged letters in their old age on this subject in 1823. Jefferson thought he could answer this question by studying tribal languages. He had thus gathered vocabulary lists of common words from each tribe that he could. By 1805, he said that he had long studied Indian languages and thought he had vocabulary lists from all the Indian Nations east of the Mississippi. One of the duties he gave Meriwether Lewis was to gather these vocabularies from every tribe he encountered on his expedition. Jefferson had about fifty of these lists by 1809. He had already done some work tabulating and comparing the lists when he retired from the White House, and he hoped to spend a significant amount of time studying these languages during his retirement and to publish his findings. Regrettably, a trunk with his life's work on this subject and all his vocabulary lists was stolen when Jefferson was moving home to Monticello.[14]

We have already seen the vast experience and knowledge Jefferson had gained about Indians, the tribal nations, and their land rights and so on while he was an attorney and politician. He was also quite knowledgeable about tribes he had not yet even encountered. When he dispatched Meriwether Lewis, for example, he sent along a metal corn grinder as a gift for the Mandan Nation because he was well aware of that nation's extensive agricultural pursuits. He also instructed Lewis in general about how to deal with Indians, and he specifically understood the importance of the Teton Sioux and directed Lewis to make them the friends of the United States. Moreover, while he was president, Jefferson met with many visiting groups of tribal leaders. He also requested that Lewis arrange for chiefs to visit Jefferson in Washington, DC. Jefferson gave speeches to these visitors and sent a few letters to tribal leaders and called them his brothers and children. In these speeches to tribes from the Louisiana Territory, Jefferson delivered the message that the French and the Spanish had left and that now the United States was their neighbor and friend. In 1804 and 1806 Jefferson told Osage chiefs, "We hope you will have no cause to regret the change." He told them that they were now one family and that Indians had things Americans wanted and Americans had items Indians wanted. Jefferson said, "We take you by your hand and I become your father." All the United States wanted, apparently, was the friendship and the commerce of the Indians.[15]

Jefferson also made several strong statements about his understanding of the humanity of Indian people. In contrast to his belief that American slaves were inferior to whites, Jefferson wrote "I believe the Indian, then, to be, in body and mind, equal to the white man." Once he qualified this statement and said they were the equal of whites in an uncultivated state. In his one book, *Notes on the State of Virginia,* he defended Indians against the charge of a European writer that America produced only weak people. Jefferson also apparently admired tribal governments. He proclaimed that Indians had the best form of government: none. This shows that his knowledge was imperfect because no group of people can live together and manage their affairs and keep order on a national and international level without governing organizations and procedures. Indian people in Jefferson's era had their own governmental structures and organizations.[16]

Jefferson also wrote and spoke of his expectation that American Indians would assimilate into American society and would become civilized, educated, and just like white citizens. He wrote to an American agent working with southern tribes in 1803 that the best outcome for Indians would be "to let our settlements and theirs meet and blend together, to intermix, and become one people. Incorporating themselves with us as citizens of the United States, this is what the natural progress of things will, of course, bring on, and it will be better to promote than to retard it. Surely it will be better for them to be identified with us, and preserved in the occupation of their lands." In an 1807 letter, President Jefferson wrote that the United States wanted to help Indians to ameliorate their poor conditions. "They are our brethren, our neighbors; they may be valuable friends, and troublesome enemies. Both duty & interest then enjoin, that we should extend to them the blessings of civilized life, & prepare their minds for becoming useful members of the American family." Apparently, he hoped that Indians would become like his beloved hardworking "yeoman farmers," tilling a small patch of land to support their families. This shows another gap, either intentional or accidental, in Jefferson's knowledge because most of the Indian groups in the eastern part of North America, and in many other parts, were already in essence "yeoman farmers" when Europeans arrived on this continent. Most American Indian Nations supported themselves by agriculture before they were ever exposed to European or American methods of farming.[17]

One of Jefferson's most surprising statements was his expectation that the assimilation of American Indians into American society would lead to the mixing of red and white blood—something that he did not approve of for black and white Americans. In his era, that was a bold and forward-looking idea. One has to wonder if he really meant these statements. Apparently, although Jefferson hoped Indians would survive, he thought that could happen only if they became American citizens and lost their tribal cultures, religions, economies, and ways of life.

JEFFERSON'S ACTUAL CONDUCT TOWARD INDIANS

Jefferson's actions regarding Indian people and governments contradicted his gentle and enlightened words. He greedily pursued his goal of acquiring all the Indian lands he could for the United States, and as fast as he could. He developed and pushed programs for removing Indians west of the Mississippi to get them out of the way of the advancing American state and society and in violation of his own stated goals to civilize, educate, and assimilate Indians into white society.

Acquiring Tribal Lands

The one thing Thomas Jefferson really wanted from Indian people was their land. There was no ambiguity in his actions and in most of his words about his greed for Indian land. Professor James Ronda stated that Jefferson made the acquiring of tribal lands "the central feature of federal Indian policy." He used every tactic he could to force tribal land sales.[18]

Under the Doctrine of Discovery and Jefferson's understanding, the only way for the United States to gain Indian lands was to buy the Indian title of occupancy and use with tribal consent. Consequently, he went about getting that "consent" in any way he could. Jefferson always reminded tribal leaders that the United States was ready to buy land whenever they were ready to sell, and he tried every ploy possible to encourage that consent. He used devious and coercive methods to encourage tribal leaders to sell land. He advocated bribing Indian political leaders; he directed executive branch employees to get tribal leaders into debt so that they would sell tribal lands to cover their personal debts; and he grabbed lands out from under tribes whenever they were available and by whatever means possible.

First, Jefferson understood the value of and often utilized the well-placed "gift" or bribe to make tribal leaders more comfortable with selling tribal lands. When he was Secretary of State in 1791, he wrote that the "most economical as well as most humane conduct towards them is to bribe them into peace, and to retain Them in peace by eternal bribes." Looking at the issue pragmatically, Jefferson stated that the military expeditions conducted against some tribes in 1790–1791 alone would have paid for presents for the tribes for the next one hundred years. During his presidency he inquired whether a Shawnee spiritual leader called the Prophet had been bribed yet or could be bribed. He also made a vague reference to whether the Prophet might be killed to stop his resistance to American expansion. In 1802 President Jefferson also directed, regarding some tribes who might be ready to sell lands, that the United States "should press again the good will of these tribes by friendly acts, and of their chiefs by largesses." Jefferson wrote that it was often easy to solicit chiefs into land sales by giving presents.[19]

Second, Jefferson was very crafty in his use of the federal "factories" or trading posts. The federal factory system was created at President Washington's suggestion in 1795 and was to be a chain of governmental trading stores across the frontier. Ultimately, 28 factories operated on the Indian frontier until the program was terminated in 1822. Washington proposed this idea to bind Indians to the United States in commerce and friendship and to keep the trade fair to avoid the friction and problems that often arose when private traders dealt with Indians and cheated them and traded alcohol and firearms.

Jefferson, however, had an entirely different take on the value of the federal factories from Washington's original idea. Jefferson increased their number and deviously and purposely used the extension of credit to get tribal leaders into debt so that they would be inclined to consent to land sales to the United States. Jefferson stated this "policy" so clearly that there is no question about his objective and his nefarious strategy for gaining "tribal consent" to land sales.

Jefferson apparently first developed this strategy in 1802 while studying the boundaries of the Indian Nations. In his private notes, Jefferson suggested that the United States should "establish among [the tribes] a factory or factories for furnishing them with all the necessaries and comforts they may wish … encouraging these and especially their leading men, to run in debt for these beyond their individual means of paying; and whenever in that situation, they will always cede lands to rid themselves of debt." In February 1803, Jefferson started to put this strategy into place. At that time, he wrote to Indiana Territory Governor William Henry Harrison, "we shall push our trading houses, and be glad to see the good and influential individuals among them run in debt, because we observe that when these debts get beyond what the individuals can pay, they become willing to lop them off by a cession of lands." Also, in November 1806, Jefferson told a prospective manager of a federal trading post in Cherokee country that getting

Indians into debt "is the way I intend to git there countrey for to git them to run in debt to the publick store and they will have to give there lands for payment."[20]

Jefferson's debt-for-land strategy was on display again in February 1803 when he exchanged very illuminating private letters with General Andrew Jackson and the U.S. Indian agent to the southeastern tribes, Colonel Hawkins. Jackson had written Jefferson because he and others were concerned that Hawkins was too friendly with Indians and was not pushing them hard enough for land sales. Jefferson answered and explained his strategy: "In keeping agents among the Indians, two objects are principally in view: 1. The preservation of peace; 2. The obtaining lands." Jefferson's idea, as he wrote Jackson, was to turn Indians to agriculture and teach them that they could give up their vast hunting grounds and live on small farming plots. They would then need to sell tribal lands to get farming implements and to get "clothes and comforts from our trading houses." He told Jackson that the United States and its agents needed to be cautious and move slowly to obtain land and to acquire influence with the tribes since his strategy rested on gaining the confidence of the Indians. But Jefferson promised Jackson that he was going to put Colonel Hawkins under "strong pressure from the executive to obtain cessions." Jefferson stated that the value of an Indian agent was not based on what they did for Indians but was to be "estimated by us in proportion to the benefits he can obtain for us." Jefferson said he was "alive to the obtaining lands from the Indians by all honest and peaceable means, and I believe that the honest and peaceable means adopted by us will obtain them as fast as the expansion of our settlements ... will require." Jefferson was certainly not bashful or reticent to state to Jackson his views on obtaining Indian lands or that he agreed with George Washington's "Savage as Wolf" policy that Indians would have to retreat before the inevitable American expansion.[21]

In another private letter two days later, Jefferson wrote the Indian agent and told Hawkins that the only way to save Indians was to teach them agriculture and how to live on smaller tracts of land. In an ironic and self-serving statement, Jefferson said, "While they are learning to do better on less land, our increasing numbers will be calling for more land, and thus a coincidence of interests will be produced between those who have lands to spare, and want other necessaries, and those who have such necessaries to spare, and want lands." What a surprising and amazing coincidence Jefferson had stumbled upon! Just when the United States found it needed more land, the Indian Nations would realize that it was also in their best interests to sell more land! Could Jefferson really have believed what he wrote?[22]

He then put pressure on Hawkins and told him it was his duty and the best for all involved to acquire as much Indian land as fast as possible. "This commerce, then, will be for the good of both, and those who are friends to both ought to encourage it. You are in the station peculiarly charged with this interchange, and who have it peculiarly in your power to promote among the Indians a sense of the superior value of a little land, well cultivated, over a great deal, unimproved, and to encourage them to make this estimate truly." Jefferson told Hawkins that people were doubting his loyalty and whether he was diligently pursuing obtaining tribal lands. But Jefferson told him, "I have little doubt but that your reflections must have led you to view the various ways in which their history may terminate, and to see that this is the one most for their happiness.... I feel it consistent with pure morality to ... familiarize them to the idea that it is for their interest to cede lands at times to the United States, and for us thus to procure gratifications to our citizens, from time to time, by new acquisitions of land." Obviously, Jefferson thought that it was best for Indians to sell their land when Americans wanted it because it was the best way "in which their history may terminate." It was, of course, also best for the United States to be allowed to buy Indian lands whenever it desired and "to procure gratifications to [U.S.] citizens."[23]

The federal government complied with these presidential directives and carried out Jefferson's policies to acquire Indian lands. And Jefferson led the way. In 1803 he personally told Choctaw tribal leaders that "we will buy your lands when you wish ... if you want to sell land for the debts you owe to merchants." In several treaties with Indian Nations, the Jefferson administration demonstrated the viability and effectiveness of his debt-for-land strategy. On June 16, 1802, the Creek Nation sold land to the United States, and the treaty recorded that it was "to satisfy certain debts due from Indians and white persons of the Creek country to the factory of the United States." In August 1804, the Delaware Nation sold land because, as the treaty said, the tribe needed to buy goods for its comfort and convenience and to introduce the civilized arts to its people. In July 1805, the Chickasaw Nation, according to the treaty, was embarrassed by debts due to merchants and traders and sold land and allowed the payments to go directly to the merchants to pay their debts. Finally, in 1805 and 1808, the Choctaw Nation sold land to the United States to pay debts its citizens owed to merchants and traders. It is apparent that the representatives of the United States obeyed the orders of Thomas Jefferson to get Indian Nations to sell their land. Jefferson used all the tools at hand, including federal treaty negotiators, territorial governors, and Indian agents, to encourage and coerce tribes to sell lands.[24]

A third manner in which Jefferson demonstrated his eagerness to get tribal lands was that he was very concerned about the ownership and occupancy of land by tribes who were decimated by disease and dwindling in numbers. He demonstrated his accurate understanding of Discovery principles in this situation when he wrote about the Cahokia Nation and stated that "we have a right to their lands in preference to any Indian tribe, in virtue of our permanent sovereignty over it." Jefferson was interested in protecting the U.S. Discovery rights of preemption and limited sovereignty over these lands as they were becoming unoccupied. He argued that when an Indian Nation became nearly extinct and was no longer occupying or using its lands, the United States should exercise its right and take possession of the territory. He was very concerned that other tribes would claim recently vacated lands, and he wanted to prevent that possibility.[25]

Jefferson also took advantage of opportunities to buy the lands of tribes who were greatly reduced in numbers. He told Governor William Henry Harrison to "claim" the land of "the Piorias [because they] have all been driven off from their country" and to conclude a treaty with the Kaskaskia Nation when it had been "reduced to a few families." Harrison followed his orders and the treaty of 1803 with the Kaskaskia was specifically agreed to because the tribe was greatly reduced in population. In that treaty, the United States bought all the tribe's land and took the tribe under its protection.[26]

Jefferson also planned for the future. In his viewpoint, Indian populations would continue to decline. Thus, in 1802, in private notes he made on the Indian Nations, he identified other tribal lands that were "not so necessary to get now," but he still ordered that the United States "inquire into titles and claim any what ever might be abandoned or lost by natives before another tribe claims." Jefferson was obviously an opportunist and a bargain hunter and was very eager when it came to acquiring Indian lands.[27]

Removal

Thomas Jefferson was the architect of the removal policy of federal Indian affairs. Removal forcibly moved most of the eastern Indian Nations west of the Mississippi River and confiscated their lands in the east for the United States. Ironically, Andrew Jackson is blamed for the Removal Era because Congress passed the Removal Act in 1830, and Jackson carried out most of the forced physical removals thereafter. But it was Jefferson who first devised this relocation program. He favored this strategy because it made more Indian lands available for purchase by the United States and then for purchase and settlement by American citizens. He tried to justify his policy by claiming it was in the best interests of Indian Nations to put some space between themselves and the land-hungry Americans.

Jefferson first raised the idea of Indian removal in 1776 and 1779 when he called for the Cherokee and Shawnee Nations to be physically driven west of the Mississippi. His first efforts as president to promote a removal policy came in 1802 when his administration made an agreement with Georgia to remove the Cherokee Nation from Georgia if the state would surrender its legal Discovery claim to the western lands. Georgia surrendered its western claim, and the Jefferson administration committed itself to removing the Cherokee Nation from Georgia as rapidly as possible even though the nation had a treaty with the United States that guaranteed it possession of its lands.

Jefferson began expressly raising the idea of removal in private letters in 1803. Of course, he did not want Indians to hear of his ultimate plans for them. In February, he wrote Indiana Territory Governor William Henry Harrison that the American settlements "will gradually circumscribe and approach the Indians, and they will in time either incorporate with us as citizens of the United States, or remove beyond the Mississippi." He also wrote Governor Claiborne in May of 1803 that the United States could tempt Indians to move west of the Mississippi by "tak[ing] by the hand those of them who have emigrated from ours to the other side of the Mississippi, to furnish them generously with arms, ammunition, and other essentials, with a view to render a situation there desirable to those they have left behind ... and thus prepare in time an eligible retreat for the whole." Finally, in July 1803, Jefferson wrote General Gates about the Louisiana Purchase, noting that it might become "the means of tempting all our Indians on the east side of the Mississippi to remove to the west." It seems quite amazing that in 1802, and in February and May of 1803, Jefferson was discussing the possibility of removing all the eastern Indian tribes west of the Mississippi into the Louisiana Territory when this region was still in Spanish and French hands. In addition, other Indian Nations already occupied and owned the land in that territory where Jefferson proposed to move eastern tribes.[28]

After the Louisiana Purchase, the territory became a more viable place to relocate the eastern tribes. Jefferson wrote in August 1803 that "the best use we can make of [Louisiana] for some time, will be to give establishments in it to the Indians on the East side of the Mississippi, in exchange for their present country ... and thus make this acquisition the means of filling up the eastern side.... When we shall be full on this side, we may lay off a range of States on the western bank ... advancing compactly as we multiply." There are two interesting points addressed here. First, Jefferson was proposing trading the eastern tribes land in Louisiana for their lands east of the Mississippi. But notice that even those lands were only to be temporary tribal holdings. As America's population increased, Jefferson fully expected to lay out states in the Louisiana Territory and fill them with Americans. The Indian people who moved to the Louisiana Territory, if any survived, would be relocated again. Plainly, Jefferson was planning by 1803 for the United States to expand westward beyond the Mississippi.[29]

Jefferson's ultimate thinking on removal and any Indians or tribal nations who resisted peaceful removal was explained to John Adams in 1812. Jefferson said that to deal with such "backward" tribes, the United States "shall be obliged to drive them, with the beasts of the forest into the Stony mountains." Thus, Jefferson had the same vision for the future of Indians as George Washington's "Savage as Wolf" policy. Indian people would just fade away or would be driven away by the inevitable expansion of the United States and its population.[30]

Assimilation

In Jefferson's idealized view of Indians, the words "assimilation," "education," and "civilization" carried the benevolent connotation of absorbing them into the American society. But in reality, Jefferson did nothing to make this eventuality occur. In fact, as we have seen, his actual tactics of taking tribal lands and removing tribes west of the Mississippi produced the exact opposite outcome. He actually resisted any real assimilation by Indians. The form of "assimilation" that Jefferson was really interested in imposing on Indians was to transform their entire way of life by encouraging them to sell their lands to the United States and to bend them to America's desires. Jefferson wanted tribal nations to sell their vast landholdings to the United States and for Indian people to farm small pieces of land. Do not forget that his real goal was obtaining Indian lands for the United States Also do not forget that Jefferson stated in 1803 that assimilation for Indians required "the termination of their history." Whatever he truly meant by that phrase, it does not sound very benevolent.

Jefferson is well known for espousing the "yeoman farmer" as the ultimate American citizen—the hardworking citizen who supports his family by farming a small plot of land, a person perhaps too busy or too smart to get involved in antisocial activities, as Jefferson defined them. Jefferson claimed to want to make Indians yeomen farmers. This was the form of assimilation he pretended to work for. But this type of assimilation was purposely designed to get Indian lands for Americans.

The evidence indicates that Jefferson was not truly interested in Indian assimilation but primarily wanted tribal lands. He ignored the fact that most American Indians were already "yeoman farmers." Almost all of the Indian Nations in the eastern United States actively practiced agriculture and had been doing so long before Europeans arrived on this continent. The eastern tribes cultivated about 80 percent of their necessary foodstuffs. For these tribal nations, hunting and gathering provided meat and foods to supplement their regular diet of crop foods. One of President Jefferson's generals even made a joke that exposed Jefferson as a hypocrite on this topic. General James Wilkinson was familiar with the agricultural tribes of the American Southeast—the Creek, Choctaw, and Cherokee, for example. He asked facetiously, weren't Indians already yeomen farmers? Why then does Jefferson want to remove them from their farming lands? The answer, of course, was that Jefferson wanted their lands and that the Indian Nations had to go whatever the justification.[31]

One powerful example demonstrates Jefferson's true ambivalence about Indian assimilation and perhaps his true hypocrisy on the topic. In 1808 a Cherokee delegation visited Jefferson in the White House to complain about another branch of the Cherokee Nation, the boundary line between the two groups, and the division of treaty payments. The first group of Cherokees offered to become American citizens to try to better protect their rights. Jefferson ostensibly approved. How could he not? Was not this the true and complete assimilation of Indian people that he had argued for? Isn't this what he meant when he said red and white blood would mix one day? Jefferson, however, placed an impossible condition on the offer that he knew the Cherokee could never fulfill. He did not really want Indian assimilation or citizenship, of course. "For Thomas Jefferson, the idea ... of United States citizenship for the Cherokees [held] no interest at all, since neither afforded any prospects of land cessions.... What he desired was Cherokee removal, since thereby the coveted Indian territory could be secured more readily and completely than by the tried methods of civilization, coercion, and corruption, although these might, and in fact did, continue to be useful as accessories."[32]

Extermination

Jefferson had an even darker side to his strategies for acquiring Indian lands. He proposed a very draconian idea for any Indian Nation that defied his plans to take their territory. Jefferson used the word "exterminate," and its synonym "extirpate," in reference to tribes that dared to fight for their homelands and presented a road-block to the American expansion Jefferson was planning. Any tribe that did not cooperate with Jefferson did so at great risk.

To be fair, Jefferson used the words "exterminate" and "extirpate" in connection with tribes that violently resisted American efforts. But could he, or would we today, expect the Indian people and their governments to have done anything less than to fight to preserve their homelands, their cultures, their religions, and their livelihoods? Should they have just passively sat back and done nothing while the United States took their lands?

As early as 1776, Jefferson called for the extermination of the Cherokee Nation and its removal west of the Mississippi because the Cherokee people fought for the British in the Revolution. Also during the Revolution, when he was the governor of Virginia, Jefferson ordered Virginia troops to exterminate the Shawnee Nation or to drive it from its lands. In 1807 President Jefferson continued to hold these genocidal views. When he learned that some tribes were preparing for war because the United States and its citizens continued to encroach on tribal lands, he said that "if ever we are constrained to lift the hatchet against any tribe, we will never lay it down till that tribe is exterminated, or driven beyond the Mississippi ... we shall destroy all of them." In 1813, when the Creek Nation fought against American encroachments into their territory, ex-President Jefferson continued to hold the same view that their "barbarities justified extermination" and that the United States must "pursue them to extermination." He also wrote that year that he could not understand the motivations of Indians who were helping the English in the War of 1812. Jefferson, of course, could not see that most tribes saw the Americans as the enemy and the English as an ally to stop U.S. expansion. Jefferson wrote Baron von Humboldt that because these tribes had taken up the hatchet against the United States, it "oblige[d] us now to pursue them to extermination, or drive them to new seats beyond our reach."[33]

Many historians and commentators have noted this aspect of Jefferson's Indian strategies. Professor Merrill Peterson, for example, stated that Jefferson's Indian policy was "[d]ivide and rule, aid the friendly in peace, exterminate the incorrigibles." Professor Peter Onuf recognized that Jefferson stated that if any tribe started a war, the United States "will extirpate [that tribe] from the earth." Historian Julius Pratt stated that Jefferson even welcomed Indian armed resistance because such actions "lay the foundation of their own destruction." This was probably one of the primary American strategies for many decades. As pioneers and settlers encroached illegally on tribal lands, tribal warriors would defend their territory and fight back. Then, as Jefferson wrote, these Indian attacks "have given us the right, as we possess the power, to exterminate or to expatriate them beyond the Mississippi." Indians who resisted assimilation and encroachment on their lands "deserved nothing less than extermination or banishment."[34]

These aggressive and militant calls for extermination of recalcitrant tribal nations and forced relocations even for compliant tribes must be considered in light of Jefferson's views on how the United States gained Indian lands. As we have seen, Jefferson and Discovery alleged that when Indian lands became vacant because a tribe moved or the majority of its population died off, the United States then gained a complete title to these lands. Jefferson's hyperaggressive policies of extermination and removal served his overriding goal of "acquiring Indian lands." As one South Carolina politician stated during the Revolutionary War, it was with "the greatest justice" that once the United States exterminated a tribe, its land became public property. Jefferson espoused the same idea. Hence, Jefferson's goals of American expansion and obtaining tribal lands were served by his aggressive policies of extermination and relocation.[35]

THOMAS JEFFERSON—HYPOCRITE OR POLITICAL SPINMEISTER?

Much has been written about Thomas Jefferson's complex and oftentimes contradictory personality and the major differences that can be perceived between his rhetoric and his actual conduct. Professor Joseph Ellis has written that Jefferson's true intentions are sometimes hard to determine. He can be, and is today, quoted by both sides to support opposite positions on various subjects. Many critics have called Jefferson a hypocrite. One of the best known biographers of Jefferson, Merrill Peterson, stated that Jefferson's actual Indian policies viewed through the lens of his benevolent statements about Indians intermixing with white Americans and being assimilated look like deviousness and even hypocrisy.[36]

Professor Peter Onuf of the University of Virginia, one of the leading Jeffersonian experts, is also conflicted about the differences he sees between Jefferson's words and conduct in certain areas. He notes that the contradiction about the Indian Nations is particularly egregious. Onuf writes that it is easy to see through Jefferson's vision and rhetoric of the expanding American empire of liberty "to the interests it so obviously served." Some of those interests were the dreams of "American policy makers ... [because] these 'Savages' threatened to deny the rising generation its birthright, preempting ... the new nation's imperial domain." Thus, Indian Nations and Indian people were obstacles to the national Manifest Destiny. Jefferson and other Founding Fathers hoped that Indians would fade away "in futile resistance to the inexorable advance of republican civilization or by assimilation with the Americans." Jefferson's vision, Onuf says, left the Indian Nations with a choice to "either ... accept the gifts of civilization and become part of the American nation, or they must face removal and extinction." Jefferson's real hypocrisy is evident, Onuf says, because Jefferson never expected Indians to assimilate or survive and he even suggested that their true nature was to resist and perish before the advance of white civilization. Yet, he wrote and spoke and pretended to work for tribal assimilation and citizenship. As Onuf concludes, Jefferson's role in "the protracted and destructive assault on Indian peoples ... raises acutely discomfiting questions about both 'progress' and 'civilization.'" It was easy to conclude, to salve one's conscience, that what "civilization" and "progress" was going to do to Indians was beyond the control of the United States, and thus "absolve[d] Americans of agency or moral responsibility for the displacement of indigenous peoples."[37]

It is impossible to psychoanalyze President Jefferson two hundred years after the fact or to accurately interpret his hidden meanings when faced with his conflicting words and deeds about Indians and Indian Nations. It is even more difficult when Jefferson himself might not have known his true motivations. Perhaps he was literally in conflict with his own personality. Consequently, it seems difficult to determine whether Jefferson was a friend or the worst enemy of Indian tribes. By his actions, he certainly became their worst enemy. His words for the most part were idealistic, but the policies he actually implemented foresaw a dismal future for Indian people and their political, commercial, and human rights. Using the rule of thumb that actions speak louder than words, I think we can rely on how Jefferson really acted toward Indian Nations and discount his words because words, after all, are cheap. We can thus gain some insight and understanding into his true intentions toward Indians and their rights.

Whether Jefferson was being hypocritical or just putting political "spin" on a situation in which he thought Indians were doomed to disappear before American Manifest Destiny, it is obvious that the strategies and actions he planned did not respect Indian human and property rights, nor does it look like he ever believed that they would survive American expansion. Jefferson was the father of Indian Removal and he worked diligently to take Indian property rights and to move Indian Nations and Indian people out of America's way. Professor Anthony Wallace stated that "the Jeffersonian vision of the destiny of the Americas had no place for Indians as Indians."[38]

I agree with these views on the contradictions in Jefferson's statements and his true intentions regarding Indians and his less-than-forthright stance. In fact, I go farther than those critics who call Jefferson just a hypocrite. He was worse than that. This conclusion is apparent in light of the evidence we have considered. To be polite, Jefferson was a political "spinmeister" of the first order. He said one thing about Indians, their governments, and their rights, and then he demonstrated what he really believed, what he really wanted, by acting in a manner diametrically opposed to his spoken and written words. Professor Ellis states that Jefferson had an amazing capacity for self-deception and self-denial and that he could straddle massive contradictions and maybe even come to believe his own lies and ignore the true ambitions in his own soul. But Ellis points out that the "most dramatic display of this Jeffersonian syndrome ... occurred in [his] treatment of Native Americans." Jefferson did all that and more in carrying out his true intentions toward Indian people.[39]

While saying and writing one thing about Indians and tribal governments and guaranteeing them their lands in legally binding treaties, Jefferson worked to reach the exact opposite result. He was smart enough, obviously, to know that he had to keep his true strategies, intentions, and lust for Indian lands private. In 1803 letters to Governors Harrison and Claiborne, when Jefferson revealed his strategy to remove all the eastern Indian Nations, he carefully instructed these gentlemen that his views had to be kept secret. He told Harrison in February 1803: "this letter is to be considered as private.... You will also perceive how sacredly it must be kept within your own breast, and especially how improper [it is] to be understood by the Indians. For their interests and their tranquility it is best they should see only the present age of their history." Harrison was to keep Jefferson's real views about removal and Indian land purchases from the attention of Indians for their own best interest! Whose interest was Jefferson really concerned with? Jefferson also wrote Governor Claiborne that his letter was "of a private character" and that the United States should "press on the Indians, as steadily and strenuously as they can bear, the extension of our purchases on the Mississippi." These views, Jefferson wrote, "are such as should not be formally declared."[40]

On January 18, 1803, Jefferson also transmitted his views about acquiring Indian lands to Congress as part of a secret message. Jefferson told Congress that many tribes were worried about the amount of land the United States was buying and had stopped selling land. Jefferson said the United States could peaceably counteract this tribal policy and continue expanding its territory by encouraging agriculture and building more federal trading houses in Indian country. Jefferson's secret message to Congress was that the real purpose behind promoting "civilization" and "assimilation" and operating the federal trading posts was to acquire Indian lands. In 1808 Jefferson sent another message to Congress about obtaining lands west of the Mississippi River "from the native proprietors." He informed Congress of his attempt "to obliterate from the Indian mind an impression deeply made in it that we are constantly forming designs on their lands." It is not difficult to imagine where Indians would have gotten that idea. So Jefferson now told Congress he "thought it best where urged by no peculiar necessity to leave to themselves and to the pressure of their own convenience only to come forward with offers of sale to the United States." Consequently, Jefferson pursued a multitude of strategies to gain Indian lands while at the same time he tried to hide his greed and his true intentions from Indian people.[41]

Jefferson also demonstrated another reason he and many American politicians were so greedy for Indian lands. The sale of the western lands, Indian lands, paid the Revolutionary War debts of the federal and state governments and continued to fund federal governmental operations for decades. Alexander Hamilton and James Madison are reported to have supported the new Constitution exactly because the federal government would assume the debts of the states. Important Southern planters also demanded new lands. Jefferson understood these needs, and he knew that it was actually cheaper to buy new land than to fertilize and revitalize old land. Jefferson's novel idea was that he had figured out how to make Indians pay for these American problems. Thus, the United States made great profits from purchasing Indian lands, often through underhanded and coercive means, and then selling the land to American settlers. During Jefferson's time, the United States usually paid tribes about 25 cents (or less) an acre for land it then immediately sold for $1.25 an acre or more. In fact, the sale of Indian lands to American settlers produced such a profit for the United States that it paid off the federal and state Revolutionary War debts and paid for the Louisiana Purchase even before the money the United States had borrowed for the Purchase had to be repaid to European bankers.[42]

In addition, Jefferson had to know at the time he made his idealistic statements about civilizing and assimilating Indians that his statements were false; they were just excuses to rationalize his true goal to obtain Indian lands and assets. Ironically, when many of the southeastern tribes were progressing toward what looked like assimilation by adopting American style constitutions, courts, and governments, a fact that Jefferson expressly recognized in 1805, 1810, and 1812, the United States and the southern states worked to remove them. The truth is that very few, if any, white Americans truly wanted to assimilate Indians into their society and to live among Indians who owned valuable property and commercial rights and assets. Acquiring Indian lands had always been the American colonial, state, and federal goals. Assimilated tribes and Indians would need to keep their lands and assets to sustain their "yeoman farmer" way of life and would want to remain on their homelands. That development would not be tolerated by Jefferson or by most other Americans of his day. A United States Court of Appeals summed up this situation exactly when it stated in 1956, "From the very beginnings of this nation, the chief issue around which federal Indian policy has revolved has been, not how to assimilate the Indian nations whose lands we usurped, but how best to transfer Indian lands and resources to non-Indians.... The numerous sanctimonious expressions to be found in the acts of Congress, the statements of public officials, and the opinions of courts ... are but demonstrations of a gross national hypocrisy."[43]

In light of the foregoing evidence, Thomas Jefferson was either lying or deluding himself when he told Congress in his Sixth Annual Message in 1806 that Indians were placing their interests under the patronage of the United States because they were inspired by "our justice and in the sincere concern we feel for their welfare." What are we to think when he told Congress in his Eighth Annual Message in 1808 "that we consider [Indians] as a part of ourselves, and cherish with sincerity their rights and interests, the attachment of the Indian tribes is gaining strength daily ... and will amply requite us for the justice and friendship practiced toward them"? He also wrote that Americans must work to convince Indians "of the justice and liberality we are determined to use toward them; and to attach them to us indissolubly." Did Jefferson truly believe his own words? How could he when his every ambition and every official action were designed to take Indian lands and their commercial, diplomatic, and political rights? One professor summarized Jefferson's attitude toward Indians this way: "Indians had only one role to play in Jefferson's vision of America. They were to get out of the way of the white people."[44]

Thomas Jefferson had several goals in mind for the future of the United States; they included expansion, growth, and prosperity. His goals conflicted with the property and human interests of Indians and Indian Nations. Jefferson definitely wanted to expand the United States across the North American continent, and he had his eyes fixed firmly on the mouth of the Columbia River and the goal of owning the Pacific Northwest territory. He was a rabid proponent of American expansion and of Manifest Destiny, and he would not tolerate Indians and Indian Nations being an obstacle to that divinely inspired destiny.

CHAPTER 5

❦

Lewis and Clark and Discovery

The dispatch of the Lewis and Clark expedition was an act of imperial policy.

Bernard DeVoto[1]

The Lewis and Clark expedition was the physical manifestation of the Doctrine of Discovery in the Louisiana and Pacific Northwest territories and of Thomas Jefferson's ambitions for a continental American empire. At least by 1803, Jefferson had set his sights on the unclaimed Pacific Northwest and on dominating and possessing that region if he could complete the United States 1792 first discovery claim to the Columbia River region. The Doctrine is plainly visible when Jefferson developed and launched the expedition because he realized the legal purpose and importance, under international law, of Lewis and Clark reaching the Pacific Ocean in the Northwest and establishing a permanent American presence there before any European country. Thereafter, Lewis and Clark performed the well-recognized rituals of Discovery in the Louisiana Territory and the Pacific Northwest, including building the "permanent" American presence of Fort Clatsop at the mouth of the Columbia River, beginning to bring the Indian Nations within the American political and commercial orbit and strengthening the United States Discovery claim. Just as Jefferson planned, the expedition became part of the evidence that the United States used for decades to prove its claim of first discovery and actual occupation of the Pacific Northwest. As historians have stated, Lewis and Clark were "agents of empire" and "the advance guard of a new American empire," and they "established a claim to the Oregon Country."[2]

The fact that the expedition operated under the Doctrine of Discovery creates an intriguing new approach for analyzing the actions of Lewis and Clark and Jefferson's motivations and objectives for the expedition. Today, many historians downplay the significance of the expedition to American history and Manifest Destiny. They argue, probably correctly, that American expansion was proceeding westward up the Missouri River before Lewis and Clark ever returned and would have occurred even without the expedition or if the expedition had failed. What this viewpoint overlooks, however, is an appreciation for the role Discovery and the expedition played in the legal arguments for U.S. territorial expansion to the Pacific Northwest and ownership of the Oregon country. This analysis opens an entirely new avenue for evaluating the importance of the expedition. In fact, Lewis and Clark were more important to the future of American expansion to the Pacific Northwest than most historians believe today, but they were important for a reason that most historians have overlooked. In operating pursuant to the Doctrine of Discovery, Lewis and Clark occupied the Northwest and greatly strengthened the United States' claim to the territory. They became a major part of the American legal argument under the Doctrine that the United States owned the Northwest.

But the Discovery aspects of the expedition have been completely ignored in all of the writings on this topic. Historians have naturally focused on the historical and not the legal facets of the expedition. Furthermore, in studying Lewis and Clark in school, Americans are primarily taught about the scientific and exploratory goals of the expedition. There is no doubt that Jefferson was very interested in the scientific aspects of the expedition. But Lewis and Clark were *not* sent west to satisfy Jefferson's scientific interests. His primary goals and justifications for the voyage involved political and commercial issues with the Indian Nations, applying the sovereign and real-property aspects of Discovery against the tribes, and the territorial expansion of the United States. Meriwether Lewis and William Clark carried out these objectives against the Indian Nations and indigenous peoples along the Missouri River from St. Louis to the Rocky Mountains and along the Columbia River system from the Rockies to the Pacific Ocean. Along the way, they claimed an empire for the United States while operating under the legal authority and the recognized rituals of the Doctrine of Discovery.[3]

PRE–LOUISIANA PURCHASE OBJECTIVES

Thomas Jefferson had long been personally interested in sending an expedition to explore the interior of North America. Certain events however prompted him, once he became president, to ensure that a voyage was undertaken. First, he received alarming news that the Scotsman Alexander Mackenzie had traveled across Canada to the Pacific Ocean in 1792–1793. This was disturbing to Jefferson because such a voyage could help England establish a Discovery claim to the Pacific Northwest and begin to occupy and exploit the region. Ultimately, it turned out that Mackenzie had not found the Columbia River or any of its tributaries, and thus his voyage did not give England any claims to the Columbia River drainage system. However, Jefferson and his personal secretary Meriwether Lewis devoured McKenzie's 1801 book about his voyage. In his book, Mackenzie recommended that England exploit the route he had pioneered, occupy the Pacific Northwest, and open a direct fur trade with Asia from a port on the Pacific coast.

This suggestion sent a chill through Thomas Jefferson. Second, Spain sold the Louisiana Territory to France in a secret treaty in 1800. Jefferson probably did not learn of this treaty for certain until 1802. This sale was an especially alarming prospect to Jefferson. He had long believed and written that the United States was content when Spain, "that feeble old man," owned Louisiana because Jefferson thought it would fall to the United States whenever the United States was ready. Now, however, France and Napoleon were a real threat to occupy Louisiana. This situation caused Jefferson to take aggressive steps to acquire Louisiana. Third, in 1802, Spain revoked the "right of deposit" and prevented Americans from storing goods at Spanish-controlled New Orleans. This cut off three-eighths of the trade of American goods and created a very serious situation. Many members of Congress called for war against Spain. Jefferson was thus provoked to undertake efforts to increase American control of the trans-Mississippi area. One of his actions was to send James Monroe to assist the American ambassador to France in buying New Orleans.[4]

In the midst of these politically charged events, Jefferson began planning an expedition with Meriwether Lewis that was aimed at the Oregon country, a territory that was not yet occupied by any Euro-American government. Jefferson personally drafted and redrafted Lewis's instructions. All of its primary purposes involved Indians, Indian governments, and various elements of the Doctrine of Discovery. On the one hand, when seeking federal funding for the expedition, Jefferson emphasized to Congress mainly the commercial purposes of the expedition and the possibilities of opening trade with the Indian Nations in the Louisiana Territory because he thought commercial activity was the constitutional link to Congress's authority to spend federal funds on the expedition. So Jefferson highlighted the objective that the expedition would search for the Northwest Passage to cross the continent to increase the American fur trade. He downplayed his own personal scientific interests in dispatching the expedition. On the other hand, Jefferson lied to France, England, and Spain about the commercial purposes of the expedition when he requested passports for Lewis and his men to pass through the territory of these nations. Jefferson falsely stated to these countries that the sole purpose of the expedition was science and exploration. The English and French ambassadors granted passports, but the French official directed that the expedition was not to engage in trade with Indians. Spain saw through Jefferson's lie, refused to issue passports, and even sent four military missions to try to stop the expedition.[5]

President Jefferson ultimately stated all the actual objectives for the expedition in three important documents. First, on January 18, 1803, Jefferson explained the commercial purposes of the voyage in a secret message to Congress in which he sought approval and funding for the expedition. A secret message was required because the expedition was an express attempt to take the fur trade away from England. In fact, even though this was a secret message to Congress, Jefferson only referred to England as that "other country." In the message, Jefferson stated that the primary objective of the expedition was commercial and was an attempt to find the elusive "Northwest Passage" across the continent to the Pacific Ocean.

Although Indian Nations would seem not to play a very large part in this goal of the voyage, it was obvious that the expedition and any Northwest Passage it might find would pass through the territory of dozens of tribes. The fur trade that this route was designed to serve would also take place in tribal territories and, hopefully, with the cooperation and active participation of Indians. So dealing with these Indian people and their governments and making them amenable to the expedition and to allowing American traders and fur trappers to travel through their territory was crucial to any possible use of a continental route if it was found. Jefferson specifically instructed Lewis and Clark to make friends of the tribes they would encounter based on this realization. "In all your intercourse with the natives, treat them in the most friendly and conciliatory manner which their own conduct will permit."[6]

Jefferson also explained the purposes of the expedition in his famous letter of instructions to Lewis dated June 20, 1803. He instructed Lewis, "The object of your mission is to explore the Missouri river ... and [its] communication with the waters of the Pacific ocean, whether the Columbia ... or any other river [that] may offer the most direct and practicable water communication across this continent for the purposes of commerce." This letter was written while American representatives were negotiating in France to buy New Orleans, but before Jefferson had any knowledge of the surprising news that would arrive in Washington, DC, around the fourth of July 1803 that France had offered the entire Louisiana Territory to James Monroe and Robert Livingstone and that they had agreed to buy it for about $15 million.[7]

The second main objective for the expedition, as explained by Jefferson to Congress and to Lewis, was to extend the commercial dealings of the United States to the Indians and their governments in the Louisiana Territory. Jefferson believed that Congress had the constitutional authority to promote commercial activity under the Interstate Commerce Clause of the Constitution. Jefferson explained to Congress that the United States was well placed to greatly expand its fur trade and the sale of American goods in the territory. This leads to an obvious question: with whom did Jefferson mean for the United States to carry on all this trade? Obviously, he meant the Indians and the native governments found there. They were the only people and the only market for American goods in the Louisiana Territory. Jefferson's hope was that Indians would trap furs to buy U.S. goods and also that American trappers would be allowed to gather furs in the territory and that the United States would become the world's biggest player in the very lucrative fur trade. A bonus to this plan, as Jefferson told Congress, was that the United States could undercut the British fur trade with China by using the Missouri, Mississippi, and perhaps the Columbia river systems to get furs to China quicker than English companies could using their northern routes to Hudson's Bay and Montreal and then to England.[8]

Moreover, Jefferson also directed Lewis to aggressively pursue the issue of American trade. Lewis was ordered to confer with Indian leaders regarding where the United States should locate federal trading posts, what kinds of goods Indians desired to buy, and what they would pay in trade. The trade goods Lewis and

Clark took with them were used as gifts in negotiations and to establish friendly relations with the tribes, but they also represented the wide range of goods the United States could provide as a trading partner. Lewis and Clark were in essence traveling salesmen.[9]

The third objective for the expedition matched up with Jefferson's personal interests in science. Jefferson instructed Lewis to make careful observations of the weather, soil, plants, and animals and to make celestial observations during his voyage and prepare a map. Lewis and Clark diligently spent hundreds of hours performing these duties. Sacagawea and other Indians helped Lewis find new plants and helped Clark with information to make his maps. In addition, a very important part of this scientific objective of the expedition included Indian people and their governments. Jefferson had long studied Indian governments, history, and cultures, and he was very interested in ethnographic information about the Indians and tribes Lewis and Clark would encounter. Jefferson helped Lewis prepare to gather this information by making suggestions for a standard questionnaire to be used with each Indian Nation encountered and for compiling vocabularies, a list of common words to be gathered from each tribe. Lewis and Clark spent a significant amount of time on these Indian vocabularies and questionnaires and gathering information about the tribes during the expedition. Some of the ethnographic information Lewis and Clark gathered could also be characterized as military intelligence because they asked tribes about their populations, number of warriors, range of territory, allies and enemies, and fighting methods, for example.[10]

The advance planning of Jefferson and Lewis demonstrates absolutely that they knew the expedition would have extensive and important contacts with Indian Nations. They also knew they would need the assistance of tribes and individual Indians to accomplish their mission, and, in fact, many Indians and tribes did assist the expedition in immeasurable ways to succeed and even to survive. Jefferson and Lewis planned all along to deal with the tribal nations in a diplomatic and friendly manner. For example, Lewis and Clark purchased, prepared, and numbered twenty-one or more gift bundles for tribes they expected to meet along their course from St. Louis to the Mandan villages in what is now North Dakota. They even prepared five gift bundles for tribes they knew they would meet beyond the Mandan villages, and Jefferson sent along a metal corn grinder for the Mandans because he was aware of their extensive agricultural lifestyle. The time, money, and thought President Jefferson and Lewis and Clark put into preparing to meet and curry favor with the Indian Nations demonstrates the absolute centrality of tribes to the expedition meeting its commercial, diplomatic, and scientific goals.[11]

The Doctrine of Discovery is also visible in other plans Jefferson had for the expedition. He wanted to use the expedition to open the Louisiana Territory to American influence and to control and dominate trade and political interactions with the tribes in the territory. But most importantly, by 1803, if not earlier, he had his sights set on the Pacific Northwest and the goal that the United States could possess that region if it could complete and perfect its 1792 first discovery claim to the area. The Lewis and Clark expedition was a crucial part of that Jeffersonian objective.

POST–LOUISIANA PURCHASE OBJECTIVES

On or about July 4, 1803, the news of the Louisiana Purchase arrived in Washington, DC. This development increased the role Discovery played in the Lewis and Clark expedition. Now that the United States had purchased France's limited sovereign, commercial, and preemption rights in the Louisiana Territory, the expedition took on a major new objective. Consequently, on January 22, 1804, Thomas Jefferson wrote another letter of instruction to Lewis and explained that he was to begin exercising America's newly acquired Discovery powers over the Indian Nations in the Louisiana Territory. Jefferson now set out a fourth major objective for the expedition.

The president's new objective was to apply the United States' newly purchased sovereign and commercial rights over the Indian Nations in the Louisiana Territory. Therefore, he wrote to Lewis that he could now more directly propose trade relations between the tribes and the United States than he could have before the purchase, when France owned these rights, and that Lewis was to proclaim the United States' sovereignty over the tribes.

> When your instructions were penned, this new position [the Louisiana Purchase] was not so authentically known as to effect the complection of your instructions. *Being now become sovereigns of the country, without however any diminution of the Indian rights of occupancy* we are authorised to propose to them in direct terms the institution of commerce with them. It will now be proper you should inform *those through whose country you will pass,* or whom you may meet, that their late fathers the Spaniards have agreed to withdraw ... that they have surrendered to us all their subjects ... *that henceforward we become their fathers and friends.* [emphasis added][12]

After the purchase, Jefferson knew that under the elements of Discovery the United States was now the predominant sovereign in the Louisiana Territory, was now in the sole possession of the Indian trade, and was now the great white father for the tribal nations. This objective solidified Lewis and Clark's role as diplomatic and political representatives of the United States who carried the news of the United States' purchase of, and sovereignty over, the territory. This objective for the expedition is less well known because it arose after the expedition had already departed. The surprising news that the United States had purchased the Louisiana Territory had not yet reached Jefferson when he issued his more well-known instruction letter to Lewis dated June 20, 1803. In June, the United States had no Discovery claim to governmental authority over the land or people in the Louisiana Territory. For that reason, Jefferson requested passports from England, France, and Spain to inform these governments that the United States was sending an expedition across their territories and to ensure them that its goal was peaceful and scientific only. Now, however, the mission of the expedition was increased in a significant way, and so Jefferson issued his new instruction in 1804.[13]

The subsequent conduct of Lewis and Clark demonstrates clearly that they carried out Jefferson's instructions and pursued his Discovery goals. We have today written proof of what they told numerous Indian Nations about the United States' authority over the tribes. Lewis wrote out a 2,500-word speech for the expedition's first tribal encounter on August 3–4, 1804, and he copied the speech into a letter that he sent to the Otoe chief Little Thief. Clark also wrote out a copy of a similar speech for the second tribal council they held with the Yankton Sioux on August 30, 1804. The letter and the speeches are worth examining closely because Lewis and Clark said they were the templates for the more than fifty tribal conferences they held during the expedition. These documents demonstrate the elements of Discovery that Lewis and Clark used in spreading the news of the new position of the United States in the Louisiana Territory.[14]

In the letter and in the speeches, Lewis repeatedly called Indians "children" and called Jefferson their new "father." He informed them that their old friends the French and Spanish were gone, never to return, and that all their citizens in the Louisiana Territory were now American citizens. In essence, Lewis was telling Indians you are now American subjects. Jefferson was now their father and was the only one they could look to for protection. Jefferson had sent Lewis and Clark to make peace between the United States and the tribes, to find out what goods the tribes wanted, and to make arrangements to deliver these goods. Lewis and Clark also distributed flags, medals, and army uniforms "as a pledge of the sincerity with which [Jefferson] now offers you the hand of friendship." Lewis pointed out that Jefferson was giving the tribes advice, which they had better take:

> [Our great chief] commanded us … to undertake this long journey … to council with yourselves and his other red-children … to give you his good advice; to point out to you the road in which you must walk to obtain happiness. He has further commanded us to tell you that when you accept his flag and medal, you accept therewith his hand of friendship, which will never be withdrawn from your nation as long as you continue to follow the councils which he may command.[15]

Lewis delivered Jefferson's message to the tribes to stop warring with other Indians and to allow American traders to enter their territory. Furthermore, Lewis warned the tribes not to displease their new great father because he "could destroy you and your nation as the fire destroys and consumes the grass of the plains." This was plainly a military threat Lewis delivered to the Indians if they ignored their new father's advice. He also threatened tribes economically because if a tribe displeased Jefferson, he would stop traders from coming. In contrast, if the tribes listened to his good advice, traders would arrive to trade for furs at the best prices Indians had ever received.[16]

Lewis also drove home the point that the United States was now the only sovereign in the Louisiana Territory that the Indian Nations could deal with, and he invited tribal chiefs to visit St. Louis and Washington, DC. They were instructed to take with them the American flags and medals Lewis and Clark gave them as evidence of invitations to peacefully visit the United States. They were also instructed to take

> all the flags and medals which you may have received from your old fathers the French and Spaniards, or from any other nation whatever, your father will give you new flags and new medals of his own in exchange.... It is not proper since you have become the children of the great chief ... of America, that you should wear or keep those emblems of attachment to any other great father but himself, nor will it be pleasing to him if you continue to do so.[17]

This letter and the identical speeches that Lewis delivered to dozens of Indian Nations drove home the elements of the sovereign and commercial Discovery powers that the United States assumed it had acquired as a result of the Louisiana Purchase. The message was crystal clear: the Indian Nations were under the sole authority and protection of and were within the political and commercial influence of the United States. Lewis recorded this idea in his journal: "we made [the Indians] sensible of their dependance on the will of our government for every species of merchandize as well for their defence & comfort."[18]

The medals, American flags, and military uniforms that Lewis and Clark referred to were "gifts" they distributed to tribal chiefs. The medals had Jefferson's image on the front and a message of peace and friendship on the back. Some historians call these items sovereignty tokens because accepting these gifts allegedly demonstrated a chief's and tribe's allegiance to the United States. Lewis and Clark also thought these objects carried this serious meaning. In his August 30 speech to the Yankton Sioux, Lewis told them that "when you accept his flag and medals, that you receive these with his hand ... so long as you continue to follow the Councils which he may command." Also, in this speech, in the August 4, 1804 letter to Little Thief, and in other speeches to numerous tribal chiefs, Lewis instructed them about the importance of divesting themselves of these sovereignty tokens from any other country and that they should only retain the American symbols. "It is not proper ... that you should wear, or keep these emblems of attachment to any other great father...." In August 1805, Lewis continued to deliver this message when he told the Shoshone Chief Cameahwait that the United States flag "was an emblem of peace [and] now that it had been received by him it was to be respected as the bond of union between us." Admittedly, Lewis and Clark took these objects with them before they knew of the Louisiana Purchase. They may have originally taken these objects solely for trading purposes with the Louisiana Territory tribes while using them for political purposes with the Indian Nations in the Pacific Northwest. But once the Louisiana Purchase was consummated, these objects took on a political Discovery symbolism, at least to the Americans, that the tribes in the Louisiana Territory were subjecting themselves to American sovereignty.[19]

Lewis and Clark repeatedly emphasized the Discovery significance of these items. They said that their "Government looked upon those things as the sacred emblems of the attachment of the Indians to their country." For example, on

November 28, 1804, they impressed upon Mandan chiefs the importance that they no longer accept any medals or flags but those of the United States. Clark recorded the message: "we had Some little talk on the Subject of the British Trader Mr. Le rock Giveing Meadils & Flags, and told those Chiefs to impress it on the minds of their nations that those Simbells [symbols] were not to be recved by any from them, without they wished to incur the displieasure of their Great American Father." The next day, the captains delivered a related order to employees of the British North West trading company. Clark wrote, "Mr. La Rock and one of his men Came to visit us we informed him what we had herd of his intentions of makeing Chiefs &c. and forbid him to give meadels or flags to the Indians, he Denied haveing any Such intention." These exchanges demonstrate the significance that Lewis and Clark placed on chiefs and tribes accepting the American sovereignty tokens.[20]

The height of ethnocentric and culturally confused thinking was demonstrated in that Lewis and Clark literally thought they were naming chiefs and apparently changing tribal governmental structures when they handed out the tokens. Lewis demonstrated this elitist, superior attitude when he advised the Yankton Sioux in his August 30 speech to "obey the councils of such chiefs as your Great father may from time to time cause to be appointed among you from your Own nation; and those particularly who are this day acknowledged by us as Chiefs." One of the expedition members also showed his apparent lack of cultural understanding when he commented after the August 3, 1804, council with the Otoe and Missouri Nations, when Lewis and Clark handed out medals, "the Indians ... appeared well pleased with the change of government, and what had been done for them. Six of them were made chiefs."[21]

Lewis and Clark also emphasized America's power and sovereign authority by performing a show at each tribal conference designed to impress the Indians. The expedition performed military maneuvers by parading and demonstrated American weapons, trade goods, and scientific instruments. This was part and parcel of Lewis's speech that tried to cajole, threaten, and intimidate Indian Nations with the strength of the United States. In fact, one reason for inviting tribal chiefs to visit the United States was to impress them with its size and strength and to demonstrate the futility of tribes trying to fight America. In total, all of the efforts that Jefferson directed Lewis and Clark to undertake were meant to enforce the United States' Discovery sovereign and commercial authority against the Louisiana Territory Indian Nations after the United States purchased the territory and the Discovery power from France.

THE DOCTRINE OF DISCOVERY IN THE PACIFIC NORTHWEST

Thomas Jefferson conceived the Lewis and Clark expedition with the legal authority of the Doctrine of Discovery in mind. Notwithstanding that the Louisiana Purchase did not occur until after the expedition was underway, Jefferson had his eyes set on a prize far afield from the Louisiana Territory from the very beginning. Jefferson had an American empire in mind that would stretch across the continent and include the Pacific Northwest. To realize his dream, he needed to perfect and complete the 1792 first discovery of the Columbia River by Robert Gray by occupying the area within a reasonable time, which is what international law required to turn a first discovery and the incomplete title that first discovery created in newly discovered lands into a recognized title. That was one of the primary reasons Jefferson created and dispatched the expedition, and it is why from the very beginning he directed Lewis and Clark to the mouth of the Columbia River where Robert Gray had first discovered the river. The Pacific Northwest was always Jefferson's primary objective for the expedition, and he was going to use the Discovery Doctrine to acquire the region for the United States.[22]

Many historians basically agree with this idea. For example, Professor Stephen Dow Beckham stated about Lewis and Clark, "The United States had embarked on the path of building a transcontinental empire," and the expedition "dramatically enhanced the United States' 'discovery rights' to what became known as the Oregon Country." A well-known Canadian historian, W. Kaye Lamb, stated that "[t]he chief purpose of the Lewis and Clark expedition was to cross this new [Louisiana] territory and bolster American claims to the further areas beyond the Rocky Mountains." Bernard DeVoto also wrote that Jefferson dispatched Lewis and Clark "to buttress the American claim to the Oregon country" and "that to secure the Columbia country ... was certainly the most urgent of Jefferson's purposes." After the expedition, the United States did exactly what these historians noted because the United States made Discovery arguments to England for four decades that Lewis and Clark were part of the evidence that the United States owned the Discovery claim to the Pacific Northwest. In 1823, for example, the United States argued that it owned the jurisdiction and sovereignty of the Northwest based "upon their first discovery of the river Columbia, followed up by an effective settlement at its mouth ... by Lewis and Clarke." In 1826 the United States also argued its ownership:

> By virtue of the first, prior discovery ... subsequent settlement within a reasonable time ... the right of occupancy, and ultimately of sovereignty ... Captains Lewis and Clark ... explored the course of the Columbia.... There they erected the works called Fort Clatsop, and wintered in 1805 and 1806.... According to the acknowledged law and usages of nations, a right to the whole country drained by that river. The United States has as strong a claim as any country ever had to vacant territory.[23]

The suggestion that Jefferson had this goal might seem startling or dubious at first, but there is no question that it is true after considering the relevant facts. First, in 1792 the private American ship captain Robert Gray was the first Euro-American to discover the mouth of the Columbia River, to sail up it, to name the river, and to publicize his discovery to the world. Under the accepted international law of Discovery, this act gave the United States a first discovery claim, "a claim recognized by the polity of nations ... [because] [d]iscovery and entrance of a river mouth gave the discovering nation sovereignty over the valley and watershed of the river and over the adjacent coast." Jefferson was Secretary of State when this event occurred and was obviously aware of this new American claim. Second, the Scotsman Alexander Mackenzie made his trip across Canada in 1792–1793, which seriously alarmed Jefferson because it posed a threat to the American claim to the Northwest. Mackenzie's trip prompted Jefferson to organize the Lewis and Clark expedition after he read Mackenzie's book about his voyage and his recommendation that England build a fur trading post in the Northwest to expand England's trade with Asia. Jefferson had long been interested in sending an exploration across North America, but it was Mackenzie's actions that finally spurred Jefferson into action. Third, Jefferson told Congress that the expedition would seek a route to the Pacific Ocean to develop the American fur trade. Fourth, Jefferson ordered Lewis that the object of the mission was to explore to "the Pacific ocean" and that Lewis was to ascertain the potential of the fur trade and the possibility that it might be conducted at the Columbia River directly with China to save the "circumnavigation now practised." The circumnavigation then practiced were the routes used by the English Hudson's Bay Company and the North West Company to take furs back to England and then to China. Lewis did ascertain the potential of an American fur trade from the Pacific coast. In fact, he told Jefferson and Congressman Mitchill in 1806 that he thought the establishment of an American trading post at the mouth of the Columbia would be the most important achievement of his expedition and that the United States would "derive the benefits of a most lucrative trade." Lewis realized better than anyone that the trip to the Pacific was difficult, but as he wrote Jefferson, he thought that within a decade a trip across the continent would become a common occurrence. Finally, Jefferson also directed Lewis to determine whether there were any ports within reach of the Columbia River that were being visited by foreign ships. Jefferson was no doubt concerned about the presence of European nations in the Pacific Northwest and the extent of their possible Discovery and occupancy claims under the Discovery element of contiguity.[24]

Jefferson was eager to get Lewis and Clark underway because ownership of the Pacific Northwest and the Oregon country was still very much in question among Europeans and the United States in 1803. Spain, Russia, and England all alleged first discovery claims to the region and to locations where they had landed and traded on the Pacific coast. The United States, of course, relied on its first discovery claim to the entire Columbia River system based on Robert Gray. Thus, the race was on between all these countries to turn their incomplete Discovery claims into actual occupancy and permanent possession as the Doctrine required. Jefferson was well aware of all these facts and of the international law Doctrine of Discovery and was actively involved in a race to occupy the Pacific Northwest before any other country.

Consequently, the Lewis and Clark expedition was a crucial part of Jefferson's strategy of solidifying America's Discovery claim to the Pacific Northwest. Jefferson coordinated the efforts of the expedition to temporarily occupy the Columbia by later encouraging American businessman John Jacob Astor to build a permanent fur trading post at the mouth of the river. Jefferson promised him all the support the executive branch could provide. Jefferson wrote later of the absolute importance of Astor's trading post to America's claim to the Northwest. The American government relied on all these facts and cited for decades Robert Gray's discovery, the Lewis and Clark expedition, and the Astoria trading post as definitive proof that the United States' Discovery claim to the Northwest was the first and that it was followed up in a timely and reasonable fashion by actual occupation and permanent possession. The United States claimed that it met all the necessary elements to turn its first discovery claim into full title and ownership of the Northwest under international law. In 1808 Alexander Mackenzie even warned his government that the United States would "claim under the right of the Discoveries of Captains Lewis and Clark" and would "found their Claims on Discovery." Mackenzie urged England to promptly occupy the Northwest before the "Americans ... take possession ... [and] set the Question fairly at rest."[25]

In light of the foregoing evidence, it should be no surprise that the expedition acted under the well-recognized rituals of the Doctrine of Discovery. Ironically, many people have called the expedition the "Corps of Discovery." This nickname might have been used by Lewis and Clark and their men, but it is not recorded in any of the official documents of the expedition. In 1807 Sergeant Patrick Gass used that name in the title of his book about the expedition. The actual nickname that is recorded in the Lewis and Clark Journals is the "Corps of Volunteers for North Western Discovery." This phrase is used at least two times in the journals by Lewis and by Clark in August and October of 1804 and a third time when Clark wrote President Jefferson in July 1803 and informed the president he was happy to join the "North Western enterprise." Clark also identified himself at least three times using different variations of the initials "NWD." These initials no doubt stood for "North Western Discovery." In August 1804, for example, he signed a document "Wm. Clark Captn. on an Expdn. for N. W. Descy." Therefore, the very name applied to the expedition by Lewis and Clark hints at what they saw as the primary goal and mission of their voyage; to discover the Pacific Northwest. Could they possibly have also had in mind the Doctrine of Discovery? They probably did not use the word "discovery" as a term of art to mean the international legal principle, but it certainly raises an interesting question. We have seen ample evidence that Discovery and its elements were common knowledge. Perhaps Lewis and Clark knew about the Doctrine. Either way, though, the nickname "Discovery" works just fine for this book's thesis.[26]

In addition to the nickname question, there is bountiful evidence of Discovery reflected in the actual conduct of the expedition. First, Lewis and Clark were dispatched by Jefferson with Discovery in mind to help establish America's claim to the Pacific Northwest. Then they followed the accepted practices and rituals of Discovery by marking the landscape and leaving symbols of their discovery and occupation of what they assumed were vacant lands available for claiming. Lewis and Clark often recorded in their journals that they carved and branded their names on trees and stones along their journey. Clark's name is still visible today on Pompey's Pillar near Billings, Montana. It is the only physical evidence of the expedition left on the landscape today. Clark also recorded carving an inscription on a tree on what is now the Long Beach Washington peninsula with "Capt William Clark December 3, 1805. By Land. U States in 1804 & 1805." This point was the farthest north the expedition traveled on the Pacific coast, and Clark wanted to leave evidence of that fact. Moreover, Lewis even carried a heavy metal branding iron on the voyage with the words "M. Lewis Capt. U.S. Army." The journals record that he "branded" his name on trees and other items many times. It is extremely doubtful that any of this marking of the landscape was merely "tourist activity," especially when viewed in light of Thomas Jefferson's Discovery goals for the expedition and his instructions regarding claiming the Pacific Northwest. It is very likely instead that the branding and marking activity was designed to have a legal significance under the Doctrine, just as were the rituals performed for centuries by European countries and sometimes by American representatives to prove Discovery claims. Historian Bernard DeVoto stated that Lewis and Clark "carved and branded trees and affixed notices to them" because "in the polity of nations this was ritual to buttress the claim which the United States had to the Columbia drainage through Robert Gray's discovery.... The ritual announced that they had traversed the country and had occupied it."[27]

A very interesting example of the American use of Discovery rituals in the Pacific Northwest dates from 1818 when American military and diplomatic personnel reasserted the United States' ownership claim to Fort Astoria and the Northwest after the War of 1812. On different occasions, an American naval captain and a diplomat reestablished American ownership by ceremonially turning the soil (like the delivery of seisin or fee title in feudal times) and by hanging lead and wooden monuments announcing the United States' ownership. The English and French had often made Discovery claims in this same fashion as discussed in chapter 2. The American representatives also raised the U.S. flag, and it was saluted by the English at Astoria. These ceremonies were recognized by both countries to have restored the United States' claim and ownership to Astoria.[28]

Lewis and Clark also spent an enormous amount of time mapping and naming the features of the landscape they observed. Jefferson told Congress that part of the commercial value of the expedition would be the accurate mapping of the route, which would make it easier for the United States and its citizens to return to claim valuable assets and land. Mapping was also a well-recognized European ritual of making Discovery claims. Explorers had to be able to prove where they had been and the new lands they had found. In addition, Lewis and Clark gathered native people to conferences to hear Jefferson's message and to observe Discovery procedures, including parading their men in military formations, and demonstrating their weapons and instruments. All of these rituals mimicked Portuguese, Dutch, and French Discovery rituals that were centuries old.[29]

Even the scientific aspects of the expedition were part of claiming new lands under Discovery. Commentators have noted that at least by the time of the English Captain George Cook in the 1770s, governmental expeditions took scientists along or undertook scientific experiments, made various studies, drew maps, and published their discoveries. One writer says that "the collection and publication of geographic information became critical to diplomatic claims to new lands." This same author claims that Alexander Mackenzie wrote his 1801 book about crossing Canada in a scientific manner and used instruments to calculate latitude and longitude, noted geologic, botanic, and ethnographic information because he had "to validate exploration in Europe's literary and official circles." In fact, Captain Cook himself asked that his Pacific discoveries be quickly "published by Authority to fix the prior right of discovery beyond dispute." Thus, publication of the voyage and discoveries of an expedition were "the ceremonies of possession expected by Enlightenment exploration." Thomas Jefferson, a man of the Enlightenment Era, ordered Lewis and Clark to perform these same tasks, and he expected them to publish their journals. He made these demands because he wanted to make diplomatic Discovery claims. "Jefferson knew that commerce and science were inextricably interdependent in the construction of a Pacific empire."[30]

In addition, Lewis and Clark did not just erect temporary winter shelters during their voyage. Instead, they built and named forts and operated them under military protocols while flying the American flag. In the winter of 1804–1805, instead of passing the freezing winter in a comfortable Mandan earthen lodge, they built the wooden Fort Mandan next to the Indian villages in modern-day North Dakota. In 1805–1806, instead of passing the rainy winter in a comfortable Chinook/Clatsop cedar long house, they built Fort Clatsop at the mouth of the Columbia River near modern-day Astoria, Oregon. The Discovery symbolism of these forts is hard to miss, especially for Fort Clatsop and the military occupation of the Pacific Northwest by the United States. The significance of Lewis and Clark occupying the Northwest and leaving a semipermanent monument to their presence and occupation is obvious. Furthermore, the significance of building forts in newly claimed areas had been demonstrated for centuries before Lewis and Clark in that England, France, and Spain had built military forts and trading posts to symbolize their occupation of various locations in North America.[31]

The evidence demonstrates that Lewis and Clark engaged in an amalgamation of all the Discovery rituals that had been practiced for centuries by England, France, Spain, Holland, and Portugal. It was as if Lewis and Clark were being extra thorough to ensure that they used all the rituals necessary to make Discovery claims. Just like European expeditions, the Lewis and Clark expedition took physical possession of land, built permanent structures, engaged in parades and formal procedures of possession and occupation, tried to obtain native consent to American possession, and engaged in mapmaking and celestial observations. Lewis and Clark also planned on publishing their journals. The expedition was the living embodiment of Discovery in the field.[32]

Finally, we arrive at the most obvious piece of evidence that Lewis and Clark operated under Discovery and that they were utilizing its rituals to claim the Pacific Northwest. On March 18, 1806, as they were about to leave Fort Clatsop on their return trip, Lewis and Clark left Discovery evidence in a document they posted at the fort. The document was nothing less than an attempt to establish "legal" evidence of the Discovery-based occupation of the Pacific Northwest by the United States. Lewis and Clark drafted this document as a memorial or declaration of their presence in the Northwest. They listed the names of all the members of the expedition and drew a rough map of their route from St. Louis to the Pacific Ocean on the back of the memorial. They hung the memorial in their room in Fort Clatsop and gave copies to various Indian chiefs and instructed them to give their copies to any passing ship captains. The document proclaimed to the world that American soldiers had traveled across the continent and lived on the Pacific coast. I do not have to interpret this document for the reader; the captains clearly explained their Discovery objective in the document:

> The object of this list is, that through the medium of some civilized person who may see the same, it may be made known to the informed world, that the party consisting of the persons whose names are hereunto annexed, and who were sent out by the government of the U' States in May 1804 to explore the interior of the Continent of North America, did penetrate the same by way of the Missouri and Columbia Rivers, to the discharge of the latter into the Pacific Ocean, where they arrived on the 14th day of November 1805, and from whence they departed the [blank] day of March 1806 on their return to the United States.

Obviously, Lewis and Clark wanted some "civilized person," that is someone other than Indians, to testify to their success at crossing the continent and living at and occupying the mouth of the Columbia River. Europeans would not have believed this story if it were told only by Indians. Lewis and Clark also wanted it to "be made known to the informed world," that is to Europeans and to any other rival for Discovery claims to the Northwest, that an American military expedition had crossed the continent, built Fort Clatsop on the Columbia, and occupied the Oregon territory. Had Lewis and Clark not lived to tell their story and publish their journals, they had at least provided evidence of their Discovery-based occupation of the Pacific coast.[33]

Amazingly, one of these memorials served the very purpose Lewis and Clark intended for them. The captain of the American ship *Lydia* arrived in the Columbia River on June 12, 1806, and was told by Indians about Lewis and Clark's visit. They gave him one of the memorials. He then transported the notice to Canton, China, where it was transferred to another ship bound for Boston, where it arrived in May 1807. This document nearly beat Meriwether Lewis back to the East Coast![34]

In conclusion, the conduct of Lewis and Clark clearly demonstrated the Doctrine of Discovery at work and Lewis and Clark's obedience to the orders of Thomas Jefferson. Jefferson had the Pacific Northwest and Discovery in mind when he first conceived and launched the expedition. This "unoccupied" country, from the Euro-American viewpoint, was ripe for the taking by the country that could actually occupy it first. Lewis and Clark occupied it for the United States.

Jefferson intended this territory to become part of the United States and he used the Lewis and Clark expedition and the Doctrine of Discovery to ensure that objective. Consequently, Lewis and Clark made Discovery claims of American sovereignty and power over the Indian Nations in the Louisiana Territory, and they also utilized the well-established rituals of the Doctrine to strengthen America's first discovery claim to the Pacific Northwest.

An understanding of the legal Doctrine of Discovery and Lewis and Clark's use of its elements helps us to see the expedition in a new light and to recognize the importance of the expedition to America's ultimate ownership of the Pacific Northwest. Historian Samuel Bemis recognized this point when he stated that the Pacific Northwest was "claimed for the United States by Lewis and Clark" and that the presence of the expedition "at the mouth of the Columbia River ... expanded the significance of the Louisiana Purchase and of the northwest boundary."[35]

Many historians, however, have stated that Lewis and Clark were not all that important to American expansion and history, that the "influence of the Lewis and Clark expedition has often been overstated," and that the "expedition was largely irrelevant because it proved premature."[36] This is probably true as far as the historical issues those statements address. When Lewis and Clark were returning to St. Louis, for example, American traders passed them on their way upriver. One trader even told Lewis and Clark that the people in the United States thought they were dead. But the commercial and territorial expansion of the United States was proceeding anyway in spite of Lewis and Clark and what might have happened to them. This viewpoint, however, ignores the Doctrine of Discovery and its significance to the successful expansion of the United States to the Pacific Northwest. Historians who discount the importance of Lewis and Clark have overlooked the very important role the expedition played in the international legal world of Discovery and to the ultimate question of ownership of the Oregon country when they traveled to the mouth of the Columbia River, built Fort Clatsop, and actually occupied the Northwest. In that realm, in the legal arena, the Lewis and Clark expedition played a crucial role and was a very significant and important part of the successful Discovery argument that resulted in the United States owning the Pacific Northwest.

CHAPTER 6

~

Manifest Destiny and Discovery

The phrase "Manifest Destiny" was apparently not used to define American expansion to the Pacific Ocean until 1845. But the idea that it was the destiny of the United States to control and dominate North America was "manifest" or clear and obvious long before 1845. Instead of being a new idea, Manifest Destiny grew naturally out of the principles and legal elements of the Doctrine of Discovery, Thomas Jefferson's ambitions, and the path-breaking work of the Lewis and Clark expedition. It was also clear, and in fact it was specifically intended, that Manifest Destiny would be a disaster for the legal, cultural, economic, and political rights of the Indian Nations and native peoples who stood in the way of this American juggernaut. This was certain because the Louisiana Purchase, the Lewis and Clark expedition to the Pacific Northwest, the Doctrine of Discovery, and Manifest Destiny virtually ensured that a wave of American expansion would sweep over the indigenous people and tribes living in those areas.

When Lewis and Clark returned to St. Louis in 1806, however, America's destiny to reach the Pacific Ocean was not so clearly visible. Many different people had the ambition and the desire to accomplish that goal, but the actual means to accomplish it were only partially visible. The 28-month voyage of Lewis and Clark and the nearly superhuman effort it took to travel from St. Louis, Missouri, to Oregon and back graphically demonstrated one undeniable fact; the United States was going to have a difficult time settling and governing the Pacific Northwest anytime soon. Moreover, the United States faced far more immediate and pressing matters than settling the Northwest. The U.S. government was still less than two decades old and was concerned with surviving as a nation and as a government. It was dealing with serious economic and political conflicts with European countries. These conflicts, and American ambitions, led the United States to declare war on England in 1812. The war was motivated by a variety of issues, but for many people it was primarily an attempt to expand

American territory by absorbing Florida, Canada, and Texas. For example, ex-president Thomas Jefferson wrote Secretary of State James Monroe on June 18, 1813, about the benefits the United States would acquire by capturing Canada. Consequently, the idea of American expansion was alive and was a hot button issue of the day. But the Pacific Northwest seemed to be beyond the technology and capabilities of the United States in that era. Could the United States ever really govern and utilize Oregon and incorporate it into the Union?[1]

Several historians do not think that Thomas Jefferson and other politicians had that goal. They cite statements by Jefferson and Senator Thomas Hart Benton of Missouri that they expected the United States' western boundary to be the Rocky Mountains. Some historians have stated that many people of that time period only hoped that the United States could somehow benefit economically from the Northwest and that perhaps those who ultimately settled the area would be the descendants of Americans and would live under a republican form of government. In sharp contrast to this interpretation, however, it is clear that one of Jefferson's primary objectives for the Lewis and Clark expedition was to reach the mouth of the Columbia River in Oregon to strengthen the United States' claim to the territory and to further his dream of the United States occupying and settling the Pacific Northwest. Senator Benton, as we will see, was a rabid supporter and one of the main spokesmen for over 30 years in the Senate for the United States to occupy and settle Oregon. He introduced numerous bills over several decades to require the United States to occupy Oregon and to make it a territory and he worked with other politicians to make this idea a reality. Why then did he make the seemingly contradictory statement that the Rockies would be our natural western boundary? Why did Jefferson reach for the Oregon country via Lewis and Clark if he did not believe that the Pacific Northwest could come within the American empire?

One answer is that both Jefferson and Senator Benton were playing politics. It is certain that Benton was just toning down his "Oregon or bust" rhetoric to mollify his opponents because he worked arduously his entire 30-year career in the Senate for the United States to occupy Oregon. It is also possible that Jefferson was just being conservative about his goals or playing politics in not letting his opponents and European nations know his true intentions and scheme to get Oregon for the United States. We should also not forget how he lied to England, France, and Spain about the Lewis and Clark expedition and its true objectives. Both Jefferson and Benton were also just being reasonable by speaking conservatively about whether the United States might expand some day to Oregon because the technology of the era made communications and travel to Oregon extremely difficult and made the idea of federal governance of Oregon from Washington, DC, seem almost an impossibility.

Jefferson, though, would have been optimistic about the ability of the United States to govern Oregon even with the technology of his time. Furthermore, since he was a man of the Enlightenment era and extremely interested in science and scientific advances, he and Senator Benton and others could hope for and foresee a day when improvements in travel and communications would make possible an American empire that stretched to the Pacific. In fact, Meriwether Lewis wrote President Jefferson on September 23, 1806, immediately after returning from Oregon, that the United States should develop the continental fur trade from a post on the Columbia River. Lewis was not deterred by the vast distance and the difficulty of the route he had just traversed. He wrote Jefferson that the United States "shall shortly derive the benefits of a most lucrative trade from this source, and that in the course of ten or twelve years a tour across the Continent by the rout mentioned will be undertaken by individuals with as little concern as a voyage across the Atlantic is at present."[2]

Jefferson and Meriwether Lewis were right to trust in technological advances that would aid American expansion. For example, the first commercial use of a steamboat by the American Robert Fulton in 1807 led to its rapid adoption throughout the United States. The first steamboat appeared on the Mississippi River and traveled as far north as St. Louis in 1817. Settlers heading west took advantage of this transportation miracle. In turn, the railroad was developed and successfully tested in England in 1825–1829. By 1830 and 1831, Americans were building their own railroads, inventing improvements, and laying tracks faster than any other country. One visionary even published a pamphlet in New York in 1830 proposing that a railroad be built to the Pacific Ocean and in 1832 a Michigan newspaper also called for a railroad to be built from New York City to the Great Lakes and on to Oregon. In 1853 Congress authorized a survey of possible transcontinental routes. In addition, in 1838 Samuel Morse demonstrated the telegraph, and five years later, Congress authorized the construction of an experimental line from Washington, DC, to Baltimore. Technological advances such as these made the dreams of a continental American empire possible. But dreams of an empire on the Pacific coast were not preposterous in 1806 because England was already developing a global economic and political empire at that time based on naval strength. England was expanding its maritime trading concerns in the Pacific Northwest, as was the United States. The United States even surged ahead of England in the Northwest sea-otter trade from the 1790s forward due to the activities of New England shipping companies. What other grand things then might the United States be able to do with the Pacific Northwest in the future?[3]

With these initial thoughts in mind, it is worthwhile to consider the inexorable march of the United States via Manifest Destiny and the Doctrine of Discovery to the Oregon country. We consider exclusively the Pacific Northwest in our analysis of Manifest Destiny. The other American territorial expansions that occurred from Jefferson's time to 1900 came at the expense of European countries and Mexico. The Doctrine of Discovery was not as heavily involved in America's conduct regarding those regions because non-Indian governments already possessed, and were considered the "owners" of, those areas. In the race for the Pacific Northwest, however, Discovery played a very active role because no non-Indian government had yet occupied the area to preempt other countries and establish its exclusive ownership under the principles of international law.

First in this chapter, we consider the development and definition of the term "Manifest Destiny." Then we examine the extensive legal and historical evidence from 1803 to 1855, which demonstrates that Manifest Destiny arose from the very elements of the Doctrine of Discovery.

Please note one point that I think proves almost on its own that Manifest Destiny grew out of Discovery. The U.S. presidents, secretaries of state, congressmen, and newspapers and citizens who advocated for Manifest Destiny and American expansion to the Pacific Ocean did so almost unanimously by invoking and using the elements of Discovery. If the modern-day reader of the evidence we will examine does not understand Discovery and the definitions of its elements, they will not comprehend the full meaning and intent of the arguments. The advocates of Manifest Destiny used the Doctrine of Discovery to prove their argument that it was America's destiny to reach the Pacific. The Doctrine of Discovery, in essence, became Manifest Destiny.

MANIFEST DESTINY

The phrase "Manifest Destiny" was apparently first applied to American territorial expansion in 1845 and was coined by the journalist John L. O'Sullivan. In July 1845, he wrote an unsigned editorial entitled "Annexation" in the monthly *United States Magazine and Democratic Review* and applied the term to America's annexation of Texas. In the editorial, O'Sullivan denounced foreign nations who were allegedly interfering with American expansion because they were "checking the fulfillment of our manifest destiny to overspread the continent allotted by Providence for the free development of our yearly multiplying millions."[4]

On December 27, 1845, O'Sullivan wrote a very influential editorial in the *New York Morning News* about the Oregon country entitled "The True Title." This editorial and its use of "Manifest Destiny" created a new slogan that justified the idea of a self-confident American expansion over the continent. The phrase became part of the national vocabulary. While the phrase was new, the idea that the United States would expand over the continent and acquire the Pacific Northwest had been alive and well since at least Thomas Jefferson's time.

Interestingly, O'Sullivan expressly utilized the Doctrine of Discovery in his argument that the United States already held legal title to Oregon. He then relied on Manifest Destiny and Divine Providence as his secondary argument that the United States owned the "True Title" to the Oregon territory:

> Our *legal title* to Oregon, so far as law exists for such rights, is perfect. Mr. Calhoun and Mr. Buchanan [U.S. Secretaries of State] have settled that question, once and for all. Flaw or break in the triple chain of that title, there is none. Not a foot of ground is left for England to stand upon, in any fair argument to maintain her pretensions.... [U]nanswerable as is the demonstration of our legal title to Oregon—and the whole of Oregon ... we have a still better title than any that can ever be constructed out of all these antiquated materials of *old*

black-letter international law. Away, away with all these cobweb tissues of *right of discovery, exploration, settlement, continuity,* &c.... were the respective cases and arguments of the two parties, as to all these points of history and law, reversed—had England all ours, and we nothing but hers—our claim to Oregon would still be best and strongest. And that claim is by the right of our *manifest destiny to overspread and to possess the whole of the continent* which Providence has given us for the development of the great experiment of liberty and federated self-government entrusted to us.... [In England's hands, Oregon] must always remain wholly useless and worthless for any purpose of human *civilization* or society.... The God of nature and of nations has marked it for our own; and with His blessing we will firmly maintain the incontestable rights He has given, and fearlessly perform the high duties He has imposed. [emphasis added]

"Black-letter international law," "civilization," the "right of discovery, exploration, settlement, continuity"—can there be any question that O'Sullivan, just a plain old newspaper man, was fully conversant with the elements of the international law Doctrine of Discovery? And can there be any dispute that he used the Doctrine and its elements of first discovery, occupation, and contiguity to justify America's legal title to Oregon?[5]

But then he found an even stronger argument for the U.S. title to Oregon: God ordained it. In fact, Providence had given Oregon to the United States to further develop "the great experiment of liberty and federated self-government" that God had "entrusted to" Americans. According to O'Sullivan, Americans would "maintain the incontestable rights" that God had given them and "perform the high duties" that God had imposed upon them. It sounds like he was making the Divine Right of Kings argument used for centuries by European monarchies to maintain their thrones. It is also reminiscent of the development of the Doctrine of Discovery and the exercise of the Church's power and the rights of European monarchs to control the lands of non-Christian, non-European peoples in the alleged service of the Christian God.

Not surprisingly, the phrase "Manifest Destiny" became very popular with many politicians, citizens, and newspapers and was widely used in the debate about Oregon. For example, the phrase was repeated almost immediately in congressional debates about the United States expanding to Oregon. An opponent of this idea, Congressman Winthrop of Massachusetts, referred to O'Sullivan's editorial on January 3, 1846, and mocked the idea that it was America's "manifest destiny to spread over this whole continent." He mocked the idea because he stated that such a claim "will not be admitted to exist in any nation except the universal Yankee nation."[6]

We know, of course, notwithstanding England's resistance and the opposition of some American citizens, that the idea of Manifest Destiny and American control of the Oregon country ultimately prevailed. This is no surprise because even though the words "Manifest Destiny" were new, the idea of American domination of the North American continent had been widely accepted from colonial times and the early days of the United States. The import of the phrase "Manifest Destiny" was that it gave a name, a cachet, a justification, to this continental ambition and it came to have its own mystical meaning and resonance in American history and in the American psyche.[7]

But what exactly did O'Sullivan and the supporters of Manifest Destiny think it meant and how do we understand its definition today? There has been extensive commentary on Manifest Destiny. Historians have for the most part agreed that there are three basic themes to Manifest Destiny.

1. The special virtues of the American people and their institutions;

2. America's mission to redeem and remake the world in the image of America; and,

3. A divine destiny under God's direction to accomplish this wonderful task.

It was pretty easy and comfortable for Americans to accept that their virtue, mission, and divine ordination mandated the expansion of America's borders because that thinking helped salve American consciences about empire building and the possibility that the Oregon country and the lands taken in the 1846 Mexican-American war were nothing more than American "colonies." Obviously, the justifying and sugar coating of this aggressive American expansion did not just begin in 1845. Historians have noted the identical process in Jefferson's vision of Manifest Destiny as he foresaw and worked toward an imperial continental American empire decreed by Providence. In fact, Jefferson stated this vision in his first Inaugural Address. On March 4, 1801, Jefferson proclaimed that the United States was a "rising nation ... advancing rapidly to destines beyond the reach of mortal eye." America was "a chosen country, with room enough for our descendants to the thousandth and thousandth generation." Thomas Jefferson plainly saw it as the destiny of the United States to expand westward under divine direction and to become "an imperial contender."[8]

Manifest Destiny also had a racial component. America's self-defined Anglo-Saxons felt they held the leading role in educating, civilizing, and conquering the continent and dominating American Indians and Mexicans. During the Manifest Destiny era, many white Americans applied the same language they had used for centuries about Indians—inferior, savage, uncivilized, and with a hopeless future—to Mexicans. In 1847, for example, one writer stated that the Mexican destiny was the same as for Indians, to assimilate into the "superior vigor of the Anglo-Saxon race, or they must utterly perish."[9]

From the early colonists to the Founding Fathers and up to 1845, Anglo-Americans assumed they were the chosen people, and they saw the proof of that ordination and mission evident in their conquest of the wilderness and of the native peoples of the American continent. The idea of an evident and divine destiny for America to dominate and control the entire continent and its non-Anglo-Saxon peoples had been American policy from the beginning of the American colonies. The idea of America's divinely inspired and foreordained expansion across the continent, Manifest Destiny if you will, was certainly a well-formulated principle in Jefferson's time. In fact, in looking west and sending Lewis and Clark west, Jefferson was just continuing the well-formulated Euro-American thinking that empire and civilization was a westward movement. "For Jefferson more than any other major figure in the revolutionary generation, the West was America's future." Jefferson was certain that the United States was the "nest" from which an empire of liberty would stretch across the continent and perhaps even farther. Thus, long before the words Manifest Destiny were coined, the idea that America's government and people were destined to control the North American continent was well established. The Doctrine of Discovery would become a very valuable tool to ensure that destiny for the United States.[10]

We now examine the factual and legal evidence that demonstrates the United States was working to expand across the continent under Manifest Destiny. In examining the development of Manifest Destiny in the forty years before it gained its own name, we see that the elements of the Doctrine of Discovery were the motivating legal principles that the United States used to formulate and to carry out its obvious or manifest destiny to expand across the continent to the Oregon country.

1803–1818

The components of Manifest Destiny on its march to Oregon included a wide array of official governmental explorations, legislative and political actions, private economic concerns, rough and tumble fur trappers, earnest missionaries, and land-hungry settlers. All of these factors helped shape American policy and history during the advance to the Pacific Ocean. These groups worked together, without even knowing it, to push and pull the United States toward Oregon and to perfect the American Discovery claim to the Columbia River region created by Robert Gray and Lewis and Clark. Here we will see how these disparate characters helped create a tide of Discovery and Manifest Destiny that won the Oregon country for the United States over the claims of rival European countries. We conclude our historical and legal examination in 1855 because in that year the United States exercised its exclusive Discovery right of preemption and signed treaties with many Northwest Indian Nations and bought more than 64 million acres of tribal land in what is now Oregon, Washington, and Idaho. That exercise of the Discovery power in 1855 and the United States' acquisition of enormous areas of land in the Northwest is an appropriate place to end our discussion of America's use of the Doctrine of Discovery and Manifest Destiny to gain the Oregon country.

Governmental Efforts to Acquire Oregon

Thomas Jefferson's desire for a continental empire was the overriding theme, the driving force that moved America toward the Pacific in this time period. He was the inspiration for the 1803 Louisiana Purchase, the architect of the 1803–1806

Lewis and Clark expedition aimed at the Columbia River in Oregon, and the promoter of American economic activity in Louisiana and Oregon. One of Jefferson's primary objectives in launching the Lewis and Clark expedition to the Pacific Northwest was unquestionably to extend American territory or at least American governmental ideals and culture to that region. As we have already noted, Meriwether Lewis's primary recommendation when he returned from his expedition was that the United States needed to establish a trading post at the mouth of the Columbia River. He thought this action would be the most important result of his expedition. Jefferson also had the Pacific Northwest in mind because we have seen that in 1804 and 1808 he believed that the Oregon country was part of American territory, and in 1812 he wrote John Jacob Astor that the Pacific Northwest was already United States territory.[11]

It is no surprise, then, that the United States began working during the Jefferson administration to bring the Oregon country under American control. The evidence also shows us that it is no surprise that Jefferson and his colleagues James Madison and James Monroe have been called "fervent expansionists" who were "willing to go to almost any length to secure additional territory" and that their goal was the "[a]nnexation of all the lands of North America." In keeping with these aggressively expansionist ideals, President Jefferson and his secretary of state, James Madison, used Discovery elements to expand American territory to the Pacific.[12]

In April 1805, for example, American diplomat James Monroe wrote a Spanish diplomat and used the elements of first discovery, possession, international law, contiguity, and preemption to argue America's right to an expansive definition of the western border of the Louisiana Territory. In 1807, Secretary of State James Madison highlighted the United States' right to the Oregon country when he wrote instructions to James Monroe regarding negotiations with England and advised him not to discuss "our [reasonable] claims ... to the Pacific Ocean" because Madison thought England was raising the issue just to inflame Spain against the United States. Madison also referred in 1806 and 1807 to a Discovery element, the United States' exclusive right to commercial and political interactions with the Indian Nations and Indians in American territory: "The privileges of British trade and intercourse with the Indians ... are not to be extended to Indians dwelling within the limits of the United States.... " Consequently, Secretary Madison and James Monroe demonstrated in 1805–1807 that they were protecting America's Discovery claims in the Louisiana Territory and the Pacific Northwest and its Discovery power over commercial and political contacts with Indians.[13]

By 1813, ex-President Jefferson was arguing that the United States owned the Oregon country because of Astoria, the permanent American trading post that John Jacob Astor had built in 1811 at the mouth of the Columbia River. Likewise, in 1814, the new secretary of state, James Monroe, argued that England had no claim on the Pacific coast because the United States had been the first to occupy the mouth of the Columbia River. Furthermore, in August–October 1814, during the negotiations to end the War of 1812, English and American diplomats engaged in remarkable discussions about the Discovery rights and powers of each country vis-à-vis the Indian Nations, their lands, their sovereignty, and their commercial rights.

In these negotiations, England tried to limit America's Discovery powers over the Indian Nations who resided within American territory. England was perhaps trying to protect its Indian allies. The American diplomats claimed that England was trying to stop the "natural growth and increase of population" of the United States. The American leaders absolutely refused to recognize any limitations on U.S. Discovery powers because it would violate the "established maxim of public law" if England was allowed any input about "Indians residing within the United States." They argued that England could not do this because "public law" held that when Europeans recognized boundaries in the New World, they gave "up to the nation in whose behalf it is made, all the Indian tribes and countries within that boundary." This public law had been "founded on principles previously and universally recognised." The public law the American diplomats were citing was, of course, the Doctrine of Discovery. According to the Americans, England was trying to take from the United States "the rights of soil and sovereignty over the territory which they inhabit" and to "preclude the United States from the right of purchasing [land] by treaty from the Indians ... by amicable treaties." The Americans strongly asserted Discovery rights and would not cede to England or to the Indian Nations the United States' preemption, sovereign, and commercial rights over the tribes and Indians within its borders. England could not prevent the United States from purchasing Indian lands by "voluntary treaty" when the tribes consented. The Americans argued indignantly that the United States was pursuing a liberal and humane policy toward Indians by introducing "civilization amongst them." Perhaps without noticing their own dishonesty, the diplomats stated that the United States was not grasping for the "progressive occupation of the Indians' territories." We know for a fact that the exact opposite was true.[14]

The diplomats argued that the United States was just insisting on the same Discovery rights that England had always exercised. They pointed out that England had assumed the rights of sovereignty and preemption over Indians and their lands in the Royal Proclamation of 1763 and in Crown and colonial treaties and land purchases. The Americans asked the English diplomats what was the meaning of the English colonial charters in America "if the Indians were the sovereigns and proprietors of the lands bestowed by those charters?" Would Great Britain have allowed another nation to deal with the Indian Nations within English territory? England's answer to these questions was clear because England always followed the Doctrine of Discovery and maintained its exclusive preemption and sovereign and commercial rights over Indians within English territory. The Americans stated that the "law of nations" and "the legitimacy of colonial settlements in America" worked to "the exclusion of all rights of uncivilized Indian tribes." Because the situation of the United States and the Indian Nations was now the same as the former English–Indian relationship, Discovery principles still controlled. The United States diplomats expressly insisted on the U.S. right of preemption because Indian Nations did not have "the right to sell their lands to whom they pleased" or "to dispose of their lands to any private persons, nor to any Power other than the United States, and to be under their protection alone."[15]

In June 1816, President Madison continued "[t]o assert American sovereignty along the [Pacific] coast." As part of his plan, Madison ordered the Navy to explore the Pacific and to land at Astoria. Events prevented this mission from proceeding, but a Pacific voyage remained a high priority of the great expansionists the new President James Monroe and Secretary of State John Quincy Adams.

Other American politicians were also very interested in the expansion of the United States during this time period and used language that linked their expansionary ideas with Manifest Destiny. For example, in 1802, Spain cut off all American trade through the port of New Orleans. This was a disaster for the United States because three-eighths of American trade passed through New Orleans at that time. Jefferson dispatched James Monroe to help the American ambassador to buy New Orleans from France. Some politicians even called for war against Spain over this issue. A committee of the House of Representatives stated that the United States should purchase or take New Orleans by military force. This committee reported to the House that New Orleans belonged to the United States because "nature had intended [it] for our own benefit." In addressing this subject, the *New-York Evening Post* gave full voice to American Manifest Destiny to dominate New Orleans, the Louisiana Territory, and all of North America. "It belongs of *right* to the United States to regulate the future destiny of *North America*. The country is *ours; ours* is the right to its rivers and to all the source of future opulence, power and happiness." Furthermore, in 1804 the House of Representatives Committee of Commerce and Manufactures reported to Congress that it "believed … [the Louisiana Territory] to include all the country … between the territories claimed by Great Britain on the one side, and by Spain on the other, quite to the South Sea [the Pacific]." This was the same claim that Jefferson hinted at in his research paper on the boundaries of Louisiana. In addition, in 1812, one congressman from Pennsylvania predicted that the United States would stretch to the Pacific Ocean one day, and in 1814 a Vermont congressman fully invoked Manifest Destiny and the Discovery element of civilization when he wrote Andrew Jackson that "[t]his Nation are destined to civilize and Govern this Continent."[16]

The Doctrine of Discovery figured prominently in incidents regarding the trading post Astoria, in the present-day state of Oregon, during and after the War of 1812. John Jacob Astor's employees and partners at Astoria were unaware of the outbreak of the war until they were so informed by members of the English fur company, the North West Company. The English informed Astor's men that a British warship was coming to seize Astoria. Astor's partners on the scene voted to sell the post to the North West Company—apparently because they feared it would soon be seized by the British navy anyway. The British ship did arrive, and the actions of the English officer seriously complicated the significance of the "voluntary sale" of Astoria.

The British ship *Raccoon* arrived at Astoria on December 1, 1814, and Captain Black reported to the Admiralty, "Country and fort I have taken possession of and left in possession and charge North West Company." He claimed this "victory" even though the North West Company had purchased the post and was flying the English flag when the *Raccoon* arrived. Captain Black, however, arranged a formal ceremony, right out of the rituals of Discovery, to demonstrate his possession of the region for the British Crown. He summoned the important tribal chiefs, raised the English flag over Astoria, broke a bottle of wine over the flagstaff, and renamed the post Fort George.[17]

This incident complicated the negotiations for the Treaty of Ghent, which ended the War of 1812. The treaty required the return of all property seized during the war. Secretary of State James Monroe wrote the American diplomat John Quincy Adams in 1814 to not forget that "the United States had in their possession at the commencement of the war a post at the mouth of the River Columbia which commanded the river" and that Adams should demand restitution of the post so that the United States could "reoccupy it without delay." The United States argued with England for years that the treaty required the return of Fort George/Astoria because it had been seized by the English naval captain. In contrast, England argued that the North West Company had purchased Astoria in a voluntary sale. Multiple issues and claims from the Doctrine of Discovery were raised in these diplomatic exchanges, but the return of possession of Astoria remained unsettled.[18]

In 1817 the new secretary of state, John Quincy Adams, and the new president, James Monroe, grew tired of this diplomatic wrangling. They unilaterally dispatched a ship and American representatives to retake possession of Astoria without English knowledge or consent. This was a bold move because it risked a military and political confrontation. It was also risky because the United States was not then in any position to physically possess or even attempt to govern the Oregon region. The task, however, was considered crucial by Adams and President Monroe because they deemed it important to undertake formal, procedural steps to reoccupy Astoria and to reassert and protect America's Discovery claims to the Northwest. Monroe and Adams discussed the Discovery implications of their action. The mission was designed, as they wrote to each other, "to assert the [American] claim of territorial possession at the mouth of [the] Columbia river." Adams also wrote that the mission was "to resume possession of that post [Astoria], and in some appropriate manner to reassert the title of the United States." The president and the secretary of state were discussing nothing less than using the elements of Discovery to reassert the United States first discovery claim to Oregon.[19]

English officials were alarmed by this action. After various diplomatic exchanges and cabinet meetings, England agreed to return Astoria to the United States. This was done over the objections of the North West Company, who claimed that it had legally purchased the post and that allowing the United States to reoccupy Astoria would allow it to enter the fur trade in the Pacific Northwest and advance American claims to the region. England had other overriding interests that led it to compromise on Astoria. The United States' position in Astoria was to be restored to what it was before the War of 1812. The English Cabinet made clear, however, that this act was not an admission of American ownership of the entire Columbia River territory. England reserved its right to make any and all Discovery arguments to its ownership of the entire region.[20]

President Monroe and Secretary Adams had the Doctrine of Discovery in mind when they dispatched the American diplomat John Prevost and the naval Captain William Biddle in September 1817 to take possession of Fort George/Astoria for the United States. It should be no surprise that the actions they took to protect America's Discovery and Manifest Destiny interests on the Pacific coast were accomplished by Discovery rituals. In fact, John Quincy Adams, the "ardent expansionist," was well aware of Discovery and its rituals. As secretary of state and later as president, he played a major role in the expansion of America's Discovery and Manifest Destiny goals. Accordingly, Monroe and Adams ordered Captain Biddle and Mr. Prevost to sail to the Columbia and to "assert there the claim of sovereignty in the name of ... the United States, *by some symbolical or other appropriate mode of setting up a claim of national authority and dominion*" [emphasis added]. This directive was nothing less than the government ordering them to perform Discovery rituals to reassert America's claim to the Northwest.[21]

Biddle and Prevost arrived at Astoria at different times. Captain Biddle arrived in the American war ship *Ontario* on August 19, 1818. He went ashore in two places and performed Discovery rituals to assert America's reoccupation and claim to the Pacific Northwest. On the north side of the mouth of the Columbia River, and in the presence of Chinook Indians, Biddle raised the U.S. flag, turned up some soil with a shovel, just like the delivery of seisin ritual from feudal times, and nailed up a lead plate that read, "Taken possession of, in the name and on the behalf of the United States by Captain James Biddle, commanding the United States ship Ontario, Columbia River, August, 1818." He then moved upriver and encountered the North West traders at Ft. George/Astoria. Inexplicably, he did not even tell them what he was doing there. He then repeated a Discovery ritual on the south side of the Columbia by nailing up a wooden sign and then sailed away. In these matters, Biddle asserted a Discovery claim in the exact same manner as European explorers had done for centuries. The performance of these Discovery rituals would not have been a surprise to the English.[22]

The diplomat John Prevost arrived at Astoria over a month later on a British ship of war, the *Blossom*. The English Captain had been instructed to cooperate fully in restoring Astoria to America. Prevost was taken to Fort George/Astoria in October 1818, and a joint Discovery ritual was staged. The English flag was lowered and the U.S. flag raised in its place. The English troops fired a salute to the U.S. flag, and papers of transfer were signed by the English Captain, the North West Company agent, and the American John Prevost. Ironically, after Prevost left, the English flag was hoisted again over Fort George/Astoria, and the North West Company resumed its activities. For the time being, the American claim of Discovery to the trading post and to the Pacific Northwest was again legally in place, but there was no American presence or permanent occupation of the region to ensure America's destiny to reach the Pacific.[23]

Congress was obviously aware of all these events. In fact, throughout this time period many congressmen kept their constituents aware of these actions through a very interesting series of what were called congressional circulars. The circulars were actually letters that congressmen wrote to individuals and that were to be shared or posted in public places or printed in newspapers to report national affairs and the activities of Congress. Many congressmen mailed hundreds of copies of these letters to their constituents. For our purpose, the circulars demonstrate clearly that members of Congress were well aware of the United States Discovery claim to the Pacific Northwest and that many of them supported the expansion of American territory with arguments based on the elements of Discovery. Congress was plainly conversant with Discovery and the idea of a continental Manifest Destiny. These circulars also demonstrate the widespread understanding of the elements of Discovery by the common voters, the use of Discovery to allege American ownership of the Pacific Northwest, and the understanding of an American destiny to absorb this area into the Union. The fact that congressmen sent letters to their constituents discussing these ideas shows that even the average citizen was informed and aware of Discovery principles.[24]

In 1807, for example, a Tennessee congressman wrote Tennesseans about the Lewis and Clark expedition and the fact that they had spent the winter of 1805–1806 on the Pacific Ocean at the mouth of the Columbia River. In language that links Manifest Destiny and elements of Discovery, the congressman wrote, "This expedition has opened to posterity an immense field for future enterprise…. [and] might procure for the people of this country the great advantages of this extensive trade; establish and preserve a passage to, and a communication with the great Pacific Ocean, and insure to the United States the ultimate possession of that vast country, formed by nature to constitute a part of the American union."[25]

Other congressmen agreed that America's border now extended to the Pacific Ocean due to the Lewis and Clark expedition and/or the Louisiana Purchase. Various congressmen informed their constituents of these facts, for example, in Tennessee, Kentucky, and North Carolina in 1805 and 1807. Apparently they were relying on the Discovery elements of first discovery and occupation to pass title to newly discovered territory to the United States. In 1805, 1806, and other years, multiple congressmen from many different states discussed with their constituents the Discovery element of Indian title and how the United States was extinguishing Indian titles through treaty purchases, only when the Indian Nations consented to the sales, and then was making the lands available for American settlers. Another congressman in 1807 informed his constituents of the progress being made toward the Discovery goal of civilizing "savage" Indians.[26]

Consequently, it is evident that federal politicians working toward expanding American territory were knowledgeable about and used the elements of Discovery in their everyday conversations and actions. The presidents, secretaries of state, and congressmen who from 1803 to 1818 discussed Manifest Destiny issues used Discovery and its elements to advance America's right to govern and own the Oregon country.

Governmental Explorations

Governmental explorations were crucial in opening the West to American expansion. These undertakings increased information about the area and its resources and increased interest and excitement in the public to gain these assets by moving west. The federal government undertook several official attempts to explore, map, and study the assets and characteristics of the West in this time period. The United States only had the ability to take minor steps toward the Pacific at this time, but it did undertake several important efforts. The most famous American exploration of this era was of course the Lewis and Clark expedition. Jefferson reported to Congress in December 1806 that in exploring the Missouri River to find the "best communication from that to the Pacific Ocean," they "had all the success which could have been expected."[27]

Jefferson's ambition for an American empire and the full utilization of the enormous Louisiana Territory, however, required more than just one expedition. He sent exploratory expeditions into different regions of the territory up the Red River and up the Washita or Ouachita River. When he sent the Freeman/Custis expedition up the Red River in modern-day Texas, he was trying to establish the southern boundary of the Louisiana Territory between Spanish territory and American Louisiana.

American General James Wilkinson, the governor of the Louisiana Territory, also sent Lieutenant Zebulon Pike on two voyages through Louisiana. In 1805, Pike ascended the Mississippi River as far as present-day Minnesota seeking to find the headwaters of the river. He was no doubt looking for the northern boundary of the Louisiana Territory. Pike kept a journal, made maps, and convinced at least one tribe to sell land for the building of a federal trading post. Additionally, Pike was sent west along the Arkansas River in 1806–1807 as far west as the Rocky Mountains and then south to the Rio Grande River, where he was detained by Spanish troops and returned to Louisiana.

These efforts demonstrated that Jefferson and Congress were interested in exploring the Louisiana Territory to discover its boundaries and the assets and possibilities it held. The United States wanted to uncover how best to exploit the purchase and how to effectively absorb the territory into the Union.

American Private Economic Forces

Even before the Lewis and Clark expedition and the Louisiana Purchase, American companies from New England had developed economic interests in the Pacific Northwest. Starting as early as 1787, the Pacific coast became a target of many New England commercial interests. They even developed a sense of ownership over this area once they established a regular route trading for and taking sea otter furs and then trading the furs in China. The New England sea-otter and whaling trade continued to expand and increase American private interests along the Oregon coast after Lewis and Clark.

Moreover, after the Louisiana Purchase and Lewis and Clark, private American economic interests did everything that Thomas Jefferson had hoped for and that he had promised Congress they would do to advance America's interests in the Louisiana Territory. The American fur trappers and traders immediately began to exploit the territory and to push American interests westward. We have already seen how Jefferson was part of this effort when he encouraged John Jacob Astor to take the American fur industry as far west as possible, to the mouth of the Columbia River, the identical spot Jefferson had targeted for Lewis and Clark.

The United States government was not in a position to immediately advance Manifest Destiny toward Oregon. But American citizens and private economic concerns were able to immediately begin pursuing the profits to be gained from furs and trade with Indian people in Louisiana and to utilize America's newly acquired Discovery interests in the territory and even to begin pushing toward Oregon.

Even before Lewis and Clark returned to St. Louis in September 1806, private American economic interests were already commencing activities in the Louisiana Territory and following the path the explorers had blazed. The American westward destiny was already in motion. In fact, one intrepid American trader followed right on the heels of Lewis and Clark up the Missouri River in 1804. He built a house in Yankton Sioux country and traded over the winter of 1804–1805. But even more impressive were the results that Lewis and Clark themselves observed as the expedition returned rapidly down the Missouri River in September 1806. They encountered American traders almost daily moving up the Missouri from St. Louis to trap furs and to trade with Indians. This American trade and commerce in the Louisiana Territory was already on the move even though Lewis and Clark had been nearly forgotten by most Americans or were presumed dead and even though the United States government was unable to immediately follow up on the expedition. America's economic destiny in the Louisiana Territory was already commencing because its traders and fur trappers were headed up the Missouri and to the west. This was exactly what President Jefferson had foreseen and hoped for, and it was what he had promised the Congress on January 18, 1803 would happen when he sought federal funding for the Lewis and Clark expedition.

The expedition did more than just provide information about the possibilities of the lucrative fur trade in the West. Two members of the expedition immediately joined this budding movement, returned to areas they had just visited, and helped to publicize and promote the trade. John Colter received permission to leave the expedition in North Dakota in August 1806 to immediately enter the fur business. He had a successful trapping career and was the first white American to see what is now Yellowstone National Park and Jackson Hole at the edge of the Rockies. He played a significant role in increasing American economic interest in the West.

In addition, the Lewis and Clark expedition's best hunter and interpreter, the half–Shawnee Indian, half-French George Drouilliard, joined the Manual Lisa Fur Company upon returning to St. Louis in September 1806. He then led fur trapping trips back to the junction of the Yellowstone and Missouri Rivers and even further into central and southwest Montana. He built several trading posts for the company, and in 1807 he led the first large-scale fur trading expedition into the territory.

These private efforts introduced Indians and Indian Nations in the Louisiana Territory to American goods and citizens and advanced American influence in the area. The fur trappers in particular explored an ever-widening arc of the territory and later the Oregon country. They pioneered for the future use of Americans the Oregon Trail and passes through the Rocky Mountains. For example, the overland expedition John Jacob Astor dispatched to build Astoria in 1810 found the South Pass through the Rockies that was later used by the Oregon Trail. Thus, private American economic interests followed the Lewis and Clark expedition westward and played an important role in advancing America's Discovery and Manifest Destiny interests in the region.

American Settlers

Even during this early time period, there were the first stirrings of American interest in migrating to the Oregon country. Notwithstanding the superhuman exertions needed by Lewis and Clark to complete their voyage and the state of technology for travel and communications, some people seemed to foresee the possibility of Americans settling Oregon. The development of technology and the increasing knowledge of the Louisiana Territory, even during this early period of American history, provided a great boost to the idea of the United States governing and settling Louisiana and even perhaps one day the Oregon country. The steamboat was the primary technical development of this period relating to travel. The American Robert Fulton first put the steamboat to commercial use in 1807, and by 1817 steamboats were being used on the Mississippi River. In fact, American military troops on their way to the Yellowstone River in Montana in 1819 traveled up the Mississippi by steamboat. The American frontier generation of 1815–1830 benefited greatly from this invention. The development was a revolution in American life and travel, and, of course, it opened up the prospect of far easier migrations to the West.[28]

1818–1827

The whole continent of North America appears to be destined by Divine Providence to be peopled by one nation, speaking one language, professing one general system of religious and political principles.

John Quincy Adams, 1811[29]

The world shall be familiarized with the idea of considering our proper dominion to be the continent of North America. From the time that we became an independent people it was as much a law of nature that this should become our pretension as that the Mississippi should flow to the sea.

John Quincy Adams, Secretary of State, 1819[30]

The preordained American momentum to control and settle the Oregon country gained enormous speed in this decade. A wide array of American governmental and private forces used Discovery and Manifest Destiny to extend America's borders to the Pacific Ocean by 1821.

Governmental efforts to acquire Oregon

John Quincy Adams was an American foreign diplomat and a one-term senator from 1793 until he served as American Secretary of State from 1817 to 1825. Adams was then the sixth president from 1825 to 1829. He was "another great expansionist" along the lines of Thomas Jefferson. The quotes at the beginning of this section demonstrate clearly his views on America's divine destiny to govern North America. We have also already seen how Adams and President James Monroe directed the United States in 1817 to reoccupy Fort George/Astoria and to reestablish its Discovery claim to the Pacific Northwest. Adams took many other dramatic and aggressive steps to protect America's claims to the West from 1818 onward. In doing so, he utilized all the elements of Discovery and helped incorporate those elements into the principle of Manifest Destiny to guarantee that America's destiny would sweep it to the Pacific Ocean.[31]

Treaties with England, 1818 and 1827

England specifically retained its Discovery claim to the Pacific Northwest even when it relinquished ownership and symbolic occupation of Fort George/Astoria to the United States. The two countries then negotiated for three decades regarding the ownership of the entire region. In official letters and diplomatic exchanges, they raised Discovery arguments about which country held the right of first discovery and which country had first actually occupied the area so as to have gained the complete title of ownership recognized under international law. The United States repeatedly argued that three points proved it held the right of first discovery and of permanent occupation of the Northwest: (1) Robert Gray's first discovery of the mouth of the Columbia River and the naming of that river in 1792; (2) Lewis and Clark's exploration of parts of that river from east to west, their building of Fort Clatsop at its mouth, and their occupation of the region in 1805–1806; and (3) John Jacob Astor's construction in 1811 of the trading post Astoria, the first permanent settlement at the mouth of the Columbia River.[32]

The English countered these Discovery arguments by asking whether "prior discovery constitutes a legal claim to sovereignty" and whether accidental discovery unattended by exploration or the taking of possession and "the discovery of the sources of the Columbia, and by the exploration of its source to the sea, by Lewis and Clark, in 1805-'6" constituted ownership. England argued that Robert Gray was only a private American sea captain, not a representative of the United States, and was unable to make official claims to territory. England also downplayed the significance of Lewis and Clark because they had not found the headwaters of the Columbia River. Instead, English citizens had found that source and had been working their way south on the Columbia for years before Lewis and Clark ever saw the river. Finally, the English discounted Astoria because the British North West Company had purchased the post.[33]

England then aggressively argued its own Discovery claim to the Oregon country by expressly relying on the Discovery elements of "first discovery," "possession," and "occupation." England claimed first discovery of the Pacific Northwest by Francis Drake's voyages in the mid-1500s (there was and apparently still is no proof that Drake ever sailed as far north as the Columbia River); the extensive trade and exploration that England had commenced in the region in the late 1700s by captains Cook, Meares, and Vancouver, to name a few; the cession by Spain to England of trading and settlement rights in the Pacific Northwest in 1790; the activities of the North West Company in western Canada and down the Columbia River; and finally, that Astor's men had sold Astoria in 1814 to the North West Company before the arrival of British military forces. England vigorously argued that it held the superior Discovery claim to the Northwest.[34]

These legal and diplomatic arguments demonstrate clearly the importance the United States and England placed on the Doctrine of Discovery in determining the future ownership of the Northwest and whether American Manifest Destiny would ever include that region. These diametrically opposed positions, however, were probably not going to be settled by lawyerly, judicial arguments in front of a court. England did, however, propose several times that a European monarch be selected to mediate this legal issue. But other political concerns weighed heavily in the balance, and it came to be in the best interests of both countries to set aside their disagreements and provide for a joint occupation and use of the region to avoid conflicts that might lead to war. Consequently, the countries agreed to a treaty in 1818 that provided both parties free use and access to the Pacific Northwest for a ten-year period for travel and trade. In essence, it was a treaty of joint occupation. England, though, had the advantageous position of already occupying the area because its citizens were encamped at Fort George/ Astoria and were expanding their fur trapping and trading activities throughout the Northwest. The United States had very little actual use or occupancy of the region at this time.

The 1818 treaty did not settle the argument over who owned Oregon. In fact, it specifically left each parties' rights intact and unresolved. John Quincy Adams and American diplomats continued to debate and negotiate with English officials about their respective Discovery claims to the Pacific Northwest for years. These extraordinary written and oral discussions demonstrate the extent to which each party understood and relied on the elements of Discovery such as first discovery, temporary and symbolic occupation, permanent and actual occupation, *terra nullius* or vacant lands, and claims to areas contiguous to discovered land and river drainage systems. In these debates, Adams, later Secretary of State Henry Clay, and other American diplomats argued that England had at most claims to land on the Pacific coast between the 51st and the 54th parallels. North of the 54th parallel, the United States recognized Russia's Discovery claim. According to Adams, the territory south of the 51st parallel "was American by prior right of discovery." The American diplomats claimed that the United States held the "absolute and exclusive sovereignty and dominion" of the Northwest based "upon their first, prior discovery" of "the mouth of Columbia river by Captain Gray [and] … the whole territory drained by that river." First discovery gave the United States "a right to occupy, provided that occupancy took place within a reasonable time, and was ultimately followed by permanent settlements and by the cultivation of the soil." The diplomats claimed the United States did actually possess and permanently occupy this "vacant territory" and owned it and the surrounding territory "on the ground of contiguity to territory already occupied." The United States claimed it held the title to this area under international law, "the established usage amongst nations." In contrast, the English foreign secretary denied the U.S. claims and told Adams that England would continue to follow the Doctrine of Discovery and considered all lands west of the Rocky Mountains to be "a vacant territory" open to all until "acquired, by actual occupancy and settlement." England went even further than just the Northwest because she considered "open ... to her future settlements or colonization, any part of the North American continent ... on the eastern coast, northern coast, or elsewhere, heretofore undiscovered and unsettled by other powers." These exchanges occurred for decades as the United States tried to get England to agree to a border between the United States and Canada in the Pacific Northwest. The United States made several offers to extend the boundary line from east of the Rockies, the 49th parallel, all the way to the Pacific Ocean. In 1823, 1826, and 1827, American diplomats made these compromise proposals, but all of the proposals were rejected.[35]

It is worthwhile to note further instructions that John Quincy Adams gave to an American diplomat and the arguments he made to English diplomats in 1823. Adams continued to rely on Robert Gray's first discovery, possession by Lewis and Clark, the construction of Astoria, its reoccupation in 1818, and contiguity to prove the United States' claim to the entire drainage system of the Columbia River. But he now added a new wrinkle to his arguments. The United States now also held Spanish Discovery rights due to the Spanish-American treaty, the Adams-Onis Treaty of 1821, which we will discuss below. Spain, Adams asserted, was "the only European power who, prior to the discovery of the [Columbia] river, had *any* pretensions to territorial rights on the NW Coast of America." As far as contiguity, Adams also relied on this element of the international law of Discovery when he argued that "[t]he waters of the Columbia river extend.... [t]o the [Louisiana] territory ... immediately contiguous to the original possessions of the United States, as first bounded by the Mississippi, they consider their right to be now established by *all the principles which have ever been applied to European settlements* upon the American hemisphere." Consequently, Adams argued the United States "absolute territorial right and inland communication" to the Pacific Northwest "is pointed out by the finger of nature." His argument was based on Discovery and Manifest Destiny. He also stated that the U.S. Congress was already exerting American jurisdiction and sovereignty over the region because it was working to establish a territorial government on the Columbia, and the settlements would be "organized as territorial Governments ... and as constituent parts of the Union, ... subject to the principles and provisions of the Constitution." Adams obviously foresaw in 1823 that Discovery and Manifest Destiny would work together to bring the Pacific Northwest into the American Union.[36]

These ongoing discussions did not settle the disputed legal question of which country owned the Pacific Northwest under Discovery. The approaching 10-year termination date of the Treaty of 1818 led the two nations to conclude a new treaty of joint occupancy of the Northwest in August 1827. This treaty continued the status quo of the joint occupancy, free travel, and free use of the Pacific Northwest by citizens of England and the United States. This treaty had no termination date. It allowed either country to opt out of the agreement by giving one year's notice.

In negotiating this treaty, the American diplomat Albert Gallatin advised Secretary of State Henry Clay in October 1826 that the United States should cede to Britain all the lands north of the 49th degree of latitude. It was better, Gallatin wrote, to establish a permanent line and to define American territory rather than to renew the Treaty of 1818 and leave the territory in joint occupancy. Gallatin worried that this situation "will leave to Great Britain for ten years longer [to] consolidate their actual possession of the whole or nearly the whole territory in dispute." President John Quincy Adams participated in these discussions and agreed to not give England any land south of the 49th parallel. Certainly, the Doctrine of Discovery played a major part in these plans to expand America's borders and to fulfill its Manifest Destiny to reach the Pacific Northwest.[37]

Treaty with Spain, 1817–1821

In 1817, Secretary of State John Quincy Adams began negotiating with the Spanish Ambassador Don Luis de Onis regarding Florida and the borders of the Louisiana Territory and ultimately about an American border on the Pacific Ocean. The negotiations were protracted and difficult both because Onis had to check repeatedly with his superiors in Spain and because both parties vigorously argued their Discovery claims to these contested areas. In just one example, in January 1818, Onis argued Spain's "rights of discovery, conquest, and possession [under] ... the law of nations." In March 1818, Adams refuted Spain's attempt to limit the western boundary of America's Louisiana Territory. Adams also invoked "the general practice of the European nations" and the elements of first discovery, possession, contiguity, the ownership of river drainage systems, and preemption rights to prove the western boundary of Louisiana was in a location favorable for the United States.[38]

In reality, Spain was mainly interested in protecting its interests in what is now Florida, Texas, and the American Southwest. After many proposals were made back and forth on boundary lines, an agreement was signed in February 1819 that granted to the United States Spain's Discovery claim to land across the continent and on the Pacific coast north of the 42nd parallel, which is now the northern border of California. Onis and Adams assumed that Spain's claim extended as far north as the 54th parallel, which was allegedly the southern edge of Russia's claim on the Pacific.

Spain delayed approving the treaty so long that President Monroe suggested to Congress in December 1819 that it should just enact laws in accordance with the terms of the treaty as if Spain had ratified it. Finally, though, Spain approved the treaty in October 1820, and the Senate quickly ratified it in February 1821. This was a very significant development in America's Discovery and Manifest Destiny claim to the Pacific Northwest. As previously discussed, Adams thereafter argued to England that this treaty greatly strengthened the U.S. claim to the Northwest. In fact, this aspect of the treaty was the most important part of the Adams-Onis treaty in regard to American Manifest Destiny in the Northwest because it gave the United States a "window on the Pacific." Adams plainly considered it a triumph and a guarantee of American Manifest Destiny because, he wrote, "the remainder of the continent should ultimately be ours" and that this treaty was "a great epoch in our history."[39]

Treaty with Russia, 1824

In 1788, Empress Catherine of Russia demonstrated her understanding of Discovery when she did not object to foreign countries trading in the Pacific Northwest notwithstanding Russia's claim to the region. She stated, "To conduct trade is one thing, to take possession is another." But by 1809, Russia was actively trying to prevent Euro-American whalers and traders from working in the Northwest. Finally in 1821, the Tsar issued an imperial order that no European or American ship could approach within 100 miles of the North American coastline claimed by Russia. This order proclaimed exclusive Russian territorial rights as far south as present-day California. This enormous land claim upset many countries and especially John Quincy Adams and President Monroe. Adams then utilized the elements of Discovery to dispute the Russian claim. In February 1822, he wrote a Russian diplomat asking for an explanation under international law to justify Russia's claim. Russia relied on "discovery, occupancy, and uninterrupted *possession*." But Adams expressly rejected these Discovery claims and any Russian claim that was based on the element of contiguity. These exchanges demonstrate once again the general knowledge and regular use of Discovery and its elements by the diplomats of many countries. Discovery and the legal rights it bestowed were common knowledge and an accepted part of international law and diplomacy.[40]

Adams did not dispute, however, that Russia could make legitimate claims under Discovery to present-day Alaska and the coast of British Columbia. Russia could even make claims to specific areas much farther south, to various points in present-day California, because Russians had established a few trading posts in these areas. But Adams would not tolerate an unbroken Russian claim from Alaska to California because that claim encompassed the very area the United States claimed under Robert Gray and Lewis and Clark and the vast area that Spain had just ceded in the 1821 treaty to the United States. Adams was not about to let Russia claim this territory. Consequently, he negotiated a treaty with Russia that not surprisingly utilized the elements of Discovery. Both parties agreed to allow the other to use the coast for fishing and trading "upon points which may not already have been occupied," and Russia conceded to restrict its claims and future settlements in North America to north of the 54th parallel. (That demarcation line probably sounds familiar because it became an American war cry in the mid-1840s for the United States to take the entire Pacific Northwest from England: "54—40 or fight.")

The main significance of the Russian and Spanish treaties to the United States was that now Secretary of State Adams had removed two of America's European rivals for ownership of the Oregon country. Only England remained.[41]

The Monroe Doctrine

President Monroe issued the Monroe Doctrine in December 1823. This policy was relevant to America's Discovery and Manifest Destiny claims. The United States now proclaimed that the era of Discovery in the Americas was at an end. No longer would the United States tolerate European countries claiming land and establishing colonies in the American hemisphere. In response to this doctrine, the English foreign secretary expressly stated that England would continue pursuing colonies and Discovery on any vacant lands to be found in the Americas.

John Quincy Adams had foreshadowed the Monroe Doctrine when he said, after finalizing the 1821 Adams-Onis Treaty, that he "considered this hemisphere closed to any new European colonial establishments." He also applied the ideas behind the Monroe Doctrine to the Northwest in July 1823 when he stated that no European nation "should entertain the project of settling a *Colony* on the Northwest Coast of America—That the United States should form establishments there with views of absolute territorial right, and inland communication is not only to be expected, but is pointed out by the finger of Nature, and has been for years a subject of serious deliberation in Congress." Adams's stance against European colonization in the Northwest relied on the United States "absolute territorial right" in Oregon, that Oregon was contiguous to the United States by "inland communication," and that "the finger of Nature" foretold that the United States would control and govern the area. These statements used both Discovery and Manifest Destiny imagery and principles. The Pacific Northwest belonged to the United States and no one else! Adams considered it a "law of nature" that the United States would possess Oregon. He had thus turned the "law of nature" and the law of Discovery into Manifest Destiny.[42]

The Monroe Doctrine and Adams statements might seem more than just a little bit ironic given that Monroe and Adams and others were interested in making an American colony out of the Oregon country and other parts of the Americas. In attempting to enforce the Monroe Doctrine, presidents Monroe and John Quincy Adams took steps to protect American rights to the Northwest. In December 1824 President Monroe asked Congress to build a military fort at the mouth of the Columbia River "within our acknowledged limits" and to "explore the coast contiguous thereto." This bold proposal provoked immediate congressional support. In December 1825, new President Adams repeated that recommendation and also asked that a government vessel be sent to explore the entire Northwest coast.[43]

United States Congress

The Congress was, of course, intimately aware of and involved in the 1818, 1821, 1824, and 1827 treaties with England, Spain, and Russia. The Constitution requires Senate ratification of treaties before they become effective. Therefore, the Senate considered, debated, and ratified these treaties. In addition, Congress became actively involved in this time period in considering American occupation of Oregon. Several individual members of Congress took important roles in pushing this idea and keeping it in the public eye for decades. They all relied heavily on the elements of Discovery in arguing that the United States already owned Oregon and ought to begin occupying it and oust England from the region.

Representative John Floyd of Virginia appears to deserve the credit for being the first member of Congress to propose legislation for the American occupation of the Oregon country. Senator Thomas Hart Benton of Missouri was a close second. He was a tireless advocate for 30 years from 1820 to 1850 for the United States to assert its Discovery rights and occupy Oregon. Another Missouri senator, Lewis Linn, also later became an advocate for an American Oregon. In fact, Senators Benton and Linn were so well known for their support of making Oregon part of the United States that two counties in the state of Oregon are named after them today.

In 1820, Congressman John Floyd, a first cousin of a member of the Lewis and Clark expedition, raised the first voice in Congress for making Oregon part of the United States. In December 1820, he offered a motion for a House committee to study the possibility of the United States occupying the Columbia River and establishing settlements there. Floyd and two others were appointed to this committee. They produced a House report on January 25, 1821, and a proposed bill to authorize the United States to occupy the Columbia River and to "extinguish the Indian title."[44]

This extraordinary report is worthy of close attention. It is filled with discussions of the elements of Discovery as justification for the United States to extend its jurisdiction and governmental control to the Pacific Northwest. In the very first paragraph, the report discussed "discovery" and concluded based upon "the usage of all nations, previous and subsequent to the discovery of America ... the title of the United States to a very large portion of the coast of the Pacific ocean to be well founded." Clearly, the House committee both understood and applied the Doctrine of Discovery in alleging that the United States owned "title" to the Northwest. It is noteworthy that this was two years before *Johnson v. M'Intosh* (1823) adopted Discovery as federal case law for how Euro-American governments acquired the lands of Native people.[45]

The House report discussed the history of European discovery in the New World and the papal division of the world into areas where Spain and Portugal gained title to the lands they discovered. This papal authority "vested in Spain a title which they deemed completely valid, and authorized her to extend her discoveries and establish her dominion over a great portion of the new world." Spain proved its title by "taking possession, according to the custom of that day." Spain took possession of lands in the New World and on the Pacific coast and "annexed them to the Crown of Spain by the triple title of conquest, discovery, and the grant of the Pope." Other Europeans recognized these rights and allowed Spain to gain by "discovery and conquest ... the undisputed possession of most of the Atlantic coast of South America."[46]

The report noted the creation, primarily by England, of a modified way to exercise "the right of annexing to their Crown all the territories discovered by their subjects." England did this by granting charters in America "extending from sea to sea, always excepting the territories of any Christian prince or people." The Native people and governments were considered "as possessing no rights ... [although] some of whom [were] as far advanced in civilization and the arts of peace, though not professing to be Christians, or skilled in war."[47]

The House report also recognized the Discovery element of contiguity as being another method for European countries to claim lands in the New World beyond conquest and discovery. The committee defined this element: "the Power which *discovered a country* was entitled to the *whole extent of soil watered by the springs of the principal river or watercourse* passing through it, *provided there was settlement made, or possession taken, with the usual formalities* ... and such right was held good to the whole extent ... and become thereby vested *with a full right of sovereignty.*" The report noted that French kings had operated under this exact method of claiming land by Discovery and contiguity when they sent Marquette, Joliet, and others to explore and claim the Mississippi River and its drainage system in the 1670s and 1680s. The French operated under these Discovery principles "taking possession, in due and solemn form, in the name of the French King. Such were the discoveries which gave to France the country called Louisiana." And all nations recognized this claim because it was based on "these settlements and discoveries of the French."[48]

The House then examined the boundaries of the Spanish and French territories claimed under Discovery and studied how England, after the French and Indian War, came to accept the contiguity element of Discovery as espoused by the French and Spanish. England did so by ceding some of its North American claims from the Atlantic to the Pacific to France and revoking some colonial charters to limit their continental claims to as far west as the Mississippi. The House further defined this Discovery element of contiguity as being "the point equidistant from" the settlements of European countries.[49]

In light of this history, the House applied the element of contiguity and concluded that the United States, "being possessed of the title of France, and, by a just application of the law of nations, that of Spain, too," owned the Pacific coast from the 60th to the 36th parallels. The House noted that the United States had used the necessary Discovery rituals to claim this area:

> [W]e know that all the formalities deemed necessary in the possession of a newly discovered country have been complied with on the part of the United States ... in 1805 Messrs. Lewis and Clark ... built Fort Clatsop ... these establishments, made by the United States not so near the settlements of California as manifestly to encroach upon them, entitle them to the whole country north of Columbia. And in applying the principle known to govern in such cases,

the point equidistant from the Spanish actual settlements and the mouth of that river is the true point at which a line drawn, separating the two countries, should commence.[50]

After proving by Discovery that the United States owned the Pacific Northwest, the House report noted the valuable economic assets of the Northwest and the potential for vast profits as recounted by Lewis and Clark and demonstrated by Astoria. This was all within U.S. grasp because the Northwest was American territory, and America could secure this vast wealth by occupying the region and putting a "guard at the mouth of the Columbia." Plainly, this committee was not worried about the distance to Oregon, a lack of technology, or the difficulty of the route that Lewis and Clark had pioneered. Instead, the committee emphasized how much easier American access was to Oregon than it had been for the English fur companies who had dealt with these issues for over 100 years and still made vast profits from the region. The committee even went beyond just crass economic interests and also noted that expanding the United States to Oregon would serve other Discovery goals of converting and civilizing Northwest natives by protecting them and providing for their instruction in agriculture and mechanic arts.

Despite this ambitious report, the House took no action at that time. Eleven months later, in December 1821, Congressman Floyd reintroduced his resolution and proposed an inquiry into the expediency of "occupying the Columbia River and the territory of the United States adjacent thereto." He not only argued for American rights to the lands contiguous to the Columbia River but he also wanted the government to look for harbors on the Pacific coast and the possibility of transporting artillery to the mouth of the river. A month later, Floyd introduced a bill in January 1822, requiring the President to occupy "that portion of the territory of the United States on the waters of the Columbia," to extinguish the Indian title, make land grants to settlers, and to form a federal territory named "Origon" when the population reached 2,000. A new House committee studied this bill and recommended that the United States occupy the Columbia.[51]

Floyd was nothing if not persistent. In December 1822, he again argued to the House the practicality of the United States settling Oregon. The distance to Oregon was not a problem. He recounted how the American population had moved westward just since 1779 and that now, with the invention of the steamboat, Oregon was no farther from the United States than St. Louis had been considered to be from Philadelphia just a few years before. He extolled the economic assets of Oregon, whaling, fisheries, agriculture, furs, timber, and the Asian trade. If America could extend as far as the Rockies, why not to the Pacific, he asked. In January 1823, he again spoke on his bill. He argued that Oregon was already part of American territory and that the United States should occupy it by building a fort, "extinguish[ing] the Indian title," and creating a District of Astoria. Other congressman joined in his call to extinguish the Indian title to land in the Northwest and give it to settlers.[52]

Representative Baylies of Massachusetts joined Floyd in his efforts in 1822, 1823, and 1826. His primary interest may have been protecting the whaling, sea-otter, and trading interests of his New England constituents, but he also foresaw the possibilities of Oregon being part of the Union and the economic benefits that would flow to the United States. He disagreed with those who argued that the United States should not grow too large. Instead, Baylies echoed Thomas Jefferson's argument that increasing the number of states and enlarging the size of American territory would create diverse interests that would cancel out competing ones and would become a security measure against disunion instead of a problem. Baylies gave full voice to Manifest Destiny in 1823 when he argued to Congress that the Rocky Mountains were not America's natural border but that "[t]he swelling tide of our population must and will roll on until that mighty ocean interposes its waters and limits our territorial empire." He also stated that the United States had "a duty to protect every part of our empire," including the Oregon country.[53]

Baylies relied on the Discovery elements of civilization and religion in his argument. He saw no problem with Americans displacing the native people of the Pacific Northwest because he claimed they had retreated to the West to avoid American settlers, the same as the fur-bearing animals. But Baylies said it would be beneficial if "savages" could learn from civilized men. If, however, they were ultimately injured by American expansion, then that was just too bad because civilization and Christianity were on the march. "To diffuse the arts of life, the light of science, and the blessings of the Gospel over a wilderness, is no violation of the laws of God; it is no violation of the rights of man to occupy a territory over which the savage roams, but which he never cultivates, and which he does not use for the purposes for which it was designed—the support of man." Baylies continued his praise of Manifest Destiny and his analogy of Indians to animals, taken straight from Washington and Jefferson: "'It is as much the order of nature that the savage should give place to the civilized man, as it is that the beast should give place to the savage man.' The stream of bounty which perpetually flows from the throne of the Almighty ought not to be obstructed in its course, nor is it right that his benevolent designs should be defeated by the perversity of man." Notwithstanding the rhetoric of Floyd and Baylies, the House rejected Floyd's bill 100 to 61 in January 1823.[54]

As you might have expected, Floyd was not deterred. In December 1823, in the new Congress, he moved for a new committee to report on occupying Oregon. In January 1824, the new committee proposed a bill to "authorize the occupation of the Columbia or Oregon River," give land grants to settlers, and form a territorial government. The House requested President Monroe to provide an estimate of the cost to send American troops to the mouth of the Columbia and the military advantages and disadvantages of this action. By February 23, 1824, the House was informed that the costs were reasonable and the proposal was entirely practicable.[55]

In December 1824, the House finally approved, 113 to 57, part of Floyd's bill and authorized the military occupation of the mouth of the Columbia. The Senate, however, tabled the bill by a 25–14 vote in March 1825. The fear of angering England and the desire to prevent the migration of American citizens and investment capital to Oregon weakened support for the bill. There was also great hope for a diplomatic settlement of the Northwest boundary issue with England because the 1818 joint occupation treaty discussed previously was then in ongoing negotiations for a new treaty.[56]

In 1826, Baylies of Massachusetts was the chair of yet another House committee to study U.S. expansion to the Pacific Northwest. On May 15, the committee issued its report in response to President Adams's message asking Congress to establish a military post at the mouth of the Columbia River and to explore the Pacific. This amazing document analyzes so many elements of Discovery that we can only note a few instances. First, the committee was investigating "the right of sovereignty and domain which appertains to the United States over the territory claimed by them on the Pacific Ocean." It did this by setting forth a "narrative of the progress of discovery, occupation, and settlement ... for the purpose of illustrating the title of the United States" and to examine "all claims to discovery and title of the territory." It then analyzed the English Discovery claim, which Captain Cook had established by taking "formal possession" of several areas in present-day Canada by burying bottles in which he "deposited coins, and papers containing the names of his ships and the date of his discoveries." After the agreement with Spain to share trading privileges along the Northwest coast, England sent representatives to "receive possession" of these Discovery rights from Spain.[57]

The committee then examined the United States' claim. Once again they relied on the actions of Robert Gray, Lewis and Clark, and John Jacob Astor and the 120 men he sent to build Astoria to make "a permanent occupation of the coast." The committee stated that this evidence proved that "[t]he American title is founded on occupation, strengthened (as the committee believe) by purchase, by prior discovery of the river, and its exploration." The committee also relied on the Discovery element of contiguity as creating an American claim to all the territory 600 miles inland from Astoria. The committee put all this evidence before the Congress "of the progress of discovery and occupation on the Northwest coast ... [to demonstrate] the claims of all civilized nations to any portions of this coast." After examining this evidence, the committee concluded that the United States held the only true claim to the Pacific Northwest: the United States

> have an incontestible claim to this coast from the 42 North nearly to the mouth of the strait called on the map the strait of John De Fuca [based on] a principle which has sometimes been operative in the adjustment of the boundaries between nations who claim sovereignty in a country inhabited by savages only, that an actual occupation of the subjects of any civilized nation on the waters of a river, shall give to that nation a preferable right to purchase of the aborigines all the lands which are watered by such river ... and beyond such waters to a point equi-distant between them and other waters which may flow in a different direction.

In this one sentence, the House committee incorporated and expressly relied on international law, first discovery, the sovereign rights granted by Discovery over "noncivilized" peoples, preemption, and contiguity to conclude that the United States held title to the Pacific Northwest. The committee then urged Congress to occupy the Northwest quickly because England's claim based on occupation was growing stronger everyday.[58]

The primary proponent in the Senate during this time period for occupying Oregon was Senator Thomas Hart Benton of Missouri. Benton had been a St. Louis newspaperman in 1819 when he began advocating for the occupation of the Oregon country and for governmental protection of the American fur trade and immigrants. He extolled the benefits to the United States of expanding to the Pacific Ocean and absorbing the assets of Oregon. When he was in the Senate from 1820 to 1850, Benton pursued his goal of acquiring Oregon for America. He told the Senate that he had received the idea of an American Oregon from Thomas Jefferson himself.[59]

In 1825, Benton explained to the Senate in the clearest and plainest terms that the United States owned the Northwest due to the Doctrine of Discovery and that he thought it was America's destiny to own the Pacific Northwest. Benton saw this affair as a contest for the Columbia that began with the discovery of the river in 1792 by an American. "The moment that we discovered it, [England] claimed it and without a color of title ... to bully us out of our discovery by menaces of war." He told Congress that the United States had taken steps to solidify its title to the Northwest after Gray's first discovery because in 1803 Lewis and Clark were sent by the United States "to complete the discovery of the whole river from its source downwards, and to take formal possession in the name of their Government." According to Benton, John Jacob Astor's permanent trading post of Astoria finalized America's Discovery ownership of the area.[60]

Benton forcefully presented to the Senate the Discovery claim of the United States. He recounted "the title of the United States" as:

consecrated by every requisite which gives validity to the claims of nations. It rested upon,

1. Discovery of the Columbia river, by Capt. Gray, in 1790. [1792]
2. Purchase of Louisiana in 1803.
3. Discovery of the Columbia, from its head to its mouth, by Lewis and Clark, in 1805. [Lewis and Clark did not find the head of the Columbia]
4. Settlement at Astoria in 1811.
5. Treaty with Spain in 1819.

By these several titles the United States have collected into her own hands all the rights conferred by first discovery and first settlement, reinforced by all the claims of France and Spain.

In his book written in 1850, Benton added a sixth factor to this list that he claimed proved the title of the United States to the Pacific Northwest as of 1819: "Contiguity & continuity of settlement & possession."[61]

Senator Benton could not have made a more correct statement of America's factual and legal Doctrine of Discovery claim to the Northwest. He relied on Robert Gray taking "possession of [the Columbia] in the name of his country, [and] bestow[ing] upon it a name." Such a discovery and naming of a river were recognized by all European countries as granting Discovery rights. He also relied on the "discoveries of Lewis & Clark" and their official, government-sponsored expedition where they "took formal possession of the whole country, and bestowed American names, badges of sovereignty, upon every considerable stream and mountain;" and the arrival of Astor's men by sea and land, which was the final "act [by which] the title of the United States was consummated." This "possession, without which discovery would confer no absolute right, now completed her title." Senator Benton was not about to surrender this overriding legal claim to England. In fact, he used Discovery arguments to discount any possible English claim to the Northwest. He argued that the English Captain George Cook "never saw, much less took possession of any part of the northwest coast of America, in the latitude of the Columbia River. All of his discoveries were far north of that point, and not one of them was followed up by possession, without which the fact of discovery would confer no title." Benton then submitted a bill to the Senate that he said would "expel the British from the Columbia river, [and] perfect our title, by reducing the disputed territory to possession." Benton was clearly a champion of Discovery and of an American Manifest Destiny aimed at Oregon.[62]

Obviously, all the senators and congressmen were aware of these legislative attempts to expand American territory to Oregon and the reliance on the elements of Discovery to do so. Many congressmen discussed Discovery elements and the expansion of American territory with their constituents during this time frame in their public letters and circulars. Congressmen also reported on the new treaties with Spain and Russia that recognized and strengthened American Discovery claims in the Pacific Northwest. For example, congressmen from Indiana, North Carolina, Tennessee, and Virginia in 1818–1819 and 1821–1824 reported that these treaties recognized a U.S. claim on the Pacific Ocean, that the lands had already belonged to the United States, and that the United States needed to establish a post at the mouth of the Columbia River. They also discussed in public letters to Indiana in 1818, North Carolina in 1823, and Tennessee in 1825 Discovery and Manifest Destiny principles such as contiguous territory, occupation of claimed lands, and the destiny of the United States to extend to the Pacific. Some congressmen were against this expansion, and they told their constituents that. Representatives from South Carolina, Indiana, North Carolina, and Missouri also wrote their constituents in 1818–1819 and 1824–1826 about Indian removal (the Jeffersonian idea to move all the eastern tribes west of the Mississippi), the definition and method of extinguishing Indian land titles, and the progress of the goal of civilizing and governing Indians.[63]

One statement from these numerous congressional circulars best exemplifies the merging of Manifest Destiny and Discovery elements in this time period. Congressman John Rhea wrote his Tennessee constituents on March 5, 1821, "The people of the United States, by treaties lately made, have their boundaries and limits defined; extending from the Atlantic ocean to the South Sea [Pacific].... They are now the sovereign of an extensive country, and their right is bottomed on irrevocable treaties made with Great Britain, with France, and with Spain. The United States, under the protection of the Almighty, are great and powerful and progressing to unknown greatness."[64]

We can also see the ugly head of Discovery racial themes and Manifest Destiny in a statement by Secretary of State Henry Clay in 1825. He opined that the future destinies of America and the Indian Nations were on a collision course. There would be no peaceful coexistence. Clay stated that it was "impossible to civilize Indians.... They were destined to extinction." This was not a new idea to many Americans; do not forget Washington's and Jefferson's analogy of Indians to wild animals. Another author states that "since the days of earliest settlement, many whites had believed that the American continent was reserved for them by Providence and that Indians should accordingly surrender it and disappear." One senator asked rhetorically in 1825 whether the West was "to be kept a jungle for wild beasts? No. It is not in the order of Providence. The earth was designed for man.... Their march onward, therefore, to the country of the setting sun, is irresistible.... our destinies, whatever they may be, were placed, in this particular context, beyond our control." Apparently, Manifest Destiny was not going to be a good thing for Indian people and their governments.[65]

Governmental Explorations

In this period the government sponsored several explorations to learn more about the West. These missions were further small steps that helped to open the American road to the Oregon country. In 1819–1820, for example, Major Stephen Long explored the Great Plains region between the Platte, Arkansas, and Canadian rivers as far west as the Rocky Mountains. In April 1819, Secretary of War John Calhoun undertook two other important governmental initiatives. First, he dispatched a military mission to the Yellowstone River in modern-day Montana that was designed to protect the American Northwest frontier and to extend the fur trade. Second, in 1825, Calhoun sent a team of surveyors to mark the Santa Fe Trail to create a national highway. In addition, the Great National Road west from Maryland reached Wheeling, Ohio, in 1818. America was headed west.

American Private Economic Forces

American maritime interests remained very active on the Pacific Northwest coast in this time period. Sea otter furs, whaling, and the Asian trade attracted the attention of many New England shipping companies. Mapping the coast and finding suitable ports became private and public concerns. But the primary private economic activity that continued to pull America overland toward Oregon were the fur trappers. They continued in this era to lead America west, following the path blazed by Lewis and Clark from St. Louis. The trappers played an important role in America's westward expansion into the Louisiana Territory and on into Oregon. Their private individual interests ultimately advanced governmental interests. While the government was undertaking the significant diplomatic steps toward gaining Oregon, as described previously, the most concrete actions performed on the ground in this era were directed by American private enterprise.

Fur trappers began to crisscross the Missouri tributaries and explore the frontier. John Jacob Astor's company, although it never returned to Astoria, was aggressively trapping and exploring the rivers of the upper Missouri. Individual mountain men also made their mark on the public's imagination and expanded the scope of American economic activity and knowledge about the West. These trappers spread the word about fertile valleys in the Louisiana Territory and in the far west from the early 1820s to the early 1840s, and they pioneered new routes through the mountains.

This advance of private American economic interests into the Louisiana Territory was exactly the result Thomas Jefferson expected and is exactly what he promised Congress. Jefferson had promised that America would take over the fur trade and the Indian trade in the Louisiana Territory largely because of the proximity of American markets and the easier travel route on the Missouri as compared with the arduous voyages faced by English companies across Canada. But the English fur companies did not just meekly surrender this lucrative business. The North West Company continued to engage in the fur trade from Fort George/Astoria through its Montreal trade route, and the Hudson's Bay Company continued its activities. In 1821 the two companies merged. They now presented a more coordinated rival to American fur interests. By 1825, Hudson's Bay abandoned Fort George/Astoria for a new post at Fort Vancouver, in present-day Vancouver, Washington.

American Settlers

The commercial activity in the Louisiana Territory and all the congressional and executive branch discussions about an American Pacific Northwest motivated many citizens to begin thinking of the possibility of immigrating to the West. Several private groups organized in 1822–1825 in Massachusetts, Ohio, and Louisiana, for example, and petitioned Congress to pass the Oregon bill for the United States to occupy the territory and distribute land grants to settlers.

1828–1843

The United States continued to use the Doctrine of Discovery and Manifest Destiny to work toward occupying and owning the Oregon country in this time period.

Governmental Efforts to Acquire Oregon

Senator Benton continued to work avidly in Congress to acquire Oregon for the United States. He was furious with President Adams's administration for signing the 1827 treaty with England that continued the joint occupation situation and really allowed England to keep the sole occupancy of Oregon. He continued to argue, as he had in 1820–1825, that the elements of Discovery granted the sole ownership of the Pacific Northwest to the United States. By 1843, he was becoming quite militant on this issue. In support of yet another bill to absorb Oregon into the Union, he told Congress he wanted to "vindicat[e] our rights on the Columbia" and that his bill would "place thirty or forty thousand rifles beyond the Rocky Mountains, which will be our effective negotiators."[66]

Benton was now joined by Senator Lewis Linn, also of Missouri, in pushing for the occupation and ownership of Oregon. In 1838–1843, Linn introduced bills to encourage American settlement in Oregon, to grant free land to settlers, to extend federal jurisdiction and laws over the area, and to use the army to prevent the region from permanently falling into England's hands. Senator Linn also relied heavily on Discovery arguments to support America's right to Manifest Destiny over Oregon. Specifically, in 1838 he told the Senate that the United States needed to occupy Oregon because "discovery accompanied with subsequent and efficient acts of sovereignty or settlement are necessary to give title." As usual, Linn relied on Robert Gray's discovery of the Columbia, on Lewis and Clark's expedition as "an important circumstance in our title ... that was notice to the world of claim," and on the idea that Lewis and Clark's "solemn act of possession was followed up by a settlement and occupation, made by ... John Jacob Astor." Linn thus believed that the United States' "right, if placed alone on the strong and certain ground of *prior discovery,* would be as immutable as the everlasting hills." The evidence of the American rights under Discovery met the very test devised by England, he said. But he also realized that under English theory, ever since the time of Elizabeth I in the late 1500s, a first discovery of new lands had to be followed within a reasonable time by actual and permanent occupation by the discovering nation to perfect the incomplete title granted by first discovery alone. Consequently, Linn wanted to provide for a permanent American occupancy of Oregon. "If we are ever to assert our rights, it must be most speedily, before they lapse into the hands of others, from long undisputed possession."[67]

Linn also wanted America to acquire the assets of the region and expand its borders to Oregon because it was an opportunity of "finding and founding empires for us." He fully expected that an American military post on the Columbia would become "a nucleus around which our infant colonies could be firmly established." Linn also talked in the imagery and fictions of Manifest Destiny because he saw God's hand behind Americans subduing the wilderness and the inherent goodness of American territorial expansion. America conquered new areas, he said, not "by physical conquests [and] fleets and armies" but because these regions and people "have sought the blessings of our institutions; not we who will have coveted the enlargement of our territory by conquering." Linn even described to the

Senate what William Clark's vision of Manifest Destiny must have been when he stood on the Pacific Ocean in 1805 and "saw through the dim vista of the future rising States of his countrymen spreading along that [Pacific] shore ... The chain is complete from the Atlantic to the Pacific ocean."[68]

Other congressmen joined in this vision and used the elements of Discovery in their attempts to make Manifest Destiny a reality. Caleb Cushing of Massachusetts explicitly relied on Discovery elements when he argued to the House of Representatives "the rights" and the "title" of the United States to "the country watered by the river Columbia." In speeches to Congress on Oregon in May 1838, he relied on "the conventional rule ... the Law of Nations" and the "principle, adopted by European nations ... that priority of discovery, followed in a reasonable time by actual occupation, confers exclusive territorial jurisdiction and sovereignty." He also relied several times on "contiguity," the Discovery element that gave the discovering country rights to an indefinite reach of land along the coast and into the interior from any spot actually discovered and occupied. Cushing said that this "general principle ... [that] discovery of the mouth of a great river, or the exploration of it, followed in a reasonable time by the actual assertion of territorial sovereignty, gives an exclusive right to all the country watered by that river." These legal principles and the facts of American explorations in the Northwest meant that "whatever rights, more or less, are derivable from *discovery*, belong to the United States alone." According to Cushing, the "[p]riority of discovery, therefore, is clearly with the United States ... the United States claim the Oregon Territory by right of discovery."[69]

Moreover, Cushing argued that contiguity extended the northwest boundary of the Louisiana Territory and gave the United States rights in the Northwest and "a claim of title superior to that of any other nation." By the Louisiana Purchase, "the United States added to *her own rights of discovery* the preexisting rights of France." He also clearly saw the Discovery significance of the Lewis and Clark expedition and the Discovery rituals they performed. He described their actions in 1805 when they "erected the works called Fort Clatsop, and in the most formal and authentic manner asserted the rights of the United States in and to the whole country." He also argued that Astor and Astoria "extended the bounds of empire." In addition, Cushing relied on the 1821 treaty with Spain and its Discovery claim from California to the 60th parallel based on its "right of early discovery and repeated explorations and acts of occupation." All of these facts added up to one point: "Here, then, we have the original title of the United States by discovery, fortified by the rights of France, continued by the exploration of Lewis and Clark, by the formal taking of possession, and by regular occupation, and completed by the recognition of Great Britain." Cushing then concluded with a confident statement that merged Discovery and Manifest Destiny and one that he claimed had proven that "the United States have a clear title to the Oregon Territory, as against any and every European Power.... Oregon is a country ours by right, ours by necessity of geographic position; ours by every consideration of national safety."[70]

In 1839, Cushing and the House Foreign Affairs Committee issued a favorable report to Congress on a bill to establish military posts on the Columbia, to defend and occupy the territory, to investigate the extent of land claimed by the United States and the evidence of "the title under which it is claimed," and to absorb Oregon as a territory. The committee report repeated much of the same Discovery analysis as Cushing's May 1838 speeches to the House. The report also submitted petitions from American citizens now living in Oregon asking Congress to appoint a civil magistrate and a governor over the region. The settlers extolled the value of the Oregon country, the mild climate, and the trade and agricultural potentials. They also petitioned the government to control the Indian trade and intercourse and to provide security for "our property.... We need a guarantee from the Government that the possession of the land we take up, and the improvements we make upon it, will be secured to us. These settlements will greatly increase the value of the Government domain in that country, should the Indian title ever be extinguished." Demonstrating the continuing influence of Jefferson's thoughts on expansion, the settlers flattered themselves by thinking that they were the "germe of a great State." This is exactly what Jefferson had stated about Astoria in 1813.[71]

Also included in the House report was a letter from the Secretary of the Oregon Provisional Emigration Society from Massachusetts. The group was interested in settling in Oregon to plant a "Christian settlement" there, "to spread civilization and Christianity among the Indians." This group was willing to immigrate and settle the "savage wilderness" if the government would grant them "a sufficient title to the land we may occupy." The House of Representatives ordered 10,000 copies of Cushing's report to be printed and distributed to the American public.[72]

Congressmen continued to report all these events to their constituents and used the widely understood language of the Doctrine of Discovery. In 1829 several wrote letters about the extinguishment of Indian titles, and in 1828 and 1829, congressmen from North Carolina, Illinois, Tennessee, and Indiana reported on the progress of bills to occupy Oregon and make it a territory. They alleged, for example, that the "claim of the United States [was] founded on prior discovery, and the purchase of Louisiana," that "the United States have the best, and ... a clear title," and that the United States should protect the valuable fur trade and oppose "our jealous rival Great Britain, who sets up a claim to a large portion of this territory." Some of these politicians were against the United States absorbing Oregon but they still reported the news and the Discovery issues involving Oregon. Other congressmen, such as future President James Polk from Tennessee, became champions for American expansion to Oregon. In 1828 Polk joined the movement in the House to acquire the Northwest by proposing to extend the jurisdiction of the territorial courts in Michigan to the Pacific between the 42nd and 54th parallels.[73]

In 1842 the secretary of war took the dramatic step of appointing Elijah White as the American Indian agent west of the Rockies. White had already been living in Oregon as part of the Methodist mission. The secretary took this step after consulting with President Tyler and Senator Linn. The action was deemed necessary because the American citizens in Oregon needed "some known agent of the government, to whom they might look for advice and some degree of protection," and the United States wanted reports on the activities of the British government and the Hudson's Bay Company.[74] Clearly, the U.S. government had its eyes firmly set on the Pacific Northwest.

Governmental Explorations

President Andrew Jackson initiated several steps that advanced Manifest Destiny. Many commentators cite his actions and his use of the phrase "extending the area of freedom" to have been part and parcel of Manifest Destiny, and his idea that this "freedom" would progress across the continent's "unsettled spaces" also raises the specter of the Discovery element of *terra nullius*. Consequently, Jackson continued the progress of Discovery ideals morphing into the new policy of Manifest Destiny.[75]

The Jackson administration dispatched several explorations that contributed to the United States' occupying and acquiring Oregon. In 1835 a cavalry unit was sent west along the Platte River to the Rocky Mountains to awe the Plains Indians and to open the trail to Oregon for settlers who were already waiting to travel west. In 1836 Jackson sent William Slacum to Oregon and the Pacific coast to report to Congress on all aspects of the country. The report Slacum filed with Congress in December 1837 sparked real interest among Americans to migrate to Oregon.[76]

In May 1836, Congress also authorized a naval expedition of six ships under Lt. Charles Wilkes to explore and chart the Pacific and the coast and rivers of the Oregon country. Wilkes ultimately proposed that Congress claim the entire Pacific Northwest because the dangers of the Columbia River bar would prevent it from being a reliable port. He suggested that the United States needed access to Puget Sound in present-day Washington State.[77]

In 1842 the United States sent Captain John Fremont on the first of his three overland expeditions in 1842–1845. These expeditions played a dramatic role in exciting the American public about Oregon and California and had a vital role in bringing about a settlement of the Oregon boundary question. One commentator states that it was "[n]ext to the Lewis and Clark expedition, and perhaps surpassing it in this respect ... [one of] the outstanding examples, in American history, of the calculated uses of exploring expeditions as diplomatic weapons." The report filed by Fremont after his first trip was used as propaganda because Congress rushed it into print and ordered 1,000 copies to be publicly distributed and immediately sent him on more expeditions.[78]

American Private Economic Forces

The fur trade continued throughout this time period to drive Americans westward, although overtrapping caused the trade to begin to die out in the mid-1840s.

Trappers continued to discover and publicize easier travel routes west and fertile lands that were apparently available for free to the first settlers. Their stories about the valuable assets of the West aroused great interest. Furthermore, the New England sea otter, whaling, and trading interests continued to utilize the Northwest coast for their very lucrative ventures. All of these American private concerns created and sustained interest in acquiring the Oregon territory.

Technological advances in the private arena in this era further spurred the United States toward Oregon. The railroad was developed and expanded rapidly in the East starting in 1830. That very same year, a pamphlet was published proposing that a railroad be built to the Pacific Ocean. In 1832 a Michigan newspaper called for a railroad to be built from New York City to Oregon. In addition, in 1838 Samuel Morse demonstrated the telegraph, and in 1843 Congress authorized the construction of a line from Washington, DC, to Baltimore. Technological advances such as these made a continental American empire more feasible.

Missionaries

American missionaries played an extremely important role in opening the Oregon Trail and working directly to extend the elements of Discovery and Manifest Destiny to Oregon from 1833 forward. After the Astorians in 1811–1814, missionaries were the first Americans to permanently occupy the region. We know the importance of permanent occupation to Discovery claims, and thus the migration of numerous Americans to Oregon was obviously a crucial element in fulfilling America's Manifest Destiny to populate and own the Pacific Northwest.

The interests of Christian missionaries in the Northwest grew out of the visit of four Nez Perce Indians to St. Louis in 1831 or 1832. The Nez Perce allegedly were seeking instruction in the Bible. A fervent call to serve the interests of Christianity among the Northwest Indians did go out, and a few hardy souls answered. In 1834 the Methodist Jason Lee traveled to Oregon and settled south of the Columbia River in the present-day Willamette Valley. He was strategically directed to settle south of the Columbia River by John McLoughlin, the Hudson's Bay Company manager at Fort Vancouver. One can only imagine that McLoughlin directed Americans south of the Columbia hoping that England would maintain its occupancy and Discovery claims to the land north of the Columbia, where Hudson's Fort Vancouver was located. In just two short years, however, the Americans who settled around Lee's church and settlement outnumbered the English in the Pacific Northwest. As noted previously, by 1839, Lee was writing Congress, asking it to establish American jurisdiction over the region. By the end of 1840, there were five hundred Americans in the Willamette Valley. The permanent occupation of the Northwest by the United States was well underway. The Hudson's Bay Company understood this threat and worried about even this first trickle of American missionaries. A company official wrote in June 1836 that these missionary immigrants were dangerous because "we have all along foreseen that ... the formation of a Colony of United States citizens on the banks of the Columbia was the main or fundamental part of their plan."[79]

The Presbyterian Church also sent missionaries to the Northwest in 1835. Henry Spaulding, Marcus Whitman, and their wives established missions in what is now eastern Washington in Cayuse country and in Idaho in Nez Perce country. Henrietta Spaulding and Narcissa Whitman were the first white women to travel to Oregon. They demonstrated the possibility of families moving permanently to Oregon.

The significance to Manifest Destiny of the American missionaries was not the small number of Indians they converted or "civilized," but the promotion of American migration and the permanent occupation of the Northwest. They pointed out the possibility of migrating—that the country was open to future immigrants—and they demonstrated that the trip and life in Oregon was feasible. They also provided knowledge of the region for future settlers, information about the Oregon Trail, exact locations for new settlers to head for, and a place they could receive assistance when they first arrived. These missionaries also provided glowing reports on the land available for free, the rich soil, and the favorable climate. They helped many Americans make up their minds to immigrate to the Northwest.

American Settlers

The executive and legislative actions to secure the Oregon country and the activities of the missionaries and private American economic interests provoked many Americans to begin immigrating to Oregon during this time period. In addition, the economic situation in the United States and especially in the Mississippi Valley was poor for many years following the Panic of 1837. The recession created enormous interest in Oregon, and many Americans were tempted to leave their problems and try their luck on the free lands readily available in the Northwest.

One person in particular is a good example of this movement and the union of Discovery and Manifest Destiny goals. Hall Kelley of Boston was allegedly talking and writing about migrating to Oregon as early as 1815–1817. He has been called the "Prophet of Oregon." Whether he was that influential or talking about immigrating to Oregon as early as 1815 is not the important point, but instead he is noteworthy because he exemplified how the idea of immigrating developed in Americans.

In February 1828, he submitted a memorial to Congress for the government to form a colony on the Pacific Northwest coast in which he relied on the elements of Discovery and Manifest Destiny. Kelley and his group wanted the government to give them land so that they could aid the government in "colonizing a part of the American territory bordering on the Pacific Ocean." They claimed they wanted to protect the American "rights and property on the North-West Coast, and [work] for the peace and subordination of the Indians." They hoped to help spread "science, the refined principles of a republican government, and Christianity"; to diffuse "light and peace over Western America"; and to "open this wilderness to the skilful and persevering industry of civilized man." That was pretty ambitious talk. To accomplish these great goals, all Kelley's group sought was for Congress to grant them jurisdiction and land rights in fee simple and to extinguish the Indian title in the Pacific Northwest. These starry-eyed believers in Manifest Destiny were convinced that "if that territory should be settled by colonists animated by the *spirit* of [American] civil and religious institutions, which constitutes the living source of our national prosperity, and which dignifies the character, and elevates the pursuits of any people, the happiest consequences must result to our country in particular and to the rest of mankind."[80]

In 1830, Kelley also wrote a notable piece about the United States occupying Oregon that helped to raise the Oregon issue in the minds of many Americans. He sent his pamphlet and letters to newspaper editors encouraging Congress to occupy and govern Oregon. His arguments resonated with Discovery and Manifest Destiny ideals. First, he worried that the advantages of the Oregon country would pass to other countries if the United States continued to hesitate. Second, he said that to protect America's legitimate rights in Oregon, the United States needed to plant a colony there. In 1831, Kelley formed a society for the "Settlement of the Oregon Territory," and by 1835 he showed up in Oregon in pursuit of his goals.[81]

Other individuals also pursued their own agendas to make Oregon part of America. Other Oregon societies formed and petitioned Congress for land. Nathaniel Jarvis Wyeth, for example, demanded that Congress make Oregon a territory. He followed up his talk by forming a company to engage in fishing and the fur trade in Oregon, and he actually led expeditions of immigrants to Oregon in 1832–1835.

The increased interest in migration led to the opening and improvement of the Oregon Trail, which created an easier route to the Northwest. In 1843, 900 Americans arrived in Oregon over the trail. Almost all of the private and public efforts at migrating west were aimed at the Oregon country because California was still owned by Mexico at this time. The natural area open for American immigration was the Pacific Northwest.

As would be expected, and as was foretold by Thomas Jefferson, the United States flag followed the American immigrants. America's Manifest Destiny to own the Oregon country was greatly strengthened by this migration and by the settlers exercising American Discovery rights to settle what they considered vacant lands and to turn those assets into their own property by cultivating the land. Furthermore, the American settlers naturally looked to the United States government and demanded that it protect them and absorb the Oregon area as a territory. Petitions demanding exactly these actions were delivered to Congress in 1838 and 1839. Other events led the ex-mountain men, the ex-Hudson's Bay Company employees, and the new arrivals to begin forming rudimentary governing bodies to keep order and to govern themselves. In February of 1841, nearly every white male south of the Columbia River met to form a probate court to operate in the Willamette Valley. By July 1843, the American settlers formed a provisional government, drafted a constitution, and called themselves the Oregon Territory. An American-style government was formed and began operating in the Pacific Northwest. It immediately called for federal jurisdiction and protection.

1844–1855

By 1855, the United States concluded its Discovery and Manifest Destiny efforts to possess and own the Pacific Northwest. In that year, the United States used its exclusive Discovery power of preemption to buy millions of acres of land from various Indian Nations in the Northwest, and in 1859 Oregon became the 33rd state of the Union.

Governmental Efforts to Acquire Oregon

Although the phrase Manifest Destiny had still not been coined, the country was gripped by an aggressive expansionist feeling by 1844. The widespread expression of Manifest Destiny ideals resulted from decades of governmental and private discussions about American Discovery rights in the Northwest. It also resulted in the United States finally settling the Oregon question, annexing Texas, and declaring war on Mexico in 1846.

The issue of annexing the independent republic of Texas had been a boiling point in American politics for more than two decades, and desires to occupy and own Oregon had been fermenting for even longer, as we have observed. The Democratic Party brought these issues to a head by including in its platform for the 1844 presidential election a Discovery demand to annex Texas and occupy Oregon. These two issues meshed nicely because they advocated admitting a new slave state, Texas, with a new non-slave territory, Oregon. The Democratic platform stated that "our title to the whole of the territory of Oregon is clear and unquestionable; that no portion of the same ought to be ceded to England or any other power; and that the re-occupation of Oregon and the reannexation of Texas at the earliest practicable period are great American measures."[82]

The Democratic candidate, James K. Polk, campaigned vigorously on this theme and on Manifest Destiny. His election slogan was the aggressive and war-like statement about the Oregon country: "54–40 or fight." Thus, Polk was claiming as American territory the Pacific Northwest coast northward into much of what is present-day British Columbia, Canada. The 1844 election was considered to be about expansion, and when Polk won, he naturally declared his election to be a mandate for American expansion. It is no surprise, then, that Texas was annexed (by President John Tyler even before Polk was inaugurated), Oregon was acquired, and a war of territorial conquest was commenced with Mexico all within less than two years.[83]

In his inaugural address on March 4, 1845, Polk addressed the Oregon question, Discovery, and Manifest Destiny. In discussing "our territory which lies beyond the Rocky Mountains," he stated that the United States' "title to the country of the Oregon is 'clear and unquestionable,' and already are our people preparing to perfect that title by occupying it." He noted that Americans were "already engaged in establishing the blessings of self-government in valleys of which the rivers flow to the Pacific. The world beholds the peaceful triumphs of our emigrants." The opening of the Northwest and the "extinguish[ing]" of the "title of numerous Indian tribes to vast tracts of country" for American settlement was a good thing, according to Polk, because Manifest Destiny and expansion strengthened the Union by not confining its population to small areas but by allowing it to "be safely extended to the utmost bounds of our territorial limits [so as to] become stronger." He warned Mexico and Great Britain not to interfere in America's expansions in North America. These were very aggressive words from a brand new president. But Polk assumed he had been elected with a Manifest Destiny mandate, and he was determined to carry out that policy.[84]

President Polk set about accomplishing his goals regarding Oregon. He met with Senator Benton in October 1845 to discuss the Northwest boundary issue. What is noteworthy about this meeting is the knowledgeable manner in which these two national politicians discussed the elements of Discovery and American Manifest Destiny rights. This conversation demonstrates clearly that both men understood and operated under Discovery principles. President Polk recorded the conversation in his diary.

Polk explained to Benton that he was going to recommend that Congress abrogate the 1827 joint occupation treaty of the Northwest with England by giving the required one-year notice, and then he would extend U.S. jurisdiction over the American citizens in Oregon. He and Benton discussed the claims of England and the United States in the Pacific Northwest. They recounted the English claim and the Discovery rituals that English citizens had performed there. Benton was worried that England had the same valid claim to a Discovery title in the area that is today British Columbia, Canada, as the United States held to the Columbia River area. England's claim, Benton stated, was based on "discovery, exploration, and settlement." The president, referring to the Adams-Onis treaty of 1821, stated that the United States claimed the entire Northwest under the Spanish Discovery title. Benton argued for an even more expansive reading of the U.S. rights. The president responded that it "would depend on the public law of nations, how far the discovery and possession of the coast would give Spain a title to the adjoining country in the interior." International law, first discovery, contiguity, discovery rituals, and occupation—they were clearly analyzing and discussing the application of Discovery.[85]

On December 2, 1845, Polk delivered his First Annual Message to Congress and discussed the Oregon question at great length. He asserted, "our title to the whole Oregon Territory ... [is] maintained by irrefragable [irrefutable] facts and arguments," and he asked Congress to decide how to maintain "our just title to that Territory." By 1845, about 5,000 Americans and perhaps 750 British citizens occupied the Oregon country. Polk explained that because of federal neglect, these American citizens had been forced to form a provisional government and had adopted "republican institutions [illustrating] that self-government is inherent in the American breast and must prevail." Polk suggested that Congress immediately provide for federal protection, laws, and civil and criminal jurisdiction to be extended to these citizens in Oregon and to control the Indian commercial and political relations in the area. He also requested the building of forts along the Oregon Trail, the creation of an overland mail service to Oregon, and landgrants to the "patriotic pioneers who … lead the way through savage tribes inhabiting the vast wilderness." He also asked Congress to give England the one-year notice required by the treaty of 1827 that the United States was abrogating the treaty.[86]

Polk briefly discussed the American title to Oregon. He referred Congress to the three decades of discussions and political negotiations between the United States and England that we have already reviewed. Polk cited the negotiations in 1818, 1824, 1826, and 1844, at least three offers by the United States to draw the boundary line on the 49th parallel, and the resulting treaties with England of 1818 and 1827. Polk was confident that the evidence of Discovery proved that "the title of the United States is the best now in existence." He also claimed under international law that England did not have a valid claim to the Pacific Northwest because "the British pretensions of title could not be maintained to any portion of the Oregon Territory upon any principle of public law recognized by nations." Polk then forcefully argued for American Manifest Destiny by noting "the rapid extension of our settlements over our territories heretofore unoccupied … the expansion of free principles, and our rising greatness as a nation." Some European countries, he explained, were talking about a "'balance of power' on this continent to check our advancement." Polk would have none of that. He expressly reaffirmed the Monroe Doctrine and stated that Europeans had no role in North America and could not interfere with any regions that might want to join the United States. He plainly threatened war if any European country interfered.[87]

This very aggressive and warlike public tone greatly concerned the English press, public, and politicians. Did President Polk really mean to go to war over the "54–40" boundary line? Was the Pacific Northwest worth a war to England? The English Cabinet ordered reports from the Hudson's Bay Company on the value of the fur trade and future prospects in the Northwest. The reports were not encouraging. The fur trade was down after 30 years of operations from Fort George/Astoria and Fort Vancouver. Even worse, in 1845 the Hudson's Bay Company had voluntarily withdrawn from Fort Vancouver, in present-day Vancouver, Washington, to Fort Victoria, on present-day Vancouver Island, Canada. This decision was made because of concerns about the growing aggressive American population in the Oregon region and declining fur production. This decision helped the English government reach a decision. England was faced with wars and important political problems elsewhere. There would be no war over a boundary line on the Columbia River, where England had argued for decades that the boundary should be drawn. But there would be no American boundary line on the 54th parallel either. Compromise was in the air. It was no surprise that the United States compromised and accepted the present-day 49th parallel boundary line between Canada and the United States despite the militant tone for "54–40." The United States had made at least four offers over several decades to settle the Northwest border issue by extending the 49th parallel boundary line from east of the Rocky Mountains to the Pacific Ocean.

During this time, Congress deliberated on Polk's suggestions about legislation on Oregon and giving England the one-year notice to abrogate the 1827 treaty and the joint occupancy of the Northwest. Discovery and Manifest Destiny continued to be dominant themes in these discussions and were raised by many politicians. In January 1846, for example, Illinois Senator Stephen Douglass stated that after terminating the 1827 treaty, the "United States will be entitled to the *actual exclusive possession of the valley of the Columbia river,* and will be entitled to continue in possession of that valley while treating the question of title." On the question of title, Douglass stated, "we do hold the valley of the Columbia in our own right by virtue of discovery, exploration, and occupation, and that we have a treaty-right in addition through the Louisiana and Florida treaty." He also expressly relied on the Discovery and Manifest Destiny goals of converting and civilizing the Indians of Oregon, and he utilized the *terra nullius* element when he claimed that the United States had rights to "the vacant and unoccupied part of North America." By 1854, Douglass was positively bursting with grandiose Manifest Destiny rhetoric when he told the Senate, "You cannot fix bounds to the onward march of this great and growing country.... He will expand, and grow, and increase, and extend civilization, Christianity, and liberal principles. I tell you, sir, you must provide for continuous lines of settlement from the Mississippi valley to the Pacific ocean."[88]

In September 1845, Polk's secretary of state, future President James Buchanan, resumed the decades-old negotiations with England on the boundary line in the Pacific Northwest. Buchanan at first argued for the 54th parallel, which had been Polk's campaign slogan, but then he agreed to the 49th parallel, where the border is today. It is entirely possible that Polk would have been satisfied with that boundary line all along and that he just sold out his "54–40" supporters or that the 54–40 claim had been political rhetoric all along. The important point for most people was that a border line was now established, England had given up its Discovery claim to the Oregon country and its insistence on the Columbia River border, and American Manifest Destiny to the Pacific Ocean was ensured! Secretary of State Buchanan now foresaw America's "glorious mission to perform ... [of] extending the blessings of Christianity and of civil and religious liberty over the whole of the North American continent."[89]

On June 15, 1846, the United States signed the treaty with England that drew the boundary line at the 49th parallel. The four-decade legal struggle between England and the United States over Discovery ownership of the Northwest was finished. The United States had now guaranteed its Manifest Destiny goal to cross the continent to the Pacific Ocean.

The United States quickly absorbed Oregon into the Union. In August 1848, Congress passed the Organic Act and created the Oregon Territory. This act applied the Northwest Ordinance of 1787 and its use of the elements of Discovery to the Oregon Territory. Thereafter, in 1849 Joseph Lane was appointed the first territorial governor, and units of the U.S. Army arrived overland. In September 1850, Congress enacted the Oregon Land Donation Act and began giving land grants to settlers as it had been requested to do for decades. In this act, Congress gave away Indian lands that had not yet had the Indian titles extinguished. Yet, strangely enough, the federal law called these lands "the public lands of the United States." This federal action and the assumption that the Indian lands were already federal property reflected the elements of Discovery and the understanding that the United States could grant away its title in these lands even while Indians occupied and used the land, and only later did the United States have to extinguish the Indian title. On February 14, 1859, Congress made Oregon the 33rd state.[90]

American Settlers

Ultimately, the physical proximity of the Pacific Northwest to the United States won the region for the United States. This proximity made it easier for American settlers to immigrate to Oregon than any other non-Indian people. Maybe this was the realistic aspect that made it America's destiny to occupy and own the Northwest. Maybe John Quincy Adams was right when he said that because of contiguity, the contiguous nature of the Oregon country to the Louisiana territory, the "finger of nature" had pointed to American ownership of the region.

But remember that even the physical proximity of the Northwest to the United States was still an enormous obstacle to American ownership of Oregon in the early 1800s. Although Jefferson and Meriwether Lewis were correct to foresee a day when the United States could utilize and govern the area, it took several decades of technological and migratory advances before the United States could reach the critical mass of population to control the Northwest. As a trickle of Americans arrived in the Northwest on the Oregon Trail, formed a government, and finally provoked the Hudson's Bay Company to withdraw to Vancouver Island, the destiny of the Pacific Northwest to be American was sealed. In 1845 a St. Louis editorial recognized this fact about American settlers: "They go to plant a new people in a new and active country—to create new states—to open a new field to the growing energies and wants of our expanding Republic—to carry civilization around the world…. It is a wonderful impulse this, combined of patriotism, curiosity, and a war-like spirit of adventure, which is pressing our people onward to the Western Seas."[91]

From 1844 onward, the trickle of American settlers to Oregon turned into a flood. In 1845, three thousand more Americans arrived in Oregon. They did what Thomas Jefferson had always predicted they would do; they immediately petitioned Congress for federal services. From 1833 forward, the American settlers had played an important role in gaining the Pacific Northwest for the United States.

Pacific Northwest Indian Treaties

Throughout North American history, the European, colonial, state, and federal governments all dealt with the Indian Nations diplomatically and on a government-to-government basis by treaty making. Issues of trade, peace, and land sales were always conducted in political conferences that resulted in the enactment of hundreds of treaties. This treaty process was carried on by the governments of England, France, Spain, the American colonies, the states, and the United States from the mid-1500s until 1871 when Congress ended treaty making with Indian Nations. Canada is still negotiating treaties with its First Nations today. The American treaty process created more than four hundred U.S.–Indian treaties that are still binding on the federal government today. The Constitution says these treaties are "the supreme Law of the Land."

It is no surprise then that the United States also entered into treaties with Indian Nations in the Pacific Northwest. In fact, the United States fully expected to exercise its Discovery power of preemption to extinguish Indian titles in the Northwest and to buy land. The United States had already been doing so since 1778 and had been dealing with the tribal nations on a sovereign-to-sovereign basis through this diplomatic process.

After enacting the 1850 act to grant land to settlers in Oregon, Congress had to begin extinguishing the Indian titles and property rights. Congress had expressly recognized Indian property rights as valid two years earlier in the 1848 Organic Act that created the Oregon Territory. Section 1 of the 1848 act stated that existing Indian property rights were not impaired "so long as such rights shall remain unextinguished by treaty between the United States and such Indians." Consequently, if the United States wanted to "impair" or purchase these property rights and grant possession of these lands to American settlers, it had to buy Indian property rights and lands via treaties. The United States started that treaty procedure with tribes in June 1850 by authorizing and appointing treaty negotiators to buy land in the Oregon Territory. Thereafter, the American negotiators met with western Oregon tribes in April and May 1851 and signed six treaties that ceded most of the tribal lands and only reserved small tracts of land for the tribes. None of these treaties were ever ratified by the Senate, and so they never became law.[92]

Anson Dart was then appointed the new United States Superintendent for Indian Affairs in 1851 for the Oregon Territory. He negotiated treaties with ten western Oregon tribes at Tansy Point at the mouth of the Columbia River wherein the tribal nations ceded large areas of their lands to the United States and reserved small reservations for themselves. Dart also negotiated three other treaties with southwest Oregon tribes. But none of the Dart treaties were approved by the Senate either. The thirteen Dart treaties and the earlier six treaties were probably not ratified because they did not remove the Indians to the eastern and arid parts of Oregon as the majority of the American settlers desired. The ultimate effect on these Indian Nations was that they lost their lands and their rights anyway and without receiving any compensation. They were just pushed aside as their populations declined drastically due to foreign diseases.

In March 1853, Congress divided the Oregon Territory into Oregon and Washington and appointed new officials. Washington Governor Issac Stevens, who was also the Superintendent for Indian Affairs, and the new Superintendent for Indian Affairs in Oregon, Joel Palmer, began negotiating new treaties with tribes. In 1853–1855, Joel Palmer negotiated treaties with southern, western, and eastern Oregon tribes that the Senate ultimately approved and made binding law.

Governor Stevens also concluded treaties in 1854 and 1855 with Washington, Idaho, and western Montana Indian Nations, which the Senate ratified. All of these treaties sold vast areas of land to the United States for various monetary payments and assistance. The Indian Nations also reserved or retained for themselves lands to be their "reservations," and they retained certain off-reservation hunting and fishing rights that have long been both exercised by Indians and challenged by non-Indians in the Northwest. The United States also promised in these treaties to protect the tribes.[93]

After buying much of the land in the Pacific Northwest through these treaties, the United States had finally fulfilled its Manifest Destiny and Thomas Jefferson's dream to control and own the Pacific Northwest. This goal was reached when the United States exercised its Discovery power of preemption as the only government with the international legal authority to buy the land in the Northwest from the Indian Nations. The United States now merged its incomplete Discovery "title" with the "Indian title," the real-property right to use and occupy the land, so that the United States now held the complete fee simple absolute title to the ceded lands.

POST-1855 DISCOVERY AND MANIFEST DESTINY

The United States continued to use the Doctrine of Discovery and Manifest Destiny after 1855. For example, in 1856 Congress enacted the Guano Island Act and utilized the Doctrine. This act relied on the familiar principles of first discovery, actual occupation, and *terra nullius*. It is still federal law and was in fact the subject of a federal court case as recently as 2000. The act provides that an American citizen who "discovers a deposit of guano on any island … not within the lawful jurisdiction of any other government, and takes peaceable possession … and occupies the same, [may request that the land] at the discretion of the President, be considered as appertaining to the United States." The Supreme Court upheld this law in 1890 by relying on the elements of Discovery:

> By the law of nations, recognized by all civiliezed states, dominion of new territory may be acquired by discovery and occupation as well as by cession or conquest; and when citizens or subjects of one nation, in its name, and by its authority, or with its assent, take and hold actual, continuous, and useful possession … of territory unoccupied by any other government or its citizens, the nation to which they belong may exercise such jurisdiction and for such period as it sees fit over territory so acquired.

This act is further evidence that the federal government has understood and used the power of Discovery from the beginning of its existence and continued to use it and to implant it into federal law.[94]

Other examples of the use of Discovery in more recent times demonstrate the modern-day relevance of the Doctrine even outside the Indian Law field. In 1872, for example, the United States argued that Haiti did not own an island it claimed in the Caribbean because it did not meet the elements of Discovery. The United States said Haiti could not demonstrate "an actual possession and use ... [or] an extension and exercise of jurisdiction and authority over" the island. Thus, Haiti's claim of ownership and sovereignty was not recognizable. On the other hand, the United States lost an international arbitration with Holland in 1928 when they made competing Discovery claims to an island in the Philippines. The American claim was based solely on Spain's first discovery of the island. But, as the arbitrator held, Spain's mere discovery of the island did not give it a complete title to the island; it only created an incomplete title. Because neither Spain nor the United States ever occupied or exercised jurisdiction over the island, the ownership of it fell to Holland, who had occupied it.[95]

In 1895 the Republican Party wrote Manifest Destiny into its official party platform. The idea was almost as popular then as in 1844–1846. In 1895 Senator Henry Cabot Lodge wrote that there could be only one flag, one country, to control all the territory in North America from the Rio Grande to the Arctic Ocean. He called for the American annexation of Hawaii, Samoa, and Cuba; note his reasoning that Cuba was only "sparsely settled." He also encouraged the United States to incorporate other lands because the "great nations are rapidly absorbing for their future expansion and their present defence all the waste places of the earth. It is a movement which makes for civilization and the advancement of the race." He clearly relied on the elements of *terra nullius* and racial justifications of Discovery to encourage American expansion.[96]

CONCLUSION

Manifest Destiny developed from the elements and the themes of the international law Doctrine of Discovery. For 40 years or more, American politicians, citizens, and newspapers used the elements of Discovery to justify Manifest Destiny and American continental expansion. Did you notice how we would not have even understood the rhetoric and the justifications for Manifest Destiny if we had not already known the definition of the elements of Discovery that were used to justify expansion?

The elements of Discovery became the rationales and justifications for the idea of a divinely inspired American expansion across the North American continent. Apparently, Euro-Americans possessed the only valid religions, civilizations, governments, laws, and cultures, and Providence intended these people and their institutions to dominate this continent. The human, governmental, and property rights of Native Americans were almost totally disregarded as Discovery and then Manifest Destiny directed the United States continental expansion. The "wild and savage" Indians and Mexicans were either to "disappear" by assimilating into white American culture or they were to become extinct. Under Manifest Destiny it was "clear" that God wanted them to get out of the way of progress—American progress. The economic and political interests of Americans and of the United States were destined to dominate the continent and to acquire almost all of its assets.[97]

The elements of Discovery and Manifest Destiny were pursued by George Washington, Thomas Jefferson, and a host of American politicians and citizens who wanted to benefit from the resources and the land that they thought was available for their taking, with God's blessing. Jefferson's ambitions and the path-breaking work of the Lewis and Clark expedition opened the American road to the Pacific Northwest. The Discovery claims the United States made against Indian Nations and Indian people in the Louisiana Territory and the Pacific Northwest limited their human, property, commercial, sovereign, and self-determination rights. The Louisiana Purchase, the Lewis and Clark expedition, and the Doctrine of Discovery nearly guaranteed that a wave of American expansion would sweep over the indigenous peoples and their governments on this continent. The Doctrine of Discovery and American Manifest Destiny were not good news, they were not divinely inspired good news, for these human beings.

Two statements aptly sum up what Discovery and Manifest Destiny meant for Indians. When Senator Benton was asked about American expansion and whether it would cause the extinction of Indian tribes if they "resisted civilization," he stated, "I cannot murmur at what seems to be the effect of divine law.... The moral and intellectual superiority of the White race will do the rest." As Manifest Destiny clashed against Indian interests in Wyoming in 1870, a newspaper wrote, "The rich and beautiful valleys of Wyoming are destined for the occupancy and sustenance of the Anglo-Saxon race.... The Indians must stand aside or be overwhelmed.... The destiny of the aborigines is written in characters not to be mistaken ... the doom of extinction is upon the red men of America."[98]

CHAPTER 7

❧

The United States' Exercise of Discovery against the Indian Nations, 1774–2005

The Doctrine of Discovery is not just an interesting relic of American history. The Doctrine is actively applied by the United States to Indians and tribal governments today and is a major component of modern-day federal Indian law. Commentators have noted, in fact, that Discovery and the Supreme Court's opinion in *Johnson v. M'Intosh* were "to influence all subsequent thinking" in federal Indian law. Consequently, the Doctrine still impacts and limits tribal sovereign, commercial, and real-property rights today. The vestiges of Discovery are reflected in far more than just the definition of the limited "Indian title," the occupancy and use right in tribal lands; they are also evident in the 200-plus years of American Indian policies and the fundamental principles of federal Indian law.[1]

FUNDAMENTAL PRINCIPLES OF FEDERAL INDIAN LAW

There are three fundamental Indian law principles that have been developed by the Supreme Court over a nearly 200-year time span. These principles still control federal Indian law to this day. They flowed naturally from the Doctrine of Discovery and reflect the Doctrine at work in modern day Indian law.

Plenary Power

The plenary power doctrine holds that Congress has very broad authority in Indian affairs. Congress, for example, has authority to enact laws that can injure Indian Nations and their citizens or that can benefit tribes and their citizens. In the late nineteenth century, Congress used this power to limit and severely harm tribal real-property rights even more than the Discovery Doctrine itself had limited those rights. On dozens of Indian reservations, Congress divided and allotted tribally owned lands to individual Indians and sold the extra or "surplus" lands to non-Indians. These actions undermined tribal ownership of communally owned property and brought many non-Indians to live on Indian reservations. The presence of non-Indians and millions of acres of non-Indian owned lands within Indian reservation borders cause tribal governments serious and nearly intractable problems that continue to this very day. The U.S. Supreme Court and President Theodore Roosevelt admitted that the Allotment Act was a congressional attempt to destroy tribal governments. Moreover, in the 1950s, Congress exercised the sovereign authority that Discovery and the Constitution apparently granted it over Indian affairs, and it terminated the legal existence and federal relationship of more than one hundred Indian Nations. In the 1970 and 1980s, Congress restored most of these tribes to federal recognition. These types of actions, however, demonstrate the nearly unchecked power Congress has in Indian affairs because of Discovery and the principle of plenary power. Only in recent times did the Supreme Court decide that congressional actions pursuant to its plenary power in Indian law require even the lowest level of judicial constitutional review. In the long history of congressional acts regarding the Indian Nations and Indian peoples, no federal law has ever been overturned because Congress exceeded its plenary power in the Indian law arena.[2]

The Supreme Court has stated that the Interstate/Indian Commerce Clause of the U.S. Constitution "provides Congress with plenary power to legislate in the field of Indian affairs." The Court has also pointed out that plenary power comes from other constitutional provisions such as the treaty making power, the Property Clause, the Supremacy Clause, and the Necessary and Proper clause, which gives the federal government the necessary authority to carry out its enumerated powers. It really does not make sense, however, to allege that the Interstate/Indian Commerce Clause created a congressional plenary power over Indian Nations because that constitutional provision addresses only commercial issues, and it concerns only the allocation of authority for dealing with tribes between the federal and state governments. That clause does not even claim to impact tribal authority or rights, nor does it expressly grant Congress a sweeping plenary power over tribes for any and all subjects.[3]

Although the Supreme Court has named several sources for plenary power, it has apparently never recognized the one source that appears obvious, the Doctrine of Discovery. In fact, it seems beyond question that Discovery and the principles and justifications behind the Doctrine helped spawn the idea that the American government held dominion and domination over the Indian Nations because they lost sovereign, diplomatic, property, and commercial rights immediately upon their first discovery by Euro-Americans. The other elements of Discovery that Christianity and European civilizations were superior and would triumph over the Indian Nations were also brought to this continent by England, France, and Spain and have remained part of the legal regime of the American colonial, state, and federal governments. As discussed previously, Discovery also created the idea that Euro-American governments held a limited fee title in the lands that Indians had lived on and owned for centuries. It appears obvious that the origin of the controversial plenary power doctrine started with Discovery principles.

The Supreme Court also developed the idea of a heightened congressional power over Indian Nations based on their alleged helpless and destitute conditions. The Court has considered the impoverished condition of Indians and their tribal governments, even when that "fact" was false, as part of the justification for a congressional duty to care for Indian tribes. In an 1886 case, the Court analyzed that the duty of the United States to protect Indians, a provision in most of the U.S.–Indian treaties, required that Congress have sufficient power over Indians and tribes to carry out its duty of protection. This overarching power is part of the plenary power doctrine. Do not forget that the idea of some kind of federal duty or guardianship over Indian Nations also came from Discovery principles and the royal charters of the early 1600s. However one examines the subject, it appears that the Doctrine of Discovery and the alleged weaknesses and subjugation of Indian Nations played large roles in the development of the plenary power principle.[4]

Trust Doctrine

The federal government also has a guardian, trustee, or fiduciary responsibility for tribes that is based on its nearly unchecked plenary power over Indians and their governments. Principles of general trust law and the alleged helplessness of tribes led to the rise of the trust responsibility as a corollary principle to plenary power. In exercising their extremely broad authority in Indian affairs, Congress and the executive branch are charged with the responsibilities of a guardian to act on behalf of the dependent Indian people and their governments. The United States has accepted this responsibility and has "charged itself with moral obligations of the highest responsibility and trust," and it judges its own conduct toward tribes "by the most exacting fiduciary standards."[5]

Many of the same justifications and Supreme Court cases that created plenary power also led to the development of the related trust doctrine. The idea of a trust relationship began developing in Supreme Court case law in 1831 when the Court considered the status of the Cherokee Nation. In that case, the Court erroneously described the thriving Cherokee Nation as being in a destitute condition and stated that the nation was dependent on the United States for its "protection" and "wants" and was in a "state of pupilage" with the federal government. The *Cherokee Nation v. Georgia* Court then went on to make the famous, or infamous, statement that the Cherokee Nation's "relation to the United States resembles that of a ward to his guardian."[6]

The next major pronouncement on the subject of the trust doctrine came in 1886 in *United States v. Kagama*. Here, the Supreme Court considered whether Congress could extend federal criminal jurisdiction into Indian country for criminal activity by Indians and what power Congress might possess to have this kind of authority. The Court expressly refused to rely on the Interstate/Indian Commerce Clause and instead started its analysis by looking at the heavy responsibility the United States has to care for Indians and their governments. Since the "Indian tribes *are* the wards of the nation … [and] communities *dependent* on the United States[,]" the Court held that "[f]rom their very weakness and helplessness" a duty arose to protect tribes under a trust responsibility, and that this duty must include whatever powers are necessary to carry out the protective duty. Thus, the United States had the authority to enact a law that federally criminalized certain Indian conduct within Indian country to fulfill the United States' protective duty towards the Indian Nations.[7]

The effect of the trust doctrine on tribes is somewhat similar to that under plenary power; sometimes the United States takes its trust responsibility seriously and engages in conduct that benefits Indians and tribal governments. Often, however, the United States has adopted a paternalistic tone, and heavily influenced by its plenary power, it has just dictated affairs to tribal governments. Only in modern times have Indians Nations been able to sue the United States for a breach of the trust doctrine and thus gained some ability to enforce this guardianship duty on the federal government.

The trust doctrine plainly had its genesis in the Discovery Doctrine. The papal bulls in the fifteenth century placed Christian guardianship duties on Spain and Portugal to convert and protect indigenous peoples. English royal charters ordered the colonists to convert and save American Indians. In colonial times and in the early American states, many colonies and states enacted laws that appointed white citizens to be trustees and guardians to manage and allegedly protect tribal rights and to civilize and convert Indians. The federal treaties with Indian Nations also contained promises by the United States to protect tribes, to control and support their commercial activities, and to provide educational and medical care. There is a long history behind the idea that Euro-Americans had a duty to care for the best interests of Indians. This thinking came largely from the Eurocentric ideas of Discovery and the notion that uncivilized, infidel savages needed to be saved by Euro-Americans. Interestingly, Chief Justice John Marshall relied on several Discovery elements when he stated in *Cherokee Nation* that Indian Nations were the wards of the United States. He pointed to the limited Indian title, the right of preemption and European title that was gained by first discovery, and issues of possession as part of the proof that tribes were in a dependent relationship. "They occupy a territory to which we assert a title independent of their will, which must take effect in point of possession when their right of possession ceases." Consequently, because Marshall relied on the Doctrine of Discovery when he initially defined the trust responsibility, there seems to be no question but that Discovery played a significant role in the development and in the modern day continuation of this basic Indian law principle.[8]

Diminished Tribal Sovereignty

The third fundamental principle of federal Indian law explicated by the Supreme Court is the diminished tribal sovereignty principle. It is closely related to the other two basic principles and also flows directly from Discovery. In fact, the

Discovery Doctrine is the origination of the idea of diminished tribal sovereignty because Indian sovereign, commercial, diplomatic, and real-property rights were assumed to have been limited automatically and immediately upon first discovery by Euro-Americans. This Eurocentric, ethnocentric thinking assumed that indigenous people were savages and inferior to "civilized" Christian Europeans.

In precontact times, the hundreds of Indian Nations in what is now the United States had a wide array of governments ranging from loosely organized political structures in small tribal bands to complex and sometimes even autocratic ruling bodies that controlled large populations. These tribes exercised nearly unlimited sovereignty over their territories, varying amounts of political control and sovereign power over their citizens, and a sovereign status that existed completely independent from the European and American governments. Yet, the third fundamental principle of federal Indian law holds, right out of Discovery, that tribal sovereignty was automatically and immediately diminished upon first contact with Euro-Americans.[9]

In spite of this principle, Indian Nations are still sovereign governments today. Even after the Supreme Court held that Discovery had limited tribal sovereign and real-property rights and stated that tribes were "domestic dependent nations" and wards of the United States, the Court still held that tribes had not lost their sovereign status and governmental authority within their own territories. In fact, the Court stated in 1832 that tribes were still "distinct, independent political communities" and that the long history of Euro-American governments repeatedly entering treaties with tribes demonstrated an ongoing acceptance of the continued sovereign, governmental status of the Indian Nations. There were, however, two factors that could diminish tribal independent sovereignty even beyond the initial impact of the Doctrine of Discovery. As the Court implied in *Worcester,* in 1832, tribes could voluntarily give up aspects of their sovereignty and sell land in treaties, and Congress could take other aspects of tribal sovereignty without tribal consent pursuant to its plenary power.[10]

After *Worcester* in 1832, the Court rarely addressed this issue again, although Congress continued full-tilt enacting laws and federal policies under its plenary power authority that limited tribal powers. Finally, in 1978 the Court returned to and expanded the principle of diminished tribal sovereignty in *Oliphant v. Suquamish Indian Tribe.*

In *Oliphant,* the Court held that the inherent sovereign authority of Indian tribes did not include the jurisdiction to criminally prosecute non-Indians. The Supreme Court relied on the principle of the diminished sovereign status of tribes and stated that Indian Nations could not have this type of criminal jurisdiction because it would be "inconsistent with their status." The Court then expanded the definition of this Indian law principle. Since *Oliphant,* the diminished sovereignty principle holds that tribes retain those aspects of their inherent sovereignty that they have not voluntarily given up, by treaty for example; that Congress has not taken pursuant to its plenary power; or, as *Oliphant* added, that they have not implicitly lost by virtue of their dependent status upon the United States.

According to the Supreme Court, then, Indian Nations are diminished sovereigns. It bears repeating that the original limitations on tribal sovereignty and the idea of the dependent status of tribes came from the European Doctrine of Discovery.[11]

FEDERAL INDIAN POLICIES

Historians recognize that there have been seven relatively distinct eras of United States Indian policy. We will briefly review some of these policy eras only to observe the exercise of Discovery powers by the United States over tribal governments and Indian people throughout American history.

The first federal Indian policy, the Trade and Intercourse era, is generally assumed to have run from 1790 to 1830 and takes its name from the congressional Trade and Intercourse Acts of 1790, 1793, 1796, 1799, and 1802 that we have discussed. In 1790, Congress moved rapidly to exercise the Discovery and preemption powers it was granted in the Constitution to control all commercial activities between Americans and Indians. The Congress enacted temporary trade and intercourse laws from 1790 to 1799 and a permanent act in 1802. Congress also enacted many other statutes to control the trade and political intercourse with tribal nations and to prevent anyone but the federal government from buying Indian lands. These policies are still mostly in effect today.

During this era, the policies of the executive branch, and George Washington and Thomas Jefferson specifically, were based on Discovery principles. The destiny of Euro-Americans to exercise the limited sovereign and property rights they gained over Indians through Discovery was correctly defined by Washington's phrase the "Savage as Wolf." In this statement, Washington and the federal government foresaw the advance of America's borders and the assumed concomitant retreat of the tribal nations. Under Discovery, once Indian Nations gave up their "Indian title," their use and occupancy rights, the ownership of the land fell to the country that held the preemption power. Thus, Washington and Jefferson and the executive branch wanted to peaceably control trade and commerce with Indians, buy Indians lands whenever they could, and await the inevitable demise of Indian people as they retreated into the forest like the "Savage as Wolf" or, as Jefferson stated, when Indians would retreat before the inevitable American advance like "the beasts of the forest." Until that time, though, the United States still wanted to control all political and commercial interactions with Indian Nations and all purchases of tribal lands. It accomplished this task by taking control of the constitutionally authorized treaty process with Indian Nations. The executive branch and Congress, then, clearly exercised the federal government's Discovery power, which consisted of a limited sovereignty over tribal governments, the right to exclude other nations and governments from dealing with tribes diplomatically and commercially, and the property right of preemption to purchase tribal lands by consent when tribes desired to sell.[12]

The relative power between Indian Nations and the United States in political and treaty negotiations quickly became one-sided in favor of the United States.

This transformation accelerated after the War of 1812 when the influence of European nations on the North American continent waned, and tribes could no longer look to European powers for support against the expansionist United States. This shift in power also created momentum for an official change in federal Indian policy. Starting with Thomas Jefferson in 1803, the plan developed to move tribes west of the Mississippi to get them out of the way of American expansion and open their lands for American settlers. The genesis of what became the removal policy and Manifest Destiny itself sprang from Washington's "Savage as Wolf" policy and Jefferson's idea that Indians would have to be removed to make room for the natural American expansion that was to come.[13]

The official Indian policy of the Removal era is considered to have run from 1830 to the 1850s. Long before 1830, of course, Washington and Jefferson were writing about Indian removal, and every president after Jefferson, from James Madison to Andrew Jackson, officially and publicly supported the policy of removing Indian tribes west of the Mississippi River as the final solution to the Indian problem. Congress gave the era its name by enacting the Removal Act in 1830. Interestingly, the act maintained on its face the elements of Discovery because consent was needed from an Indian Nation before the United States could buy its land. The Act required tribal consent both for removal and for tribes to sell their original lands east of the Mississippi. It also required that "the Indian title ha[d] been extinguished" to the lands where the tribes were to be moved west of the Mississippi. Thus, the elements of Discovery still played an important role in the Removal era. However, removal was ultimately enforced in fact as a coercive, mandatory policy. Many tribes, especially the Cherokee Nation, were forcibly removed from their homelands and marched on the Trail of Tears to what is now Oklahoma.

The rapid growth of the United States in 1846–1848 as a result of American victory in the Mexican–American War quickly required a modification of the removal policy. The mass migration of Americans resulting from the 1849 California gold rush and the expansion of the Oregon Trail in the mid-1840s prevented any hopes of an orderly removal process of all the Indian Nations in North America to the Indian Territory in what is now Oklahoma. Of course, the United States did not abandon its goals of Manifest Destiny or the "Savage as Wolf" policy because these newly encountered Indian tribes stood in the way of the foreordained American expansion. Therefore, in Texas in 1849 and in California in the 1850s and elsewhere, federal officials developed the idea of separating Indians from American gold miners and settlers onto small and often remote reservations so as to confine Indians to limited territories and to hopefully prevent conflicts. This policy began what was called the Reservation era, which ran roughly from 1850 to 1887. The United States continued to exercise its Discovery powers by completely controlling Indian affairs and using its constitutional Discovery authority through treaty making and otherwise to keep the states out of Indian issues and to totally dominate the Indian Nations. In addition, the United States continued to exercise its preemption power to buy land from tribes with their putative consent through the treaty process. The very powerful United States treated the Indian Nations like the limited sovereigns Discovery defined them as being.

The increasing domination of the United States over Indian Nations became evident in what is called the Allotment and Assimilation era, which is considered to have run from 1887 to 1934. The United States now more strongly than ever exercised its authority over Indians with very little, and then later no, tribal input or consent. Moreover, Congress radically altered the policies of the treaties and the Reservation era and breached the limits of its alleged Discovery power over Indian property by unilaterally altering the nature of tribal real-property rights under the General Allotment Act of 1887. The goal of this legislation was to break up tribal ownership of land, open the reservations for non-Indian settlement, and end tribal existence, all without tribal consent. Congress accomplished this task by dividing or allotting many tribally owned reservations into 160- and 80-acre plots that were then granted in individual ownership to family heads and individual adult tribal members. Any reservation land in excess of what was needed to allot a share to each tribal citizen was called "surplus" and was sold to non-Indian settlers who then moved onto the reservations. In addition, a significant amount of the land allotted to tribal citizens was ultimately lost from Indian ownership by voluntary sales and state tax foreclosures. The Allotment era resulted in a loss of about two-thirds of all tribally owned lands from 138 million acres in 1887 to 48 million acres by 1934. In addition, nearly 20 million acres of the remaining 48 million acres of tribally owned lands in 1934 were arid or semi-arid.[14]

The Allotment era was a disaster for tribal governments and their communities. The United States dealt their cultures, governments, and people a near-fatal blow. In doing so, the federal government unilaterally expanded its Discovery rights of preemption and limited sovereignty over tribes. The forced allotments of communally owned tribal lands into individual ownership and the confiscation of "surplus lands" and their sales to non-Indians were conducted almost completely without tribal consent and in fact went against the active opposition of most tribal governments. That policy was a violation of the element of Discovery, as Jefferson often explained to tribal leaders, that they could occupy, use, and live on their lands forever if they wished. The Allotment Act is a dramatic example of the United States exercising and, in fact, expanding its Discovery power far beyond the legal definition of the Doctrine. The United States radically limited and changed tribal real-property rights without the consent of tribes, in violation of Discovery.

Furthermore, Allotment continues to have a major impact in Indian country today. Indian tribes now own about 45.2 million acres of land in tribal communal ownership. Individual Indians own about 10.2 million acres of land on reservations left over from the individual allotments of the Allotment era. All of these parcels of land are held in trust status, with the tribe or Indian person being the beneficial owner of the land and the United States being the legal owner. This ownership pattern gives the United States a major role in decisions about developing or selling these lands. Moreover, the "checkerboarded" status of many reservations today with numerous non-Indians owning land in fee simple and living on reservation and tribes and Indians owning trust land causes tribal governments all sorts of criminal, civil, regulatory, and adjudicatory jurisdictional problems. The Allotment Act and its illegally expanded definition of the United States Discovery power continue to adversely effect Indians and their governments today.[15]

Also during this era, the United States exercised its Discovery sovereign authority over tribes and Indians by arbitrarily deciding to force assimilation on Indians by bringing them into the American "melting pot." Straight out of the fifteenth-century papal bulls and the sixteenth- and seventeenth-century English colonial charters, civilization, citizenship, education, and religious conversion of Indians became federal objectives. As early as 1870, President Grant handed control of many reservations to various religious denominations, and the federal government even deeded Indian land to these religions to operate missions and schools. In the 1880s, the federal government commenced operating boarding schools to educate and civilize Indians. The goal of these schools was aptly summed up by the creator of the very first one: Captain Henry Pratt said the goal was "to kill the Indian, save the man." During this same time period, the Bureau of Indian Affairs attempted to take absolute control of Indian life and to squeeze out Indian government, religion, and culture.[16]

The United States continued its Discovery domination of Indian tribes in what is called the Termination era, which ran roughly from 1945 to 1961. Under this official policy, the United States sought to end as rapidly as possible the federal–tribal political relationship and to terminate the authority and legal existence of tribal governments. As a result, more land was lost from communal tribal ownership, and federal responsibilities for Indians and their governments under various treaties and federal laws were lessened. Tribal governments were not consulted nor was consent secured about the termination policies, and the vast majority of tribes and Indians were against the policy. This one-sided domination of the federal–tribal relationship by the United States demonstrates its aggressive exercise of the sovereignty aspect of the Discovery power.

Currently, the United States pursues a more respectful approach to its use of Discovery against tribal governments and Indian people. Starting in the early 1960s, when termination was phased out, the United States began formulating what is now called the Self-Determination era of Indian policy. The era was named by President Nixon when he stated that termination would no longer be federal policy and that Indian people had the "right of self-determination." The principal legislative initiative of this era is the Indian Self-Determination and Education Assistance Act of 1975, which was designed to create a fundamental, philosophical change in the federal administration of Indian affairs. This act allows Indian Nations to contract with the federal government for the delivery of federal services, and although the programs continue to be federally funded, the tribes can administer the programs themselves. Federal domination of Indian services is supposed to end.[17]

The elements of Discovery, however, are still ever-present in federal Indian law, even in the Self-Determination era. Discovery is present in the fundamental principles of federal Indian law; in the dominant control the United States continues to exercise over tribal political, commercial, and real estate issues; and in regard to the sale or use of allotted lands held by individual Indians. The United States continues to maintain its Discovery preemption right in tribal lands and to enforce its Discovery sovereign power over tribal governments. Consequently, the Doctrine of Discovery continues to be the controlling legal precedent for American interactions with Indian Nations. From the days of the European explorers to the colonies, to the American states, and to the present-day United States government, Discovery remains an active and important part of American Indian affairs, federal law, and the lives of Indian people and the Indian Nations.

Conclusion

T he elements and objectives of the Doctrine of Discovery have dominated the history of North American native people since the arrival of Europeans on this continent. First, the international legal principles of Discovery were used by European countries to claim and capture property, sovereign, and human rights over the indigenous peoples and their governments. The Doctrine was then used by the European colonists to define and limit the governmental and property rights of America's native people to acquire them as cheaply as possible. The elements of Discovery permeated colonial history and law, and the new American states and their federal governments greedily adopted the principles of Discovery for their own benefit. The Doctrine is plainly visible throughout U.S. history and in federal Indian law and policies.

Thereafter, President Thomas Jefferson played a major role in applying Discovery against native governments and peoples all across the continent. He plainly understood and utilized Discovery in the Louisiana and Oregon Territories when he launched the Lewis and Clark expedition; when he made the Louisiana Purchase, even though he thought his actions were unconstitutional; and when he took steps to acquire the Pacific Northwest for the United States. Lewis and Clark then used the well-recognized legal principles and rituals of Discovery to help the United States exercise its Discovery powers and claims across the continent. The elements of Discovery were then readily adopted into Manifest Destiny, the new name for the very old idea of American continental expansion, and the United States was then able to exercise its Discovery sovereign and commercial powers and the right of preemption to dominate tribal nations across the continent. In consequence, the "divine mandate" was fulfilled, and American government and citizens overspread the entire continent, just as Thomas Jefferson had hoped and foretold.

We have now looked at a mountain of evidence regarding American expansion and Manifest Destiny under the microscope of Discovery. This book is apparently the first attempt to examine this evidence in light of the legal Doctrine of Discovery. The value of this effort is that an understanding of the international legal principles under which Euro-Americans dealt with Indian Nations sheds a new light on the conduct of Thomas Jefferson and Lewis and Clark and on many other events in American history and law. A knowledge of the impact of Discovery on American and Indian history leads us to a fuller and more diverse understanding of many of these historic events. We can thus perceive more clearly how tribal governments and individual Indians lost many of their property and human rights, and their sovereign, self-governing powers.

Hopefully, this book has proven to the reader the pervasive presence of Discovery in the past 400 years of Euro-American interactions with the indigenous people of North America and has shown that the Doctrine continues to play a major role in the federal–tribal relationship today. As a consequence, American Indians lost valuable natural-law rights of self-determination, sovereignty, and real-property ownership without their knowledge or consent. The confiscation of these rights by Euro-Americans was not justified by any rational, legal, free exchange of rights, but was just presumed because of the ethnocentric assumption of the "superior genius" of Europeans. The resulting purchases of the "Indian title" by colonial and American governments were tainted by Discovery and were often conducted in an atmosphere of coercion and enforced by the "sword." In adopting the Doctrine, the U.S. Supreme Court stated in 1823,

> On the discovery of this immense continent, the great nations of Europe were eager to appropriate to themselves so much of it as they could respectively acquire. Its vast extent offered an ample field to the ambition and enterprise of all; and the character and religion of its inhabitants afforded an apology for considering them as a people over whom the superior genius of Europe might claim an ascendancy. The potentates of the old world found no difficulty in convincing themselves that they made ample compensation to the inhabitants of the new, by bestowing on them civilization and Christianity.[1]

This statement makes it clear that religious, cultural, and racial prejudices led to the development and application of the Doctrine against American Indian governments and their citizens. We can see in that quotation the outrageous idea that European religions and civilizations were a "fair trade" for the sovereignty, human, and property rights of North American natives. The Supreme Court has reemphasized several times that religious and cultural biases are at the root of federal power over Indian people. In 1877, for example, the Court stated that "[i]t is to be presumed that ... the United States would be governed by such considerations of justice as would control a Christian people in their treatment of an ignorant and dependent race." In 1913 the Court stated that the Pueblo people of New Mexico practiced "debauchery," "intemperance," and "heathen customs,"

were governed "by superstition," and were an "uninformed and inferior people …
intellectually and morally inferior."[2]

The Supreme Court recognized the ridiculousness of Discovery and its rationales
even while it was adopting the Doctrine in 1823. The Court even ignored its own
opinion that Indians possessed natural rights to their lands. It said that the idea
that Indians were mere occupants and incapable of transferring their lands to
individuals might well "be opposed to natural right." The Court also raised a very
good question, which it did not answer: why do American farmers, "merchants
and manufacturers have a right, on abstract principles, to expel hunters from the
territory they possess" or to limit tribal rights? Yet in spite of these concerns, the
Court adopted Discovery as federal law.[3]

The goal of this book is to increase public knowledge of the Doctrine of
Discovery and how American history and law can take on a richer meaning and
understanding when one sees the legal background and justifications for various
historical, law-related, and political principles. I also hope to start a careful
examination of Discovery's modern-day effects on Indian tribal governments
and its metamorphosis into the plenary power, the trust responsibility, and
the diminished tribal sovereignty doctrines of federal Indian law. It should be
obvious from our review of federal policies and basic Indian law principles that
Discovery has worked primarily if not totally to the detriment of Indian people
and their governments. As one professor stated, "the rule profoundly harmed
the Indians," and as the Supreme Court said in *Johnson v. M'Intosh,* tribal rights
were "to a considerable extent, impaired" by Discovery. The ultimate question,
then, is whether this relic of colonialism and feudalism, and racial, religious, and
cultural domination should be relegated to the dustbin of history. Must Americans
and American Indians tolerate the Doctrine of Discovery in our present and our
future; is it unchangeable, immutable? Is there anything that can be done to erase
a "legal doctrine" that has been enshrined in American culture and law for four
hundred years?[4]

Some of the leading commentators in the Indian law field think that it is
improbable that the Supreme Court would, or even should, reconsider Discovery
and the basic principles of federal Indian law. They point out that it is possible
that the current Supreme Court would not do a better job than the Court did
nearly two hundred years ago in setting out the principles that control the interactions between tribal, federal, and state governments and that determine the rights
of Indian people and their governments. This concern could very well be true. On
the other hand, some authors argue that the medieval, feudal, ethnocentric, and
racial Doctrine of Discovery must be destroyed, and the sooner the better.[5]

I take a middle ground between these two positions. I offer a modest proposal
that could start the United States down the road to making the fundamental
principles of American Indian law more just for the U.S. citizens who are also
citizens of Indian Nations. This idea could also help the United States better fulfill
its trust responsibility for Indians and tribes and keep its treaty promises to tribal
governments. I do this because the United States and American citizens should

not ignore the Doctrine of Discovery, its origination, and its impact on Indians and tribal governments any more than the United States could have permanently ignored slavery or the exclusion of women from voting, for example.

My proposal does not rely on the federal courts. Instead, my suggestion relies on Congress and the idea that positive law, law enacted by the federal legislature, could provide the answer. Congress could consider after lengthy deliberation and with ample tribal input and direction viable ways to make concrete changes in federal Indian law that could begin to rectify some of the damage Discovery has inflicted on tribal and Indian rights. This certainly seems to be a superior method in lieu of relying on the whims of litigation and the United States Supreme Court.

My suggestion is not really radical or dangerous, I hope. I only suggest that Congress purposely extend more completely the commendable goals of the self-determination era of federal Indian policy, which already includes the objective to end the "prolonged Federal domination of Indian service programs." This goal, enunciated in 1975 when the Indian Self-Determination and Education Assistance Act was passed into law by Congress, and the policies that have developed since that time, such as the Tribal Self-Governance Act, demonstrate promising avenues for continuing to lessen the federal domination of tribal affairs and intrusions into the personal lives of American Indians and for freeing them from the medieval restraints of the Doctrine of Discovery.[6]

As we have reviewed, Congress has extensive power in the Indian law arena because of the plenary power doctrine. The Supreme Court has already recognized that Congress has broad authority to exercise this power in significant ways that benefited Indians and their governments as long as the congressional actions "are tied rationally to the fulfillment of Congress's unique obligation toward the Indians [and are] reasonable and rationally designed to further Indian self-government." Congress could utilize this very authority and extend the implementation of its Self-Determination and Self-Governance goals by undertaking even more steps to limit the Doctrine of Discovery.[7]

An example of just such a congressional action occurred in 2000. At that time, Congress lessened the federal authority to approve contracts with tribes. Congress amended an 1871 statute and, in essence, voluntarily ceded to tribal governments the federal Discovery authority to approve contracts that encumber tribal lands if the contracts are less than seven years long. This was just a minor step compared with the enormous powers granted to the United States by Discovery, and in fact, the amendment apparently was not even noticed by Congress or by others as being a lessening of Congress's Discovery powers. The intent of the amendment was not directed at Discovery at all, but the amendment was instead designed to improve economic development in Indian country. This is an example, however, of a limitation of the United States' Discovery power and decision-making authority over tribal lands and commercial dealings. This is a perfect demonstration of the small, incremental steps that a congressional committee, with active tribal participation, or a congressional–tribal blue ribbon commission could formulate and suggest to Congress to enact as laws to reduce the Discovery burden on Indians and their governments.[8]

Congress could authorize a congressional committee or a commission to engage in a government-to-government political dialogue with Indian governments about further changes in federal Indian policies and laws to reduce the effects of Discovery. Congress could then consider enacting into federal law the jointly drafted agreements these efforts produced. Congress has already followed this procedure; for example, numerous times in water-rights agreements that the federal executive branch, Indian governments, and states have negotiated in the past. This kind of political interaction between tribes and the federal government could be used to further rid tribal governments and Indians of the constraints of federal domination and plenary power, and to increase Indian Self-Determination rights. This would in essence be a partial return to the bilateral treaty making relationship that existed between Euro-American governments and Indian Nations for 250 years when these governments negotiated and traded their rights and interests in a political and diplomatic setting. This could give tribal governments a real decision-making role and a real voice in how the United States treats them instead of tribes just suffering under the heavy hand of the all-powerful "Discovering" nation and federal paternalism.

One cautionary note is in order. In the past, some politicians and people intent on acquiring tribal lands and property rights have used congressional policies to the detriment of American Indians while pretending to be concerned for Indian interests. I am well aware that the Allotment and Termination eras of federal Indian policy, which we discussed briefly, seriously injured Indian governmental and property rights, and yet were partially justified by arguments that they would free Indians from the restraints of communal land ownership and the onerous burden of their tribal governments. Hopefully we can learn from the mistakes of those eras, avoid the hidden agendas of the advocates of those kinds of policies, and instead work to lessen the bonds of federal control over Indians and their governments without destroying the treaty promises, the trust responsibility, and the political status of Indian tribes.

I am also aware of the significant concerns of Indian Nations that any discussion of lessening the power of Discovery could turn to the topic of somehow lessening the federal trust responsibility. I do not propose any changes to this protective trust duty, and I do not believe that examining and trying to lessen the evils of the Doctrine of Discovery requires a reevaluation of the trust doctrine. That principle arises from Supreme Court cases that are still the law today and from express promises in hundreds of treaties the United States entered with tribal governments from 1785 to 1871. According to the U.S. Constitution, those treaty promises to protect tribes are the "supreme Law of the Land" and the United States must keep those promises and obey its own law. The United States should be able to continue complying with its trust responsibility and its treaty promises and maintain its government-to-government political relationship with Indian Nations while still searching for ways to lessen the onerous aspects of Discovery in tribal and Indian life. In fact, would not the United States better fulfill its trust responsibility by working to lessen the constraints Discovery places on the lives and the governmental and property rights of American Indians?

Proposing such a change in 200-year-old policies and laws requires serious thought, consideration, and tribal consultation and input. This book has presented the legal and historical evidence on the Doctrine of Discovery and Manifest Destiny and their impact on American history and law and on America's native peoples. But what are we to do with this information, and what are we to do about Discovery? One thing seems clear: the United States and its citizens must face squarely the fact that many of the principles of federal Indian law and the modern-day treatment of Indian Nations and Indians are based on the Doctrine of Discovery and on religious, racial, cultural, and ethnocentric prejudices that are many centuries old. These lamentable relics of our past should not and cannot continue to be perpetuated and tolerated in modern-day America. They should have no place in the modern-day relationship between Indian Nations, Indian people, and the United States. Native people and their governments should no longer be controlled by the principles of their "discovery" under the Doctrine of Discovery.

Notes

INTRODUCTION

1. *City of Sherrill v. Oneida Indian Nation of N.Y.*, 544 U.S. 197 (2005); *Delgamuukw v. British Columbia*, 3 S.C.R. 1010 (1997); *Guerin v. The Queen*, 2 S.C.R. 335 (1984); *Calder v. Attorney General for British Columbia*, S.C.R. 313 (1973); *Mabo v. Queensland*, 107 A.L.R. 1 (1992) (Australian High Court).

2. Robert J. Miller, "The Doctrine of Discovery in American Indian Law," 42 *Idaho L. Rev.* 1, 21–75 (2006).

3. *Id.* at 21–103.

4. *Johnson v. M'Intosh*, 21 U.S. (8 Wheat.) 543, 587–92 (1823).

5. Donald Jackson, *Thomas Jefferson & the Stony Mountains* (Urbana, Chicago, and London: University of Illinois Press, 1981), p. 298.

6. Felix S. Cohen, "Original Indian Title," 32 *Minn. L. Rev.* 28, 48 (1947).

7. Cornelius J. Moynihan & Sheldon Kurtz, *Introduction to the Law of Real Property*, 4th ed. (St. Paul, MN: Thomson/West, 2005), pp. 212–213.

CHAPTER 1

1. *Johnson v. M'Intosh*, 21 U.S. (8 Wheat.) 543, 573–74, 584, 588, 592, 603 (1823).

2. *Johnson*, 21 U.S. at 573–75, 578–79.

3. *Johnson*, 21 U.S. at 584, 587–88, 592, 596–97, 603.

4. *Id.* at 573–74, 579, 584–85, 587–88, 592; Eric Kades, "The Dark Side of Efficiency: Johnson v. M'Intosh and the Expropriation of American Indian Lands," 148 *U. Pa. L. Rev.* 1065, 1078, 1110–31 (2000); Terry L. Anderson & Fred S. McChesney, "Raid or Trade? An Economic Model of Indian-White Relations," 37 *J. L. Econ.* 39 (1994).

5. "The History and Influence of the Puritans," *The Miscellaneous Writings of Joseph Story*, ed. William W. Story (1852; Reprint, Union, NJ: Lawbook Exchange, 2001), p. 459.

6. Robert J. Miller, "Agents of Empire: Another look at the Lewis and Clark Expedition," *Or. St. Bar Bull.* 35 (Feb. 2004); Vine Deloria Jr. & David E. Wilkins, *Tribes,*

Treaties, & Constitutional Tribulations (Austin: University of Texas Press, 1999), p. 4; Henry Wheaton, *Elements of International Law,* 6th ed., ed. William B. Lawrence (Boston: Little, Brown, 1855), pp. 219, 225–26; *Johnson,* 21 U.S. at 588; Story, pp. 460, 464–65.

7. Anthony Pagden, *Lords of all the World: Ideologies of Empire in Spain, Britain and France c. 1500-c. 1800* (New Haven, CT: Yale University Press, 1995), pp. 8, 24, 126; Robert A. Williams, Jr., *The American Indian in Western Legal Thought: The Discourses of Conquest* (New Haven, CT, and Oxford: Yale University Press, 1990), pp. 14, 29–31; *The Expansion of Europe,* ed. James Muldoon (Philadelphia: University of Pennsylvania Press, 1977); Carl Erdmann, *The Origin of the Idea of Crusade,* trans. Marshall W. Baldwin & Walter Goffart (Princeton, NJ: Princeton University Press, 1977), pp. 155–56.

8. Wheaton, pp. 226–39; Williams, p. 13 & n.4, 14–17, 45–47, 49, 66.

9. Williams, pp. 58–63, 65–67; James Muldoon, *Popes, Lawyers and Infidels* (Philadelphia: University of Pennsylvania Press, 1979), pp. 109–19; Pagden, pp. 24, 126; Steven T. Newcomb, "The Evidence of Christian Nationalism in Federal Indian Law: The Doctrine of Discovery, Johnson v. McIntosh, and Plenary Power," 20 *N.Y.U. Rev. L. & Soc. Change* 303, 316 (1993); *Johnson,* 21 U.S. at 572–73.

10. *Expansion of Europe,* p. 47–48, 54–56; Edgar Prestage, *The Portuguese Pioneers* (London: A. & C. Black, 1966), pp. 8–9, 27, 38–41, 43–50, 54–59, 96–97, 100–102; James Muldoon, *Popes, Lawyers and Infidels* (Philadelphia: University of Pennsylvania Press, 1979), pp. 119–21; Williams, p. 69–71.

11. *Church and State through the Centuries,* ed. & trans. Sidney Z. Ehler & John B. Morrall (New York: Biblo and Tannen, 1967), pp. 146–53; Williams, pp. 71–72; Muldoon, pp. 126–27; *European Treaties Bearing on the History of the United States and Its Dependencies to 1648,* ed. Frances G. Davenport (Washington, DC: Carnegie Institution of Washington, 1917), p. 23.

12. Williams, pp. 74–78; Samuel Eliot Morison, *The European Discovery of America: The Southern Voyages,* Vol. 2 (New York: Oxford University Press, 1974), pp. 27–44; Samuel Eliot Morison, *Admiral of the Ocean Sea* (Boston: Little, Brown, 1942), pp. 105, 229; *European Treaties,* pp. 9–13, 23, 53–56.

13. *Church and State,* p. 156; Morison, *Admiral,* pp. 368–73; *Foundations of Colonial America: A Documentary History,* Vol. 3, ed. W. Keith Kavenagh (New York: Chelsea House, 1973), p. 1684; Pagden, p. 47; Williams, p. 80.

14. Pagden, pp. 31–33; Muldoon, p. 139; Morison, *Admiral,* p. 368.

15. Patricia Seed, *Ceremonies of Possession in Europe's Conquest of the New World, 1492–1640* (Cambridge, England, and New York: Cambridge University Press, 1995), pp. 9 & n.19, 69–73, 101–02; James Simsarian, "The Acquisition of Legal Title to Terra Nullius," 53 *Pol. Sci. Q.* 111, 113–14, 117–18, 120–24 (March 1938); Friedrich August Freiherr von der Heydte, "Discovery, Symbolic Annexation and Virtual Effectiveness in International Law," 29 *Am. J. Int'l L.* 448, 450–52 (1935).

16. Williams, pp. 89–91, 97, 99–101; Franciscus de Victoria, *De Indis et de Iure Bellie Relectiones,* ed. Ernest Nys & trans. John Pauley Bate (Washington, DC: Carnegie Institution, 1917), pp. 115, 123, 125–31, 135–39, 151, 153; Pagden, p. 46; Lewis Hanke, *The Spanish Struggle for Justice in the Conquest of America* (1949), pp. 17–22, 113–32.

17. Williams, pp. 98, 101–03; Victoria, pp. 54–55, 151–61; Arthur Nussbaum, *A Concise History of the Law of Nations* (New York: Macmillan, 1947), pp. 61–62; Seed, pp. 88–97; Pagden, pp. 93, 97–98; Hanke, pp. 133–46, 156–72.

18. Muldoon, pp. 141–42; Seed, pp. 69–73; Hanke, p. 33; *The Spanish Tradition in America,* ed. Charles Gibson (New York: Harper & Row, 1968), pp. 59–60; Pagden, p. 91.

19. Pagden, p. 90; Williams, pp. 161, 170, 177–78; *Early American Indian Documents: Treaties and Laws, 1607–1789,* Vol. 7, ed. Alden T. Vaughan & Barbara Graymont (Washington, DC: University Publications of American, 1998), pp. 30–32.

20. Pagden, p. 34; Joseph Jouvency, *An Account of the Canadian Mission,* Vol. 1 (1710; reprinted in *Jesuit Relations,* ed. Rueben Gold Thwaites, 1896), pp. 179, 205; *Travels and Explorations of the Jesuit Missionaries in New France,* Vol. 2, ed. Reuben Gold Thwaites (New York: Pageant Book Co., 1959), pp. 33, 127, 199, 203; *Id.,* Vol. 3, pp. 33, 39, 41; *Id.,* Vol. 34, pp. 217–19; *Id.,* Vol. 55, pp. 95–97, 105–15; *Id.,* Vol. 41, pp. 245–47; *Id.,* Vol. 47, pp. 259–71; Fred Anderson, *Crucible of War: The Seven Years' War and the Fate of Empire in British North America, 1754–1766* (New York: Knopf, 2000), pp. xv & xix; Jack M. Sosin, *Whitehall and the Wilderness: The Middle West in British Colonial Policy, 1760–1775* (Lincoln: University of Nebraska Press, 1961), pp. 21–22, 73.

21. *Foundations of Colonial America,* Vol. 1, pp. 18, 22–29; *Foundations,* Vol. 3, pp. 1690–98; Williams, pp. 126–225; Heydte, pp. 450–54; *Select Charters and Other Documents Illustrative of American History 1606–1775,* ed. William MacDonald (London: MacMillan, 1906; Reprint, Littleton, CO: Rothman, 1993), pp. 2–3, 18, 24–25, 37–39, 51–52, 59, 121–26, 184, 205; Samuel Smith, *History of New Jersey* (Burlington, VT: James Parker, 1765; Reprint, Philadelphia: David Hall, 1890), p. 16.

22. Williams, pp. 126–225; Heydte, pp. 450–54; Francis Jennings, *The Invasion of America: Indians, Colonialism and the Cant of the Conquest* (Chapel Hill: University of North Carolina Press, 1975), pp. 132–33.

23. Heydte, pp. 450–52, 458–59; Williams, p. 133; Hyde, *Treatise on International Law,* Vol. 1 (Boston: Little, Brown, 1922), p. 164; *European Treaties,* p. 219.

24. Heydte, pp. 460–61; Pagden, p. 81.

25. Anderson, pp. 25–26; "Journal of Captain Fitch's Journey to the Creeks" (May 1756), *Colonial Indian Documents Microfilm Collection, Instances of Encroachment made by the French upon the Rights of the Crown of Great Britain in America,* ed. Randolph Boehm, microformed on Records of the British Colonial Office, Part 1, Class 5: Westward Expansion 1700–1783, Reel I, Vol. 12, Frame 0158 (1972); Thomas Maitland Marshall, *A History of the Western Boundary of the Louisiana Purchase, 1819–1841* (Berkeley: University of California Press, 1914), p. 12; Donald Jackson, *Thomas Jefferson and the Stony Mountains* (Urbana, Chicago, and London: University of Illinois Press, 1981), p. 3; *A Voyage Round the World: Which Was Performed in 1785, 1786, 1787, and 1788, by M. De La Peyrouse* (Edinburgh: J. Moir, 1798), pp. 70–71.

26. Cornelius J. Moynihan & Sheldon Kurtz, *Introduction to the Law of Real Property,* 4th ed. (St. Paul, MN: Thomson/West, 2005), pp. 212–13.

27. Henry Reynolds, *The Law of the Land* (New York: Viking Penguin, 1987), p. 173; Lynn Berat, *Walvis Bay: Decolonization and International Law* (New Haven: Yale University Press, 1990), p. 118; Colin G. Calloway, *Crown and Calumet: British-Indian Relations, 1783–1815* (Norman: University of Oklahoma Press, 1987), p. 9; Alex C. Castles, "An Australian Legal History," reprinted in *Aboriginal Legal Issues, Commentary and Materials,* ed. H. McRae et al. (Holmes Beach: Wm. W. Gaunt 1991), pp. 10, 63.

28. Thomas L. Purvis, *Colonial America to 1763* (New York: Facts on File, 1999), pp. 43, 207–08; Charles R. Boxer, *The Dutch Seaborne Empire 1600–1800* (New York: Knopf, 1970), pp. 228–29, 296; *Early American Indian Documents,* Vol. 7, pp. 30–31.

29. Howard R. Berman, "Perspectives on American Indian Sovereignty and International Law, 1600 to 1776," in *Exiled in the Land of the Free,* ed. Oren Lyons & John Mohawk (Santa Fe, NM: Clear Light Publishers, 1992), p. 140 & nn.68–72; *Foundations,* Vol. 2, p. 1266; Purvis, pp. 43, 207–08.

30. Berman, p. 136 & nn.43–46; *Early American Indian Documents,* Vol. 7, pp. 30–31, 122–23, 127; *Foundations,* Vol. 2, pp. 766 & 1260; *Early American Indian Documents,* Vol. 1, p. 18.

31. Simsarian, pp. 111, 113, 115–17; *Early American Indian Documents,* Vol. 7, pp. 30–31.

32. *Select Charters and Other Documents Illustrative of American History,* pp. 44, 48–50.

33. Daniel Philpott, *Revolutions in Sovereignty: How Ideas Shaped Modern International Relations,* p. 157 (Princeton, NJ, and Oxford: Princeton University Press, 2001).

34. Berat, pp. 118–20, 156; "Sovereignty Over Unoccupied Territories—The Western Sahara Decision," 9 *Case W. Res. J. Int'l L.* 135, 137–43 (1977); The Western Sahara Advisory Opinion, *I.C.J.* 14 (1975).

35. *The Island of Palmas Case,* 2 R.I.A.A. 829, in *Hague Court Reports* , ed. James Brown Scott, (New York: Oxford University Press, 1928), p. 83; "Sovereignty Over Unoccupied Territories—The Western Sahara Decision," 9 *Case W. Res. J. Int'l L.* 135 n.2 (1977).

CHAPTER 2

1. *The Records of the Virginia Company of London,* Vol. 3, ed. Susan Myra Kingsbury (Wilmington, DE: Scholarly Resources, 1933), pp. 541–43; *Early American Indian Documents: Treaties and Laws, 1607–1789,* Vol. 4, ed. Alden T. Vaughan & W. Stitt Robinson (Washington, DC: University Publications of America, 1983), p. 112; Samuel Smith, *The History of the Colony of New Jersey* (Burlington, NJ: James Parker, 1765; Reprint, Trenton, NJ: William S. Sharp, 1890), pp. 7–8; *The Papers of Benjamin Franklin,* Vol. 5, ed. William B. Wilcox (New Haven, CT: Yale University Press, 1959–93), p. 368; *The Papers of George Mason,* Vol. 2, ed. Robert A. Rutland (Chapel Hill: University of North Carolina Press, 1970), p. 751.

2. Robert J. Miller, "American Indian Influence on the U.S. Constitution and Its Framers," 18 *Am. Indian L. Rev.* 133, 135–38 (1993); *A Bibliography of the English Colonial Treaties with the American Indians,* ed. Henry F. De Puy (Mansfield, CT: Martino Publishing, 1917, reprinted 1999); *Thompson v. Johnston,* 6 Binn. 68, 1813 WL 1243, at *2 (Pa. Sup. Ct. 1813); *Sacarusa & Longboard v. William King's Heirs,* 4 N.C. 336, 1816 WL 222, at *2 (N.C. Sup. Ct. 1816); Shaw Livermore, *Early American Land Companies: Their Influence on Corporate Development* (New York: The Commonwealth Fund, 1939), pp. 20, 31; *Early American Indian Documents,* Vol. 15, pp. 47–48; *Id.,* Vol. 8, pp. 576–77; *Id.,* Vol 1, p. 57; Thomas L. Purvis, *Colonial America to 1763* (New York: Facts on File, 1999), p. 188; *Foundations of Colonial America: A Documentary History,* Vol. 1, ed. W. Keith Kavenagh (New York: Chelsea House, 1973), pp. 96, 102; *Laws of the Colonial and State Governments Relating to Indians and Indian Affairs, from 1633 to 1831* (Washington, DC: Thompson and Homans, 1832; Reprint, Stanfordville, NY: Coleman, 1979), pp. 41, 52, 133–34, 178.

3. *Foundations,* Vol. 2, p. 1267.

4. *The Papers of James Madison,* Vol. 8, ed. Robert A Rutland et al. (Charlottesville: University Press of Virginia, 1983), p. 156; *Id.,* Vol. 14, p. 442; *Foundations,* Vol. 1, pp. 194, 413, 601; *Id.,* Vol. 2, pp. 925–31, 1282; *Early American Indian Documents,* Vol. 15, pp. 46–48, 153–54, 259, 268; *Id.,* Vol. 14, pp. 20–21, 170–71, 295–96, 406; *Id.,* Vol. 4, pp. 93–94; *Id.,* Vol. 20, p. 597; *Colony Laws of Virginia,* Vol. 2, pp. 467–68; *George Washington Writings,* ed. John Rhodehamel (New York: Literary Classics of the U.S., 1997), pp. 779, 903, 919, 923; Jack M. Sosin, *Whitehall and the Wilderness: The Middle West in British Colonial Policy, 1760–1775* (Lincoln: University of Nebraska Press, 1961), pp. 108–09, 122; *The Earliest Acts and Laws of the Colony of Rhode Island and*

Providence Plantations: 1647–1719, ed. John D. Cushing (Wilmington, DE: M. Glazier, 1977), p. 139; *Acts and Laws of New Hampshire 1680–1726,* ed. John D. Cushing (Wilmington, DE: M. Glazier, 1978), p. 142; *The Colony Laws of North America Series* (Wilmington, DE: M. Glazier, 1977), pp. 35–36; *The World Turned Upside Down: Indian Voices from Early America,* ed. Colin G. Calloway (Boston: St. Martin's Press, 1994), p. 78; *The Writings of George Washington,* Vol. 27, ed. John C. Fitzpatrick (Washington, DC: U.S. Government Printing Office, 1931), p. 140.

5. *Early American Indian Documents,* Vol. 15, pp. 80–81; *Id.,* Vol. 4, pp. 92–93, 110–14; Peter S. Onuf, *Jefferson's Empire: The Language of American Nationhood* (Charlottesville: University Press of Virginia, 2000), p. 81; Niall Ferguson, *Empire: The Rise and Demise of the British World Order and the Lessons for Global Power* (New York: Basic Books, 2002), pp. 54–55.

6. *Early American Indian Documents,* Vol. 4, pp. 51, 70–71; *The Writings of Thomas Jefferson,* Vol. 12, ed. Andrew A. Lipscomb & Albert Ellery Bergh (Washington, DC: Jefferson Memorial Assoc. of the U.S., 1903), p. 100; Francis Paul Prucha, *The Great Father: The United States Government and the American Indians* (Lincoln: University of Nebraska Press, 1995), pp. 116, 120.

7. Anthony Pagden, *Lords of all the World: Ideologies of Empire in Spain, Britain and France c. 1500–c. 1800* (New Haven, CT: Yale University Press, 1995), pp. 34–35; *Select Charters and Other Documents Illustrative of American History 1606–1775,* ed. William MacDonald (London: MacMillan, 1906; Reprint, Littleton, CO: Rothman, 1993), p. 131; *Early American Indian Documents,* Vol. 16, pp. 295–96; *Id.,* Vol. 20, p. 597; *Laws of the Colonial and State Governments,* pp. 12, 16–17, 22, 37, 45, 59, 136, 142, 146, 150, 154; *The Livingston Indian Records, 1666–1723,* ed. Lawrence H. Leder (Gettysburg, PA: The Pennsylvania Historical Assoc., 1956; Reprint, Stanfordville, NY: Coleman, 1979), p. 98.

8. *Early American Indian Documents,* Vol. 15, pp. 40–41, 47–48, 153, 283, 306–07; *Id.,* Vol. 16, pp. 46–48; *Id.,* Vol. 29, pp. 30, 176–78, 406–12, 436, 525, 538–39; *Id.,* Vol. 4, pp. 70–71; *The Livingston Indian Records,* pp. 65, 86, 89, 117, 182.

9. *Bibliography of the English Colonial Treaties,* p. 17; *The Writings of Benjamin Franklin,* ed. Albert Henry Smyth (New York: Macmillan, 1907), pp. 481–82, 488–89; *Early American Indian Documents,* Vol. 11, p. 202; Joseph Henry Smith, *Appeals to the Privy Council from the American Plantations* (New York: Columbia University Press, 1950), pp. 418–42; Vine Deloria Jr. & David E. Wilkins, *Tribes, Treaties, & Constitutional Tribulations* (Austin: University of Texas Press, 1999), p. 11.

10. George Lewis Chumbley, *Colonial Justice in Virginia* (Richmond, VA: Diety Press, 1971), p. 5; *County Court Records of Accomack-Northampton, Virginia 1632–1640,* ed. Susie M. Ames (Charlottesville: University Press of Virginia, 1954, reprint 1975), pp. lxi, lxv, 56–57; Smith, p. 165.

11. 77 *Eng. Rep.* 377, 378, 397 (K.B. 1608); Robert A. Williams, Jr., *The American Indian in Western Legal Thought: The Discourses of Conquest* (New Haven, CT, and Oxford, England: Yale University Press, 1990), p. 199.

12. Smith, pp. 418–42; *Bibliography of the English Colonial Treaties,* p. 21; *Johnson v. M'Intosh,* 21 U.S. (8 Wheat.) 543, 598 (1823).

13. Smith, pp. 115, 122, 124; *Early American Indian Documents,* Vol. 4, pp. 27–28, 62, 110–11, 114–15; *Id.,* Vol. 19, p. 506; *The Records of the Virginia Company of London: The Court Book,* Vol. 2 (Washington, DC: U.S. Government Printing Office, 1906), p. 94; Williams, pp. 214–17; *The Records of the Virginia Company,* Vol. 1, ed. S. M. Kingsbury (Washington, DC: U.S. Government Printing Office, 1933), pp. 71–87.

14. Dorothy V. Jones, *License for Empire: Colonialism by Treaty in Early America* (Chicago: University of Chicago Press, 1982), p. 36; Sosin, pp. 28–31, 45–46, 48–49, 51, 56, 79–83; Fred Anderson, *Crucible of War: The Seven Years' War and the Fate of Empire in British North America, 1754–1766* (New York: Knopf, 2000), pp. xv & xix, 85, 221, 565–57.

15. Sosin, pp. 80–98; Anderson, pp. 85, 221, 565–57; "The Declaration of Independence," in, *Basic Writings of Thomas Jefferson,* ed. Philip S. Foner (New York: Willey Book, 1944), pp. 21, 23–24.

16. Henry Steele Commager, *Documents of American History,* 8th ed., Vol. 1 (New York: Appleton-Century-Crofts, 1968), pp. 47, 48; Sosin, pp. 21–22, 73; *Select Charters and Other Documents,* pp. 261–62, 266.

17. *George Washington Writings,* p. 125; *The Writings of Benjamin Franklin,* pp. 488–89.

18. *The First Laws of the State of Virginia,* p. 35.

19. N.Y. Const. art. 37 (1777); N.Y. Act of March 18, 1788, Sess. 11, ch. 85; 2 Greenl. ed. Laws 194.

20. N.C. Const. art. I, § 25 (1776); Tenn. Const. art. XI, § 32 (1796).

21. GA. Const. art. I, § 23 (1798).

22. Onuf, p. 83; *First Laws of the State of Virginia,* pp. 103–04; *Marshall v. Clark,* 8 Va. 268, 1791 WL 325, at *3 (Va. Sup. Ct. 1791); *Papers of George Mason,* Vol. 2, pp. 746, 752.

23. *Laws of the Colonial and State Governments,* pp. 18, 34, 50, 65–71, 148, 171–73; *The First Laws of the State of Connecticut,* ed. John D. Cushing (Wilmington, DE: M. Glazier, 1982), pp. 101–02; *Danforth v. Wear,* 22 U.S. (9 Wheat.) 673, 677–78 (1824); *Sacarusa & Longboard v. William King's Heirs,* 4 N.C. 336, 1816 WL 222 (N.C. Sup. Ct. 1816) (1802 law); *Patterson v. The Rev. Willis Jenks et al.,* 27 U.S. (2 Pet.) 216, 234 (1829); *The First Laws of the State of Georgia,* Vol. 1, ed. John D. Cushing (Wilmington, DE: M. Glazier, 1981), p. 288; *The First Laws of the State of Rhode Island,* Vol. 1, p. 10; *Thompson v. Johnston,* 6 Binn. 68, 1813 WL 1243, at *2 (Pa. Sup. Ct. 1813); *Blair v. McKee,* 6 Serg. & Rawle 193, 1820 WL 1846 (Pa. Sup. Ct. 1820); Niall Ferguson, *Colossus: The Price of America's Empire* (New York: Penguin Press, 2004), p. 35.

24. *Tennessee v. Forman,* 16 Tenn. 256 (1835); Tim Alan Garrison, *The Legal Ideology of Removal: The Southern Judiciary and the Sovereignty of Native American Nations* (Athens and London: University of Georgia Press, 2002), pp. 103–124, 151, 228; *South Carolina v. Catawba Indian Tribe,* 476 U.S. 498 (1986); *County of Oneida v. Oneida Indian Nation,* 470 U.S. 226 (1985); *Seneca Nation of Indians v. New York,* 382 F.3d 245 (2d Cir. 2004); *Oneida Indian Nation v. New York,* 860 F.2d 1145 (2d Cir. 1988); N.Y. Act of April 2, 1813, Sess. 36; N.Y. Act of April 12, 1822, Sess. 45, ch. CCIV.

25. *Forman,* 16 Tenn. 256, 258–85, 287, 332–35, 339–45 (1835); Robert J. Miller, "A New Perspective on the Indian Removal Period," 38 *Tulsa L.J.* 181, 192–94 (2002).

26. *Arnold v. Mundy,* 6 N.J.L. 1, 1821 WL 1269 at *10, *53, *56 (N.J. 1821). See also *Caldwell v. Alabama,* 2 Stew. & p. 327, 396, 408, 413–16 (Ala. 1831); *Georgia v. Tassels,* 1 Dud. 229, 231–32, 234, 237–38 (Ga. 1830); *Jackson, ex dem. Smith v. Goodell,* 20 Johns. 188 (N.Y. Sup. Ct. 1822); *Jackson v. Sharp,* 14 Johns. 472 (N.Y. Sup. Ct. 1817); *Sacarusa & Longboard v. William King's Heirs,* 4 N.C. 336 1816 WL 222, at *3 (N.C. 1816); *Strother v. Martin,* 5 N.C. 162, 1807 WL 35, at *2–3 (N.C. 1807).

27. *Strother v. Martin,* 5 N.C. 162, 1807 WL 35, at *4 (N.C. 1807); *Thompson v. Johnston,* 6 Binn. 68, 1813 WL 1243 *2 & 5 (Pa. 1813).

28. *Fletcher v. Peck,* 10 U.S. (6 Cranch.) 87, 142–44 (1810); *Jackson, ex dem. J. G. Klock v. Hudson,* 3 Johns. 375, 1808 WL 477, at *5, 3 Am. Dec. 500 (N.Y. Sup. Ct. 1808).

29. *Marshall v. Clark,* 8 Va. 268, 1791 WL 325 *4 (Va. Sup. Ct. 1791); *Fletcher v. Peck,* 10 U.S. at 142–44; *Writings of Thomas Jefferson,* Vol. 3, pp. 19–20.

30. *Select Charters and Other Documents,* pp. 253–56.

31. *Early American Indian Documents,* Vol. 18, pp. 4, 39, 43, 59, 63, 65, 70, 84, 98, 124, 203; Miller, 18 *Am. Indian L. Rev.* p. 137; *Colonial Series: The Papers of George Washington,* ed. W. W. Abbot, Vol. 4, pp. 192–94 (Charlottesville, VA: University press of Virginia,1988); *Cherokee Nation v. Georgia,* 30 U.S. (5 Pet.) 1, 34 (1831) (Baldwin, J., concurring); Treaty with the Delawares, Sept. 17, 1778, 7 Stat. 13; *Indian Affairs: Laws and Treaties,* Vol. 2, ed. Charles J. Kappler, pp. 3–5 (Washington, DC: U.S. Government Printing Office, 1904).

32. *Articles of Confederation* art. IX (1781); Miller, 18 *Am. Indian L. Rev.* pp. 151–52; Phillip B. Kurland & Ralph Lerner, *The Founder's Constitution,* Vol. 2 (Chicago: University of Chicago Press, 1987), pp. 145, 529 (1784 letters between Monroe and Madison); *Cherokee Nation v. Georgia,* 30 U.S. (5 Pet.) 1, 64 (1831) (Thompson, J., dissenting); *Worcester v. Georgia,* 31 U.S. (6 Pet.) 515, 559 (1832).

33. *George Washington Writings,* pp. 536–41.

34. Francis Paul Prucha, *Documents of United States Indian Policy,* 3rd ed. (Lincoln: University of Nebraska Press, 2000), pp. 1–2; *Writings of George Washington,* Vol. 27, pp. 136–37, 139; *George Washington Writings,* p. 529.

35. Prucha, *Documents,* pp. 3–4; *The World Turned Upside Down: Indian Voices from Early America,* ed. Colin G. Calloway (Bedford/St. Martin's: Boston, MA,1994), p. 9; *Early American Indian Documents,* Vol. 18, p. 278; *The American Indian and the United States: A Documentary History,* Vol. 3, ed. Wilcomb E. Washburn (New York: Random House, 1973), pp. 2140–42; *Laws of the Colonial and State Governments,* pp. 16, 20, 23, 29.

36. Deloria Jr. & Wilkins, p. 11; 34 *Journals of the Continental Congress* 124–25 (May 1788); Colin G. Calloway, *Crown and Calumet: British-Indian Relations, 1783–1815* (Norman: University of Oklahoma Press, 1987), pp. 9–10.

37. *Documents of American Indian Diplomacy,* Vol. 1, p. 14; Catherine Bowen, *Miracle at Philadelphia* (Boston: Little, Brown, 1966), pp. 168–70; *The Papers of Alexander Hamilton,* Vol. 3, ed. Harold C. Syrett & Jacob E. Cooke (New York: Columbia University Press, 1962), p. 702; *Journals of the Continental Congress,* Vol. 33 (Library of Congress Records, 1786), p. 623; *Fletcher v. Peck,* 10 U.S. (6 Cranch.) 87, 142 (1810); Jones, pp. 147–48, 170; Deloria Jr. & Wilkins, p. 81; *Papers of George Mason,* Vol. 2, pp. 655–63.

38. *The Territorial Papers of the United States,* Vol. 2, ed. Clarence E. Carter (Washington: U.S. Government Printing Office, 1934), pp. 6–9; *The Papers of Thomas Jefferson,* Vol. 6, ed. Julian P. Boyd et al. (Princeton, NJ: Princeton University Press, 1952), pp. 571–600; *Papers of George Mason,* Vol. 2, p. 794–95.

39. Merrill Peterson, *Thomas Jefferson & The New Nation* (New York: Oxford University Press, 1970), pp. 266, 281–82; Peter S. Onuf, *Statehood and Union: A History of the Northwest Ordinance* (Bloomington: Indiana University Press, 1992), pp. xiv–xix, 3, 15, 25, 46; Anthony F.C. Wallace, *Jefferson and the Indians* (Ann Arbor: University of Michigan Press, 1999), pp. 162–63; *Writings of Thomas Jefferson,* Vol. 6, p. 79.

40. Prucha, *Documents,* p. 9; Onuf, p. xiii; Wallace, p. 163; 9 Stat. 323 § 14 (1848).

41. Treaty with the Wyandot, Etc., Jan. 9, 1789, Art III, 7 Stat. 28; Treaty with the Six Nations, Oct. 22, 1784, Art. III & IV, 7 Stat. 15; II Kappler's, pp. 5–25.

42. Treaty with the Cherokee, Nov. 28, 1785, Art. III & IX, 7 Stat. 18; Treaty with the Choctaw, Jan. 3, 1786, Art. II & VIII, 7 Stat. 21; Treaty with the Chickasaw, Jan. 10, 1786, Art. II & VIII, 7 Stat. 24; Treaty with the Wyandot, Etc., Jan. 9, 1789, Art I, VII, XIII 7 Stat. 28;

Treaty with the Wyandot, Etc., Jan. 21, 1785, Art. II & VI, 7 Stat. 16; Treaty with the Shawnee, Jan. 31, 1786, Art. II & V; Treaty with the Six Nations, Oct. 22, 1784, Art. III & IV, 7 Stat. 15; Treaty with the Six Nations, Jan. 9, 1789, Art. 1 & 2, 7 Stat. 33; II Kappler's, pp. 5, 7, 9–10, 12–21, 24.

43. Miller, 18 *Am. Indian L. Rev.* pp. 151–52; *The Records of the Federal Convention of 1787,* Vol. 1, ed. Max Farrand (New Haven, CT: Yale University Press, 1937), p. 316; Max Farrand, *The Framing of the Constitution* (New Haven, CT: Yale University Press, 1913), pp. 47–48; U.S. Constitutional Convention, *Journal of the Federal Convention,* ed. E. H. Scott (Chicago: Albert, Scott, 1893), p. 47; *The Federalist Papers,* No. 3 & 42, ed. Clinton Rossiter (New York: New American Library, 1961), pp. 44 (John Jay), 268–69; 33 *Journals of the Continental Congress* 455–63 (1787); Peterson, p. 119; Curtis G. Berkey, "United States-Indian Relations: The Constitutional Basis, in *Exiled in the Land of the Free: Democracy, Indian Nations, and the U.S. Constitution,* ed. Oren Lyons & John Mohawk (Santa Fe: Clear Light Publishers, 1992), pp. 208–09, 213, 218.

44. U.S. Const. art. I, § 8; *Worcester v. Georgia,* 31 U.S. (6 Pet.) 515, 559 (1832); *Cotton Petroleum Corp. v. New Mexico,* 490 U.S. 163, 192 (1989).

45. Act of July 22, 1790, ch. 23, 1 Stat. 137, 138, § 4, Prucha, *Documents,* p. 15; *Oneida Indian Nation v. New York,* 860 F.2d 1145, 1159 (2d Cir. 1988).

46. 25 U.S.C. § 177 (2000) (codified as amended); Act of March 1, 1793, ch. 19, 1 Stat. 329; Act of May 19, 1796, ch. 30, 1 Stat. 469; Act of March 3, 1799, 1 Stat. 743; Act of March 30, 1802, ch. 13, 2 Stat. 139.

47. Robert J. Miller, "Economic Development in Indian Country: Will Capitalism or Socialism Succeed?" 80 *Or. L. Rev.* 757, 808–09 (2002); Prucha, *The Great Father,* pp. 116, 120.

48. *Writings of George Washington,* Vol. 35, pp. 299–302; *The Works of John Adams, Second President of the United States,* Vol. 10, ed. Charles Francis Adams (Boston: Little, Brown, 1856), pp. 359–60; Charles Royce, *Indian Land Cessions in the US,* Bureau of American Ethnology, Eighteenth Annual Report, 1896–1897, part 2, pp. 536–37 (1899).

49. Prucha, *Documents,* p. 12.

50. *Papers of Alexander Hamilton,* Vol. 14, pp. 89–91; *Id.,* Vol. 3, pp. 702–15.

51. Treaty with the Cherokee, July 2, 1791, Art. II, 7 Stat. 39; Treaty with the Six Nations, Nov. 11, 1794, Art. III, 7 Stat. 44; Treaty with the Wyandot, Etc., Aug. 3, 1795, Art. V, 7 Stat. 49; Treaty with the Sauk and Foxes, Nov. 3, 1804, Art. 4, 7 Stat. 84; Treaty with the Osage, Nov. 10, 1808, Art. 10, 7 Stat. 107; II Kappler's, pp. 29, 35, 42, 75, 97.

52. Treaty with the Cherokee, July 2, 1791, Art. II, 7 Stat. 39; Treaty with the Wyandot, Etc., Aug. 3, 1795, Art. V & VIII, 7 Stat. 49; Treaty with the Creeks, June 29, 1796, Art. III & IV, 7 Stat. 56; Treaty with the Creeks, Aug. 7, 1790, Art. II, 7 Stat. 35; Treaty with the Sauk and Foxes, Nov. 3, 1804, Art. 1, 7 Stat. 84; Treaty with the Piankashaw, Dec. 30, 1805, Art. II, 7 Stat. 100; Treaty with the Osage, Nov. 10, 1808, Art. 10, 7 Stat. 107; Treaty with the Wyandot, Etc., July 22, 1814, Art. III, 7 Stat. 118; Treaty with the Winnebago, June 3, 1815, Art. 3, 7 Stat. 144; II Kappler's, pp. 25, 29, 30, 42–43, 47, 74, 89, 97, 105, 130.

53. 10 U.S. (6 Cranch.) 87, 139, 142 (1810).

54. *Id.* at 121–24, 140–42, 146–47.

55. *Id.* at 142–43.

56. 13 U.S. (9 Cranch) 11, 16 (1815).

57. *Johnson,* 21 U.S. (8 Wheat.) 543, 550–51, 555, 557 (1823).

58. *Id.* at 567–69.

59. *Id.* at 572, 582, 584.

60. *Id.* at 584–85, 588.

61. *Id.* at 573–74.

62. *Id.* at 604–05.

63. *Id.* at 587–90.

64. *Id.* at 574, 587. *Compare Fletcher,* 10 U.S. at 142–43; *Meigs,* 13 U.S. at 17–18.

65. *Cherokee Nation v. Georgia,* 30 U.S. (5 Pet.) 1, 17–18 (1831).

66. *Id.* at 22–23, 26–27, 33–35, 37–40, 45, 48–49.

67. 31 U.S. (6 Pet.) 515, 537–38, 542–49, 551–52, 559–62 (1832).

68. 38 U.S. (13 Pet.) 195, 201 (1839).

69. *Martin v. Waddell's Lessee,* 41 U.S. 367, 409 (1842); *United States v. Rogers,* 45 U.S. 567, 572 (1846).

70. 348 U.S. 272, 277 (1955).

71. *Id.* at 279. See, for example, *County of Oneida v. Oneida Indian Nation,* 470 U.S. 226, 234–35 (1985); *Mitchel v. United States,* 34 U.S. (9 Pet.) 711, 746 (1835).

72. 348 U.S. at 279.

73. 348 U.S. at 289–90.

74. 348 U.S. at 291.

75. *Oneida Indian Nation of New York v. The City of Sherrill, New York, et al.,* 145 F.Supp.2d 226, 233–36 (N.D. N.Y. 2001), aff'd in part, vacated and remanded in part, *Oneida Indian Nation of New York v. City of Sherrill, New York,* 337 F.3d 139 (2d Cir. 2003), *rev'd,* 125 S. Ct. 1478 (2005); *Oneida Indian Nation of New York v. City of Sherrill, New York,* 337 F.3d 139, 146–50, 158–65 (2d Cir. 2003), *rev'd,* 544 U.S. 197 (2005).

76. *City of Sherrill v. Oneida Indian Nation of New York,* 544 U.S. 197 (2005).

CHAPTER 3

1. Robert J. Miller, "The Doctrine of Discovery in American Indian Law," 42 *Idaho L. Rev.* 1, 76–103 (2006).

2. Frank. L. Dewey, *Thomas Jefferson Lawyer* (Charlottesville: University Press of Virginia, 1986), pp. xi, 14–15, 22, 25, 30–31, 33, 35–36; Edward Dumbauld, *Thomas Jefferson and the Law* (Norman: University of Oklahoma Press, 1978), pp. 26–27, 89, 157 n.5, 180 n.114, 216 n.14; Merrill Peterson, *Thomas Jefferson & The New Nation* (New York: Oxford University Press, 1970), p. 22; *The Works of John Adams,* ed. Charles Francis Adams (Boston: Little, Brown, 1856), p. 359.

3. Dewey, pp. 22, 30–31, 33, 35–36; Dumbauld, at 26–27, 89, 157 n.5, 180 n.114; 216 n.14; *The Writings of Thomas Jefferson,* Vol. 2, ed. Andrew A. Lipscomb & Albert Ellery Bergh (Washington, DC: U.S. Government Printing Office, 1903), pp. 188–89.

4. Dewey, pp. 30–31.

5. *Writings of Thomas Jefferson,* Vol. 2, pp. 131–33, 187–89; Peterson, pp. 118, 121.

6. *Writings of Thomas Jefferson,* Vol. 13, p. vii; James P. Ronda, "Introduction," in *Thomas Jefferson and the Changing West,* ed. James P. Ronda (St. Louis: Missouri Historical Society Press, 1997), p. xiv; Anthony F. C. Wallace, "'The Obtaining Lands': Thomas Jefferson and the Native Americans," in *Thomas Jefferson and the Changing West,* ed. James P. Ronda (St. Louis: Missouri Historical Society Press, 1997), p. 27; Dorothy V. Jones, *License for Empire: Colonialism by Treaty in Early America* (Chicago: University of Chicago Press, 1982), p. xi.

7. *The First Laws of the State of Virginia,* ed. John D. Cushing (Wilmington, DE: M. Glazier, 1982), pp. 103–04; Peter S. Onuf, *Jefferson's Empire: The Language of American*

Nationhood (Charlottesville: University Press of Virginia, 2000), p. 37; Peterson, pp. 118–21; *The Papers of Thomas Jefferson,* Vol. 1, ed. Julian P. Boyd (Princeton, NJ: Princeton University Press, 1950), pp. 337–86.

8. Dumbauld, p. 180 n.114.

9. *The Papers of George Mason,* Vol. 1, ed. Robert A. Rutland (Chapel Hill: University of North Carolina Press, 1970), pp. 313, 424, 746, 748–49; Peterson, pp. 280–81.

10. *Writings of Thomas Jefferson,* Vol. 3, p. 19.

11. *Fletcher,* 10 U.S. at 139–43; *Meigs,* 13 U.S. at 17–18.

12. *Writings of Thomas Jefferson,* Vol. 3, p. 19.

13. *Writings of Thomas Jefferson,* Vol. 3, p. 19; *Fletcher,* 10 U.S. at 139–43.

14. *Writings of Thomas Jefferson,* Vol. 8 pp. 99–101.

15. *Writings of Thomas Jefferson,* Vol. 3, pp. 218–19.

16. *Writings of Thomas Jefferson,* Vol. 3, pp. 164, 168, 175, 220; *Id.,* Vol. 8, pp. 220, 226–27.

17. *Writings of Thomas Jefferson,* Vol. 17, pp. 328–29, 333.

18. *Writings of Thomas Jefferson,* Vol. 17, p. 333.

19. *Writings of Thomas Jefferson,* Vol. 9, p. 102.

20. David J. Weber, *The Spanish Frontier in North America* (New Haven, CT, and London: Yale University Press, 1992), p. 252.

21. Bernard DeVoto, *The Course of Empire* (Boston: Houghton Mifflin, 1952), pp. 323–28; *Writings of Thomas Jefferson,* Vol. 8, pp. 416–17.

22. *Writings of Thomas Jefferson,* Vol. 1, pp. 337–38, 340–41.

23. Ronda, "Introduction," p. xiv; Joseph J. Ellis, *American Sphinx: The Character of Thomas Jefferson* (New York: Knopf, 1998), p. 212; Drew R. McCoy, *The Elusive Republic: Political Economy in Jeffersonian America* (Chapel Hill: University of North Carolina Press, 1980).

24. *Writings of Thomas Jefferson,* Vol. 10, pp. 294–96.

25. *Annals of Congress,* 8th Congress, 1st Session, p. 486 (1803).

26. Thomas Jefferson, "The Limits and Bounds of Louisiana," in *Documents Relating to the Purchase & Exploration of Louisiana* (Boston and New York: Houghton, Mifflin, 1904), pp. 24–37.

27. *Id.*

28. *Id.* at pp. 40–45.

29. See, for example, "Lewis and Clark: 'We proceeded on,'" *The Economist* 30 (15 May 2004); Ellis, p. 101; Esmond Wright, *A History of the United States of America: An Empire for Liberty; From Washington to Lincoln,* Vol. 2 (Oxford and Cambridge: Blackwell, 1995), p. 20; Saul K. Padover, *Jefferson* (New York: Harcourt, Brace, 1942), pp. 313–14.

30. Felix S. Cohen, "Original Indian Title," 32 *Minn. L. Rev.* 28, 35 (1947).

31. *A Compilation of Messages and Papers of the Presidents,* Vol. 1, ed. James D. Richardson (Washington, DC: Bureau of National Literature, 1913), pp. 360, 363–65, 421, 422, 426.

32. *Id.* at p. 436.

33. See, for example, *Writings of Thomas Jefferson,* Vol. 16, pp. 394–95, 398–99, 400–02, 467, 472.

34. *Letters of the Lewis and Clark Expedition with Related Documents 1783–1854,* 2nd ed., Vol. 1, ed. Donald Jackson (Urbana, Chicago, and London: University of Illinois Press, 1978), p. 61; Anthony F. C. Wallace, *Jefferson and the Indians: The Tragic Fate of the First Americans* (Ann Arbor: University of Michigan Press, 1999), pp. 224, 255.

35. *The Works of Thomas Jefferson,* Vol. 10, ed. Paul Leicester Ford (New York: G.P. Putnam's Sons, 1905), p. 14; *Compilation,* p. 346.

36. *Letters of the Lewis and Clark Expedition,* Vol. 1, pp. 61–65, 165.

37. *Writings of Thomas Jefferson,* Vol. 16, p. 472.

38. William Plumer, *Memorandum of Proceedings in the U.S. Senate, 1803–1807,* ed. Everett Somerville Brown (December 2, 1806; New York: Macmillan, 1923) p. 520.

39. James P. Ronda, *Astoria & Empire* (Lincoln and London: University of Nebraska Press, 1990), pp. xii, 44; Grace H. Flandrau, *Astor and the Oregon Country* (St. Paul, MN: Great Northern Railway, 1922), p. 7; *Writings of Thomas Jefferson,* Vol. 12, p. 28.

40. Ronda, *Astoria & Empire,* p. xii.

41. *The Writings of Thomas Jefferson,* Vol. 6, ed. H.A. Washington (New York: H.W. Derby, 1861), pp. 55–56.

42. *Writings of Thomas Jefferson,* Vol. 13, pp. 432–34.

43. *Writings of Thomas Jefferson,* Vol. 10, p. 93.

CHAPTER 4

1. *A Compilation of the Messages and Papers of the Presidents,* Vol. 1, ed. James D. Richardson (Washington, DC: Bureau of National Literature, 1913), pp. 309, 311; James P. Ronda, *Finding The West: Explorations with Lewis and Clark* (Albuquerque: University of New Mexico Press, 2001), p. 64; William Earl Weeks, "New Directions in the Study of Early American Foreign Relations," in *Paths to Power: The Historiography of American Foreign Relations to 1941,* ed. Michael J. Hogan (Cambridge, England: Cambridge University Press, 2000), p. 26; Robert W. Tucker & David C. Hendrickson, *Empire of Liberty: The State-craft of Thomas Jefferson* (New York and Oxford: Oxford University Press, 1990), pp. 20, 159; Joseph J. Ellis, *American Sphinx: The Character of Thomas Jefferson* (New York: Knopf, 1998), p. 212.

2. Donald Jackson, *Thomas Jefferson and the Stony Mountains* (Urbana, Chicago, and London: University of Illinois Press, 1981), p. 298; *The Writings of Thomas Jefferson,* Vol. 10, ed. Andrew A. Lipscomb & Albert Ellery Bergh (Washington, DC: U.S. Government Printing Office, 1903), pp. 294, 445; *The Writings of Thomas Jefferson,* Vol. 6, ed. H.A. Washington (New York: H.W. Derby, 1861), p. 248.

3. *Writings of Thomas Jefferson,* Vol. 12, pp. 275, 277; *Id.,* Vol. 9, p. 218; *Writings of Thomas Jefferson,* Vol. 1, ed. Washington, p. 518.

4. *Compilation,* pp. 309, 311; Peter S. Onuf, *Jefferson's Empire: The Language of American Nationhood* (Charlottesville: University Press of Virginia, 2000), p. 15; *Writings of Thomas Jefferson,* Vol. 6, ed. Washington, p. 55.

5. Robert J. Miller, "The Doctrine of Discovery in American Indian Law," 42 *Idaho L. Rev.* 1, 76–98 (2006); James P. Ronda, "Introduction," in *Thomas Jefferson and the Changing West,* ed. James P. Ronda (Albuquerque: University of New Mexico Press, 1997), p. xiv; Ellis, p. 212; Bernard DeVoto, *The Course of Empire* (Boston: Houghton Mifflin, 1952), pp. 323–28, 420, 430, 512, 527–28; Merrill Peterson, *Thomas Jefferson and the New Nation* (New York: Oxford University Press, 1970), p. 746; *The Journals of Lewis and Clark,* ed. Bernard DeVoto (Boston: Houghton Mifflin, 1953), pp. xxxiii–xxxiv.

6. Tucker, pp. 164–65, 168, 234–35.

7. *Journals of Lewis and Clark,* pp. xxxiii–xxxiv; *Writings of Thomas Jefferson,* Vol. 9, p. 218; *Writings of Thomas Jefferson,* Vol. 1, ed. Washington, p. 518; Ellis, pp. 92–93; Peterson, pp. 746–50.

8. Ellis, pp. 92–93, 206; Tucker, pp. 108–29; Peterson, pp. 747–52; *Compilation,* pp. 330–31; Saul K. Padover, *Jefferson* (New York: Harcourt, Brace, 1942), pp. 314–16; *The Writings of Thomas Jefferson,* Vol. 8, ed. Paul Leicester Ford (New York: G.P. Putnam's' Sons, 1892–99), pp. 144–45.

9. *Annals of Congress,* 8th Congress, 1st Session, p. 1124 (March 8, 1804); Jackson, pp. 108–09; Thomas Maitland Marshall, *A History of the Western Boundary of the Louisiana Purchase, 1819–1841* (Berkeley: University of California Press, 1914), p. 14 & n.30; *Writings of Thomas Jefferson,* Vol. 4, ed. Washington, pp. 515–17; Robert Greenhow, *The History of Oregon and California,* 4th ed. (Boston: Freeman and Bolles, 1847), pp. 281–82; William Earl Weeks, *John Quincy Adams and American Global Empire* (Louisville: The University Press of Kentucky, 1992), pp. 26–28.

10. *William Plumer's Memorandum of Proceedings in the U.S. Senate, 1803–1807,* ed. Everett Somerville Brown (New York: Macmillan, 1923), p. 520; Jackson, pp. 200, 280; *Writings of Thomas Jefferson,* Vol. 10, p. 93; *Id.,* Vol. 12, p. 28; *The Writings of Thomas Jefferson,* Vol. 6, ed. Washington, pp. 55–56.

11. Jackson, pp. 297, 300; Richard W. Van Alstyne, *The Rising American Empire* (New York and London: Norton, 1960), pp. 88, 101, 146; Julius W. Pratt, *Expansionists of 1812* (Reprint, Gloucester: Peter Smith, 1957), pp. 12, 14, 261; *Writings of Thomas Jefferson,* Vol. 6, ed. Washington, p. 131; Weeks, "New Directions," p. 30.

12. Jackson, pp. 297–98; Tucker, p. 160; *Writings of Thomas Jefferson,* Vol. 8, ed. Ford, p. 24.

13. Reginald Horsman, *Expansion and American Indian Policy 1783–1812* (East Lansing: Michigan State University Press, 1967), p. 108; Peterson, pp. 284, 745; Ronda, p. 62.

14. *Writings of Thomas Jefferson,* Vol. 14, pp. 401–02; *Id.,* Vol. 11, pp. 79–80 (1805); *Id.,* Vol. 12, pp. 312–13; Peterson, pp. 258–59; Jackson, p. 19; Bernard W. Sheehan, *Seeds of Extinction: Jeffersonian Philanthropy and the American Indian* (Chapel Hill: University of North Carolina Press, 1973), pp. 46–48.

15. *Writings of Thomas Jefferson,* Vol. 16, pp. 406–09, 417–20.

16. *Writings of Thomas Jefferson,* Vol. 5, p. 6; Ellis, p. 101; *The Papers of Thomas Jefferson,* Vol. 8, ed. Julian P. Boyd (Princeton, NJ: Princeton University Press, 1950), p. 185, *Id.,* Vol. 11, pp. 48–50, 92–93; Sheehan, p. 124; Jenry Morsman, "Jefferson's Fluid Plans for the Western Perimeter," in *Across the Continent: Jefferson, Lewis & Clark, and the Making of America,* ed. Douglas Seefeldt, Jeffrey L. Hantman & Peter S. Onuf (Charlottesville and London: University of Virginia Press, 2005), pp. 71–72; Reginald Horsman, *Race and Manifest Destiny: The Origins of American Racial Anglo-Saxonism* (Cambridge and London: Harvard University Press, 1981), p. 101.

17. *Writings of Thomas Jefferson,* Vol. 10, p. 363; *Id.,* Vol. 16, p. 289; Horsman, *Race and Manifest Destiny,* p. 107.

18. Ronda, "Introduction," p. xiv; Tucker, pp. 160–62; Vine Deloria Jr. & David E. Wilkins, *Tribes, Treaties, and Constitutional Tribulations* (Austin: University of Texas Press, 1999), p. 89.

19. *Writings of Thomas Jefferson,* Vol. 8, pp. 177–78; *Id.,* Vol. 11, pp. 25, 325; *Id.,* Vol. 17, pp. 376–77; Anthony F. C. Wallace, *Jefferson and the Indians: The Tragic Fate of the First Americans* (Cambridge: Belknap Press of Harvard University Press, 1999), pp. 310–13; Sheehan, p. 172.

20. *Writings of Thomas Jefferson,* Vol. 17, p. 374; R. S. Cotterill, *The Southern Indians before Removal* (Norman: University of Oklahoma Press, 1954), p. 140 n.2; Anthony F. C. Wallace, "The Obtaining Lands': Thomas Jefferson and the Native Americans," in *Thomas*

Jefferson and the Changing West, ed. James P. Ronda (Albuquerque: University of New Mexico Press, 1997), p. 30; *Documents of United States Indian Policy,* 3rd ed., ed. Francis Paul Prucha (Lincoln: University of Nebraska Press, 2000), p. 22; Colin G. Calloway, *The American Revolution in Indian Country: Crisis and Diversity in Native American Communities* (Cambridge, England, and New York: Cambridge University Press, 1995), p. 242; Roger G. Kennedy, *Mr. Jefferson's Lost Cause: Land, Farmers, Slavery, and the Louisiana Purchase* (Oxford and New York: Oxford University Press, 2003), p. 163 & n.26.

21. *Writings of Thomas Jefferson,* Vol. 10, pp. 357–59.

22. *Id.* at pp. 357–63.

23. *Id.*

24. *Writings of Thomas Jefferson,* Vol. 16, pp. 394–95, 400–02, 472; Treaty with the Creeks, June 16, 1802, Art. I & II, 7 Stat. 68; Treaty with the Delaware, Aug. 18, 1804, Art. III & IV, 7 Stat. 81; Treaty with the Chickasaw, July 23, 1805, Art. II, 7 Stat. 89; Treaty with the Choctaw, Nov. 16, 1805, Art. II, 7 Stat. 98; *Compilation,* pp. 422–23, 425–26.

25. *Writings of Thomas Jefferson,* Vol. 17, pp. 375–76.

26. *Writings of Thomas Jefferson,* Vol. 10, pp. 371–72; Treaty with the Kaskaskia, Aug. 13, 1803, Art. 1, 7 Stat. 78.

27. *Writings of Thomas Jefferson,* Vol. 17, pp. 375–76; *Id.,* Vol. 10, p. 371.

28. *Writings of Thomas Jefferson,* Vol. 10, pp. 371, 391, 393–94, 401–02; Jon Kukla, *A Wilderness So Immense* (New York: A.A. Knopf, 2003), p. 302; Jackson, p. 112.

29. *Writings of Thomas Jefferson,* Vol. 4, ed. Ford, pp. viii, 244, 500; *Writings of Thomas Jefferson,* Vol. 16, p. 285; Ronda, *Finding The West,* p. 62.

30. *The Adams-Jefferson Letters,* Vol. 2, ed. Lester J. Cappon (Chapel Hill: University of North Carolina Press, 1959), p. 308.

31. *Writings of Thomas Jefferson,* Vol. 17, p. 374; Kennedy, p. 155.

32. Cotterill, pp. 158–59; Kennedy, p. 194; *Compilation,* p. 442.

33. *The Papers of Thomas Jefferson,* Vol. 3, ed. Boyd, pp. 259, 276 n.7; *Writings of Thomas Jefferson,* Vol. 2, pp. 344–45; *Id.,* Vol. 11, p. 345; *Id.,* Vol. 14, p. 23; Sheehan, p. 244 & n.2; 169; Calloway, pp. 53, 172; Wallace, pp. 65 & n.32, 71.

34. Peterson, p. 193; Onuf, *Jefferson's Empire,* p. 47 & n.66; Pratt, pp. 247–48; Ellis, p. 202; *Writings of Jefferson,* Vol. 6, ed. Washington, p. 273; Horsman, *Race and Manifest Destiny,* p. 103; Jeffrey Ostler, *The Plains Sioux and U.S. Colonialism from Lewis and Clark to Wounded Knee* (Cambridge: Cambridge University Press, 2004), p. 13.

35. Calloway, p. 197.

36. Ellis; Peterson, p. 774.

37. Onuf, *Jefferson's Empire,* pp. 2, 3, 16–17, 20–21, 49.

38. Wallace, p. 11.

39. Joseph J. Ellis, *Founding Brothers: The Revolutionary Generation* (New York: Vintage Books, 2000), pp. 197–98, 210–11, 219–20; Ellis, p. 200.

40. *Writings of Thomas Jefferson,* Vol. 10, pp. 373, 391–92.

41. *Compilation,* pp. 340, 422, 425; Wallace, p. 222; Tucker, p. 17.

42. *Writings of Thomas Jefferson,* Vol. 6, p. 79; Van Alstyne, p. 82; Kennedy, pp. 17, 36, 68, 152–54, 251–52; *Compilation,* p. 367.

43. Wallace, "The Obtaining Lands," p. 34; *United States v. Ahtanum Irr. Dist.,* 236 F.2d 321, 337–38 (9th Cir. 1956); *Adams-Jefferson Letters,* Vol. 2, p. 307; *Compilation,* pp. 367, 431–32; Ostler, pp. 13, 17 & n.5, 40; Sheehan, p. 265; Patricia Nelson Limerick, *The Legacy of Conquest: The Unbroken Past of the American West* (New York: Norton, 1987), p. 190; Kennedy, pp. 36, 125.

44. *Compilation,* pp. 395–96, 442; *Writings of Thomas Jefferson,* Vol. 11, p. 81; Robert A. Williams, Jr., "Thomas Jefferson: Indigenous American Storyteller," in *Thomas Jefferson and the Changing West,* ed. James P. Ronda (Albuquerque: University of New Mexico Press, 1997), pp. 95–96.

CHAPTER 5

1. Bernard DeVoto, *The Course of Empire* (Boston: Houghton Mifflin, 1952), p. 411.

2. Peter S. Onuf & Jeffrey L. Hantman, "Introduction: Geopolitics, Science, and Culture Conflicts," in *Across the Continent: Jefferson, Lewis & Clark, and the Making of America,* ed. Douglas Seefeldt, Jeffrey L. Hantman & Peter S. Onuf (Charlottesville and London: University of Virginia Press, 2005), p. 4; Stephen Dow Beckham, *Lewis & Clark: From the Rockies to the Pacific* (Portland, OR: Graphic Arts Center Publishing, 2002), pp. 11, 92, 139; James P. Ronda, *Finding The West: Explorations with Lewis and Clark* (Albuquerque: University of New Mexico Press, 2001), pp. 62–64, 71; Joseph J. Ellis, *American Sphinx: The Character of Thomas Jefferson* (New York: Knopf, 1998), p. 212; Esmond Wright, *A History of the United States of America: An Empire for Liberty; From Washington to Lincoln,* Vol. 2 (Oxford and Cambridge: Blackwell, 1995), pp. 22, 243; Albert Furtwangler, *Acts of Discovery* (Urbana: University of Illinois Press, 1993), pp. 77–79, 90; James P. Ronda, *Astoria & Empire* (Lincoln and London: University of Nebraska Press, 1990), pp. 43, 327; Roy E. Appleman, *Lewis & Clark: Historic Places Associated with Their Transcontinental Exploration* (Washington, DC: U.S. National Park Service, 1975), p. 39; Merrill Peterson, *Thomas Jefferson and the New Nation* (New York: Oxford University Press, 1970), pp. 746, 904; DeVoto, pp. 420, 430, 512, 527–28, 538–39, 549; *The Journals of Lewis and Clark,* ed. Bernard DeVoto (Boston: Houghton Mifflin, 1953), pp. xxxiii–xxxv, l; *The Writings of Thomas Jefferson,* Vol. 10, ed. Andrew A. Lipscomb & Albert Ellery Bergh (Washington, DC: U.S. Government Printing Office, 1903), pp. 445–46; *American State Papers: Documents, Legislative and Executive, of the Congress of the United States,* Vol. 6, pp. 666–70; *Id.,* Vol. 5, pp. 533–58.

3. Robert J. Miller, "The Doctrine of Discovery in American Indian Law," 42 *Idaho L. Rev.* 1, 86–103 (2006); Robert J. Miller, "The Doctrine of Discovery," *We Proceeded On* 24–29 (August 2004).

4. Onuf & Hantman, p. 8; Anthony F. C. Wallace, *Jefferson and the Indians: The Tragic Fate of the First Americans* (Cambridge, MA: Belknap Press of Harvard University Press, 1999), p. 241; Stephen E. Ambrose, *Undaunted Courage: Meriwether Lewis, and the Opening of the American West* (New York: Simon & Schuster, 1996), pp. 68–70, 73–75; Saul K. Padover, *Jefferson* (New York: Harcourt, Brace1942), pp. 314–16; DeVoto, pp. 337, 386; Ronda, *Finding The West,* p. 64; Alan Taylor, "Jefferson's Pacific: The Science of Distant Empire, 1768–1811," in *Across the Continent: Jefferson, Lewis & Clark, and the Making of America,* ed. Douglas Seefeldt, Jeffrey L. Hantman & Peter S. Onuf (Charlottesville and London: University of Virginia Press, 2005), pp. 34, 37; *Journals of Lewis and Clark,* p. xl; Ellis, pp. 92–93, 206, 242–45; *A Compilation of the Messages and Papers of the Presidents,* Vol. 1, ed. James D. Richardson (Washington, DC: Bureau of National Literature, 1913), pp. 330–31, 338, 346; Peterson, pp. 746–50, 755, 758.

5. James P. Ronda, *Lewis & Clark among the Indians* (Lincoln and London: University of Nebraska Press, 1984), pp. 3, 9; Ambrose, pp. 76–78, 81–84; *Letters of the Lewis and Clark Expedition with Related Documents 1783–1854,* 2nd ed., Vol. 1, ed. Donald Jackson (Urbana: University of Illinois Press, 1978), pp. 10–13, 19–20, 173–75, 183–89.

6. *Letters*, Vol. 1, ed. Jackson, pp. 10–13, 64; *Journals of Lewis and Clark*, pp. xxxiii–xxxv; Jon Kukla, *A Wilderness So Immense* (New York: Knopf, 2003), p. 261.

7. *Letters*, Vol. 1, ed. Jackson, p. 61.

8. *Compilation*, p. 346; *Letters*, Vol. 1, ed. Jackson, pp. 12 & 13, 64; Ronda, *Lewis & Clark among the Indians*, pp. 9, 19–23.

9. *Letters*, Vol. 1, ed. Jackson, p. 64; Ronda, *Lewis & Clark among the Indians*, p. 9.

10. *Letters*, Vol. 1, ed. Jackson, pp. 62, 64, 157; Ronda, *Lewis & Clark among the Indians*, pp. 1, 113–32; 6 *The Definitive Journals of Lewis & Clark*, ed. Gary E. Moulton (Lincoln and London: University of Nebraska Press, 1987), pp. 289–301, 320–26, 369–71, 417–24; *Id.*, Vol. 3, pp. 333–505; *Id.*, Vol. 6, pp. 445–96; Furtwangler, pp. 87, 161; Frank Lawrence Owsley, Jr. & Gene A. Smith, *Filibusters and Expansionists: Jeffersonian Manifest Destiny, 1800–1821* (Tuscaloosa: University of Alabama Press, 1997), pp. 12–13.

11. Robert J. Miller, *We Proceeded On*, pp. 25–26; Ronda, *Lewis & Clark among the Indians*, pp. 9–10, 14; *Letters*, Vol. 1, ed. Jackson, p. 62; Ambrose, p. 84; 3 Moulton, pp. 492–505.

12. *Letters*, Vol. 1, ed. Jackson, p. 165.

13. Robert J. Miller, *We Proceeded On*, pp. 25–26; Ronda, *Lewis & Clark among the Indians*, p. 133; Ambrose, pp. 76–78, 154.

14. *Letters*, Vol. 1, ed. Jackson, p. 203; Ambrose, p. 156; Ronda, *Lewis & Clark among the Indians*, pp. 20–21, 79, 81; Moulton, Vol. 3, at 156.

15. *Letters*, Vol. 1, ed. Jackson, pp. 205–07; George Berndt, "Comparing Lewis & Clark's speeches to the Otos and the Yankton Sioux," *We Proceeded On* 38 (August 2005) (Lewis Speech, Second Tribal Council, 30 August 1804, Yankton Sioux Nation) (U.S. National Park Service, mnrr_interpretation@nps.gov).

16. *Letters*, Vol. 1, ed. Jackson, pp. 205–07; George Berndt, "Comparing Lewis & Clark's speeches to the Otos and the Yankton Sioux," *We Proceeded On* 38 (August 2005) (Lewis Speech, Second Tribal Council, 30 August 1804, Yankton Sioux Nation) (U.S. National Park Service, mnrr_interpretation@nps.gov).

17. *Letters*, Vol. 1, ed. Jackson, p. 208; Lewis Speech at Second Tribal Council; Moulton, Vol. 5, p. 111.

18. *Letters*, Vol. 1, ed. Jackson, p. 208; Lewis Speech at Second Tribal Council; Moulton, Vol. 5, p. 111.

19. Moulton, Vol. 5, pp. 79–80; R. B. Bernstein, *Thomas Jefferson* (Oxford: Oxford University Press, 2003), p. 144; Ronda, *Finding The West*, p. 71; Ronda, *Lewis & Clark among the Indians*, pp. 92 & 193; Francis Paul Prucha, *Indian Peace Medals in American History* (Madison: State Historical Society of Wisconsin, 1971), pp. xiv, 8, 11, 13, 91; *Letters*, Vol. 1, ed. Jackson, p. 205; Lewis Speech at Second Tribal Council.

20. Prucha, *Indian Peace Medals*, p. 20; Moulton, Vol. 3, p. 242.

21. Lewis Speech at Second Tribal Council; Moulton, Vol. 10, p. 25 (Patrick Gass).

22. Robert J. Miller, "The Doctrine of Discovery in American Indian Law," 42 *Idaho L. Rev.* 1, 76–97 (2006); Robert J. Miller, *We Proceeded On*, pp. 25–26; Thomas P. Slaughter, *Exploring Lewis and Clark: Reflections on Men and Wilderness* (New York: Knopf, 2003), pp. 161, 172, 188; Friedrich August Freiherr von der Heydte, "Discovery, Symbolic Annexation and Virtual Effectiveness in International Law," 29 *Am. J. Int'l L.* 448, 453–55 (1935).

23. Beckham, pp. 11, 92, 139; *Journals of Lewis and Clark*, pp. xxxv & l; W. Kaye Lamb, "Introduction," in *The Journals and Letters of Sir Alexander Mackenzie*, ed. W. Kaye Lamb (London: Cambridge University Press, Hakluyt Society, 1970), pp. 1, 42, 518 n.4;

Ronda, *Finding the West,* pp. 62–64; Furtwangler, pp. 77–79, 90; DeVoto, pp. 420, 430, 512, 527–28, 538–39, 549; Appleman, p. 39; *American State Papers,* Vol. 6, pp. 666–70; *Id.,* Vol. 5, pp. 533–58.

24. Ronda, *Finding the West,* p. 64; Elliott West, "Finding Lewis and Clark by Stepping Away," in *Finding Lewis & Clark: Old Trails, New Directions,* ed. James P. Ronda & Nancy Tystad Koupal (Pierre: South Dakota State Historical Society Press, 2004), p. 177; Donald Jackson, *Thomas Jefferson and the Stony Mountains* (Urbana, Chicago, and London: University of Illinois Press, 1981), pp. 200, 280; *Letters,* Vol. 1, ed. Jackson, pp. 61, 62, 65; Frederick Merk, *The Oregon Question: Essays in Anglo-American Diplomacy and Politics* (Cambridge, MA: The Belknap Press of Harvard University Press, 1967), pp. 4, 42, 47, 51, 110, 156, 165; DeVoto, pp. 323–38.

25. *Writings of Thomas Jefferson,* Vol. 13, pp. 432–34; Peterson, p. 904; Grace H. Flandrau, *Astor and the Oregon Country* (St. Paul, MN: Great Northern Railway, 1922), p. 7; Merk, pp. 4, 14–15, 29, 399; *The Journals and Letters of Sir Alexander Mackenzie,* pp. 517–18.

26. David L. Nicandri, "The Columbia Country and the Dissolution of Meriwether Lewis," 106 *Oregon Historical Quarterly* 8 & n.4 (Spring 2005); Stephen Dow Beckham et al., *The Literature of the Lewis and Clark Expedition: A Bibliography and Essays* (Portland, OR: Lewis & Clark College, 2003), pp. 104–05; *Letters,* Vol. 1, ed. Jackson, pp. 113, 210; Moulton, Vol. 3, pp. 14, 152–53, 170 & n.10 (Clark listed self as "Capt or [on?] E. N W D;"); Lewis Speech at Second Tribal Council, 30 August 1804 (Clark signed "Wm Clar (Capt?) Expd For N W D").

27. Moulton, Vol. 6, pp. 81, 106–07; *Id.,* Vol. 4, p. 276; *Id.,* Vol. 11, pp. 192–93; Robert A. Saindon, "They Left Their Mark: Tracing the Obscure Graffiti of the Lewis and Clark Expedition," in *Explorations Into the World of Lewis & Clark,* Vol. 2, ed. Robert A. Saindon (Great Falls, MT: Lewis and Clark Trail Heritage Foundation, 2003), pp. 492, 496; DeVoto, p. 512.

28. Thomas Maitland Marshall, *A History of the Western Boundary of the Louisiana Purchase, 1819–1841* (Berkeley: University of California Press, 1914), p. 12; Donald Jackson, *Thomas Jefferson and the Stony Mountains* (Urbana, Chicago, and London: University of Illinois Press, 1981), p. 3; Merk, pp. 22–23; DeVoto, p. 512.

29. Slaughter, pp. 161, 172, 188; Patricia Seed, *Ceremonies of Possession in Europe's Conquest of the New World, 1492–1640* (Cambridge and New York: Cambridge University Press, 1995), pp. 1–2, 5–6, 17–19.

30. Taylor, pp. 19–20, 30, 32, 39; Onuf & Hantman, p. 6.

31. Seed, pp. 17–19; Edmond Atkin, "Reasons for French Success in the Indian Trade," in *Major Problems in American Indian History,* ed. Albert L. Hurtado and Peter Iverson (Lexington, KY, and Toronto, ON: Heath and Company, 1994), p. 143 (a 1755 report stated "Forts really are for establishing between the Crowns of Great Britain and France marks of Possession"); Beckham, *Lewis & Clark,* pp. 11, 92 (Forts Mandan and Clatsop "buttressed American claims of 'discovery' and arguments for possession"); Arthur Young, *Political Essays Concerning the Present State of the British Empire* (1772; New York: Research Reprints, 1970), p. 472; "Journal of Captain Fitch's Journey to the Creeks" (May 1756), *Colonial Indian Documents Microfilm Collection,* ed. Randolph Boehm, microformed on Records of the British Colonial Office, Vol. 1, Class 5: Westward Expansion 1700–1783, Reel I, Vol. 12, Frame 0158 (1972).

32. *See* Seed, pp. 1–2, 5–6, 9–14, 67, 179–86; M. De La Peyrouse, *A Voyage Round the World: Which Was Performed in 1785, 1786, 1787, and 1788* (Edinburgh: Abridged translation, J. Moir, 1798), pp. 70–71.

33. Moulton, Vol. 6, pp. 429, 430–31.

34. Moulton, Vol. 6, p. 432 n.1; *Letters,* Vol. 1, ed. Jackson, p. 300; Saindon, p. 501; Mary Malloy, *"Boston Men" on the Northwest Coast: The American Maritime Fur Trade 1788–1844,* ed. Richard A. Pierce (Kingston, ON: Limestone Press, 1998), pp. 53, 169.

35. Samuel Flagg Bemis, *John Quincy Adams and the Foundations of American Foreign Policy* (New York: Knopf, 1949), pp. 174, 281.

36. James P. Ronda, "Introduction," in *Finding Lewis & Clark,* p. xii; Onuf & Hantman, pp. 5, 7; West, pp. 180–81, 185–86, 188.

CHAPTER 6

1. Julius W. Pratt, *Expansionists of 1812* (Gloucester: Peter Smith, 1957), pp. 12–14, 261; William Earl Weeks, *Building the Continental Empire: American Expansion from the Revolution to the Civil War* (Chicago: Ivan R. Dee, 1996), pp. 28–29; *Overland to the Pacific: Where Rolls the Oregon: Prophet and Pessimist Look Northwest,* Vol. 3, ed. Archer Butler Hulbert (Denver, CO: Denver Public Library, 1933), pp. xiii & 5.

2. Donald Jackson, *Thomas Jefferson and the Stony Mountains: Exploring the West from Monticello* (Chicago and London: University of Illinois Press, 1981), p. 200; *Letters of the Lewis and Clark Expedition with Related Documents 1783–1854,* 2nd ed., Vol. 1, ed. Donald Jackson (Urbana, Chicago, and London: University of Illinois Press, 1978), p. 320.

3. Stephen E. Ambrose, *Nothing Like It in the World: The Men who Built the Transcontinental Railroad 1863–1869* (New York: Simon & Schuster, 2000), pp. 26–31; Weeks, *Building the Continental Empire,* pp. 83–86; Julius W. Pratt, "John L. O'Sullivan and Manifest Destiny," 12 *New York History* 213, 220 (1933); Alan Taylor, "Jefferson's Pacific: The Science of Distant Empire, 1768–1811," in *Across the Continent: Jefferson, Lewis & Clark, and the Making of America,* ed. Douglas Seefeldt, Jeffrey L. Hantman & Peter S. Onuf (Charlottesville and London: University of Virginia Press, 2005), p. 27.

4. "Annexation," 17 *United States Magazine and Democratic Review* 5 (July 1845) (quoted in Julius W. Pratt, "The Origin of 'Manifest Destiny,'" 32 *The American Historical Review* 795, 798 [July 1927]).

5. *New York Morning News,* 27 December 1845 (quoted in Julius W. Pratt, "The Origin of 'Manifest Destiny,'" pp. 795, 796).

6. *Congressional Globe,* 29th Congress, 1st Session, appendix 99 (quoted in Pratt, "The Origin of 'Manifest Destiny,'" p. 795.); *Congressional Globe,* 29th Congress, 1st Session, p. 207 & appendix 79–80, 92, 96, 99, 104, 110.

7. Robert W. Johannen, "The Meaning of Manifest Destiny," in *Manifest Destiny and Empire American Antebellum Expansionism,* ed. Sam W. Haynes & Christopher Morris (College Station: Texas A&M University Press, 1997), pp. 9, 13; David S. Heidler & Jeanne T. Heidler, *Manifest Destiny* (Westport, CT, and London: Greenwood Press, 2003), p. xv; *Reprint of Documents: Manifest Destiny and the Imperialism Question,* ed. Charles L. Sanford (New York and London: John Wiley, 1974), p. 8; Esmond Wright, *A History of the United States of America: An Empire for Liberty; From Washington to Lincoln* Vol. 2. (Oxford and Cambridge: Blackwell, 1995), p. 426.

8. Weeks, *Building the Continental Empire,* pp. 60–61, 110; Johannen, p. 10; *Reprint of Documents,* p. 10; Deborah L. Madsen, *American Exceptionalism* (Jackson: University Press of Mississippi, 1998), pp. 1–2; Sam W. Haynes, *James K. Polk and the Expansionist Impulse* (New York: Longman, 1997), pp. 87–90, 99; Bernard DeVoto, *The Course of Empire* (Boston: Houghton Mifflin, 1952), p. 411; Reginald Horsman, *Race and Manifest Destiny: The Origins*

of American Racial Anglo-Saxonism (Cambridge and London: Harvard University Press, 1981), p. 86; Anders Stephanson, *Manifest Destiny: American Expansion and the Empire of Right* (New York: Hill and Want, 1995), pp. 21–27, 46–47, 55–60; *A Compilation of the Messages and Papers of the Presidents,* Vol. 1, ed. James D. Richardson (Washington, DC: Bureau of National Literature, 1913), pp. 309, 311; James P. Ronda, *Finding the West: Explorations with Lewis and Clark* (Albuquerque: University of New Mexico Press, 2001), pp. 63–64.

9. Thomas R. Hietala, "'This Splendid Juggernaut:' Westward a Nation and Its People," in *Manifest Destiny and Empire,* p. 53; Horsman, pp. 1, 3, 5, 82–85, 89–93, 207–08; Stephanson, pp. 54–57.

10. Horsman, pp. 1, 3, 5, 82–85; Joseph J. Ellis, *American Sphinx: The Character of Thomas Jefferson* (New York: Knopf, 1998), p. 212.

11. Jackson, pp. 200, 280; Thomas Jefferson, "The Limits and Bounds of Louisiana," in *Documents Relating to the Purchase & Exploration of Louisiana* (Boston and New York: Houghton, Mifflin, 1904), pp. 24–37; William Earl Weeks, *John Quincy Adams and American Global Empire* (Louisville: University Press of Kentucky, 1992), p. 26.

12. Frank Lawrence Owsley, Jr. & Gene A. Smith, *Filibusters and Expansionists: Jeffersonian Manifest Destiny, 1800–1821* (Tuscaloosa and London: University of Alabama Press, 1997), pp. 1–2, 183; *The Writings of Thomas Jefferson,* Vol. 6, ed. H.A. Washington (New York: H.W. Derby, 1861), pp. 55–56.

13. *Congressional Globe,* 25th Congress, 2nd Session, p. 566 (May 1838); *American State Papers: Documents, Legislative and Executive, of the Congress of the United States: Foreign Relations,* Vol. 2, pp. 662–65; *Id.,* Vol. 3, pp. 85–86, 126, 185–86.

14. James P. Ronda, *Astoria & Empire* (Lincoln and London: University of Nebraska Press, 1990), pp. 309–10; *American State Papers,* Vol. 3, pp. 706, 712–16, 720, 724, 731.

15. Ronda, *Astoria & Empire,* pp. 309–10; *American State Papers,* Vol. 3, pp. 706, 712–16, 720, 724, 731.

16. *Annals of Congress,* 8th Congress, 1st Session, p. 1124 (March 8, 1804); Albert K. Weinberg, *Manifest Destiny: A Study of Nationalist Expansionism in American History* (Gloucester: Peter Smith, 1958), pp. 30–31 (quoting *New-York Evening Post,* 28 January 1803, and *Annals of Congress,* 7th Cong., 2nd Sess., at 372–73); Owsley, pp. 9–10, 82.

17. Michael Golay, *The Tide of Empire: America's March to the Pacific* (New York: John Wiley, 2003), p. 63; William Goetzmann, *When the Eagle Screamed: The Romantic Horizon in American Expansionism, 1800–1860* (New York: John Wiley, 1966; Reprint, Norman: University of Oklahoma Press, 2000), p. 11.

18. *American State Papers,* Vol. 3, p. 731; *Id.,* Vol. 4, pp. 377, 852.

19. *The Writings of John Quincy Adams 1816–1819,* Vol. 6, ed. Worthington Chauncey Ford (New York: Macmillan Co., 1916; Reprint, New York: Greenwood Press, 1968), pp. 204–05, 366, 372–73.

20. Ronda, pp. 244–45, 307; Frederick Merk, *The Oregon Question: Essays in Anglo-American Diplomacy and Politics* (Cambridge: The Belknap Press of Harvard University, 1967), pp. 15–24; Joseph Schafer, "The British Attitude Toward the Oregon Question, 1815–1846," 16 *The American Historical Review* 283–84 (Jan. 1911).

21. Merk, *The Oregon Question,* pp. 17–18, 22–23; DeVoto, p. 512; Weeks, *Building the Continental Empire,* p. 50; Weeks, *John Quincy Adams,* p. 50; Ronda, pp. 310–15, 308–10.

22. Merk, *The Oregon Question,* pp. 22–23; 3 *Oregon Historical Quarterly* 310–11 (Sept. 1902); 19 *Oregon Historical Quarterly* 180–87 (Sept. 1918); 20 *Oregon Historical Quarterly* 322–25 (Dec. 1919); Golay, p. 15.

23. Ronda, pp. 314–15; Merk, *The Oregon Question,* pp. 23–24; *House Document No. 112,* 17th Congress, 1st Session, pp. 13–19; *Annals of Congress,* 17th Congress, 2nd Session, p. 246; Golay, p. 65.

24. *Circular Letters of Congressmen to Their Constituents 1789–1829,* Vol. 1, ed. Noble E. Cunningham, Jr. (Chapel Hill: University of North Carolina Press, 1978), pp. xv–xxviii.

25. *Circular Letters,* Vol. 1, p. 496.

26. *Circular Letters,* Vol. 1, pp. 376, 381, 386, 401–03, 405–07, 415, 423, 439, 484–85, 501, 571; *Id.,* Vol. 2, p. 997; *Id.,* Vol. 3, pp. 1515, 1551.

27. *Compilation,* p. 396.

28. *Circular Letters,* Vol. 3, pp. 1047; William H. Goetzmann, *Exploration and Empire: The Explorer and the Scientist in the Winning of the American West* (New York: Knopf, 1966), p. 159; Ray Allen Billington, *The Far Western Frontier, 1830–1860* (Evanston & London: Harper & Row, 1956), pp. 70–71.

29. Stephanson, p. 59.

30. Richard W. Van Alstyne, *The Rising American Empire* (New York and London: Norton, 1960), p. 96; Weeks, *John Quincy Adams,* p. 19.

31. Robert W. Tucker & David C. Hendrickson, *Empire of Liberty: The Statecraft of Thomas Jefferson* (New York and Oxford: Oxford University Press, 1990), p. 162.

32. *American State Papers,* Vol. 3, p. 185, 731; *Id.,* Vol. 4, pp. 377, 381, 452–57, 468–72; Merk, *The Oregon Question,* pp. 4, 14–23, 42, 47, 51, 110, 156, 165–66, 399; *Writings of John Quincy Adams,* Vol. 6, p. 400; Schafer, pp. 285–86.

33. *American State Papers,* Vol. 5, pp. 555–57; *Id.,* Vol. 6, pp. 663–66; Merk, *The Oregon Question,* p. 403.

34. *American State Papers,* Vol. 5, pp. 555–57; *Id.,* Vol. 6, pp. 663–66; Merk, *The Oregon Question,* p. 403.

35. Van Alstyne, pp. 97, 98; *American State Papers,* Vol. 4, pp. 331, 377, 452–57, 468–72; *Id,.* Vol. 5, pp. 436–37, 446–47, 449, 554–58, 791; *Id.,* Vol. 6, pp. 644, 652–53, 657, 661–70; Merk, *The Oregon Question,* pp. 4, 14–35, 42, 47, 51, 68–69, 110, 156, 164–66, 185–88, 395–412.

36. *American State Papers,* Vol. 5, pp. 446–47; Weinberg, p. 136.

37. *The Papers of Henry Clay,* Vol. 5, ed. James F. Hopkins & Mary W.M. Hargreaves (Louisville: The University Press of Kentucky, 1973), pp. 596, 843.

38. *American State Papers,* Vol. 4, pp. 455, 470.

39. Dale L. Walker, *Pacific Destiny: The Three-Century Journey to the Oregon Country* (New York: Forge, 2000), p. 385; *The Diary of John Quincy Adams 1794–1845,* ed. Allan Nevins (New York: Charles Scribner's Sons, 1951), p. 211; Weeks, *John Quincy Adams,* pp. 73, 119–20; *Compilation,* Vol. 1, p. 626.

40. Jackson, p. 53; *American State Papers,* Vol. 5, pp. 436–37, 446, 449, 791; *Writings of John Quincy Adams,* Vol. 7, pp. 212–15; Weeks, *John Quincy Adams,* pp. 79–81.

41. *American State Papers,* Vol. 5, pp. 583–84.

42. Van Alstyne, pp. 58, 116; Walker, p. 385.

43. Frederick Merk, *History of the Westward Movement* (New York: Knopf, 1978), p. 314; *Overland to the Pacific,* Vol. 3, pp. 87–88; *Debates,* 18th Congress, 2nd Session, appendix 7; 1 *Cong. Deb.* 705–06, appendix 7 (1825).

44. *Annals of Congress,* 16th Congress, 2nd Session, p. 679; *Overland to the Pacific,* Vol. 3, p. 42, 45; *American State Papers,* Vol. 2, pp. 629–34; Charles H. Ambler, *The Oregon Country, 1810–1830: A Chapter in Territorial Expansion,* 30 *The Mississippi Valley Historical Review* 8 (June 1943).

45. *Annals of Congress,* 16th Congress, 2nd Session, p. 679; *Overland to the Pacific,* Vol. 3, p. 42, 45.

46. *Annals of Congress,* 16th Congress, 2nd Session, p. 679.

47. *Id.*

48. *Id.*

49. *Id.*

50. *Id.*

51. Edward Gaylord Bourne, "Aspects of Oregon History Before 1840," 6 *Oregon Historical Quarterly* 264 (1906); Ambler, pp. 12–13.

52. Ambler, pp. 14–16; *Overland to the Pacific,* Vol. 3, p. 52; *Annals of Congress,* 17th Congress, 2nd Session, p. 396–409.

53. *Annals of Congress,* 17th Congress, 2nd Session, pp. 682–83.

54. *Id.*

55. Ambler, pp. 16–17.

56. Van Alstyne, p. 96; Merk, *The Oregon Question,* p. 7; Ambler, p. 19.

57. *House Report No. 213,* 19th Congress, 1st Session, pp. 5–6, 8 (1826).

58. *House Report No. 213,* 19th Congress, 1st Session, pp. 5–6, 8–12 (1826); *Overland to the Pacific,* Vol. 3, p. 12.

59. *Overland to the Pacific,* Vol. 3, p. 42; Thomas Hart Benton, *Thirty Years' View; or, A History of the Working of the American Government for Thirty Years, From 1820–1850,* Vol. 1 (New York: Appleton and Company, 1856; Reprint, Greenwood Press, 1968), p. 14.

60. *Gales & Seaton's Register,* 699–700; *Cong. Debates,* Vol. 1, 705–06 (1825).

61. *Gales & Seaton's Register,* 699–700; *Register of Debates,* 18th Congress, 2nd Session, pp. 700, 705; Benton, Vol. 1, p. 54.

62. William Nisbet Chambers, *Old Bullion Benton: Senator from the New West* (Boston and Toronto: Atlantic Monthly Press, 1956), pp. 82–84; Ambler, p. 22; *Overland to the Pacific,* Vol. 3, p. 101; *Register of Debates in Congress,* Vol. 1, pp. 711–13; Benton, Vol. 1, p. 52.

63. *Circular Letters,* Vol. 3, pp. 1016, 1018, 1036, 1040, 1047, 1155–54, 1059, 1082, 1138, 1158, 1267, 1281, 1284, 1295, 1300, 1326, 1339, 1344.

64. *Circular Letters,* Vol. 3, p. 1146.

65. Harry L. Watson, *Liberty and Power: The Politics of Jacksonian America* (New York: Farrar, Straus and Giroux, 1990), pp. 53, 105; 1 *Cong. Debates* 689 (1825).

66. *Congressional Globe,* 27th Congress, 3rd Session, p. 117 (February 2, 1843).

67. *Senate Document, No. 25–470,* 5–6 (1838); *Congressional Globe,* 27th Congress, 3rd Session, pp. 79, 153 (January 9, 1843); Mirth Tufts Kaplan, "Courts, Counselors and Cases: The Judiciary of Oregon's Provisional Government," 62 *Oregon Historical Quarterly* 124 (June 1961).

68. Billington, pp. 83–88 & n.37; *Congressional Globe,* 27th Congress, 3rd Session, appendix p. 152; *Congressional Globe,* 27th Congress, 2nd Session, pp. 736–37.

69. *Congressional Globe,* 25th Congress, 2nd Session, p. 566 (May 1838).

70. *Congressional Globe,* 25th Congress, 2nd Session, p. 566–70 (May 1838); John Belohlavek, "Race, Progress, and Destiny: Caleb Cushing and the Quest for American Empire," in *Manifest Destiny and Empire,* p. 32.

71. *House Report No. 25–101,* 3–5, 25–27 (1839); 6 *Oregon Historical Quarterly,* at p. 271.

72. *House Report No. 25–101,* 3–5, 25–27 (1839); 6 *Oregon Historical Quarterly,* at p. 271.

73. *Circular Letters,* Vol. 3, pp. 1409, 1465, 1478, 1491, 1499, 1506, 1521, 1544, 1551.

74. Kaplan, p. 123.

75. Major L. Wilson, *Space, Time and Freedom: The Quest for Nationality and the Irrepressible Conflict 1815–1861* (Westport and London: Greenwood Press, 1974), p. 12.

76. *Report on the Territory of Oregon to Accompany House Bill No. 976,* 25th Congress, 3rd Session, House Report, p. 101 (1839); Goetzmann, p. 168; Billington, p. 83.

77. Johannen, pp. 3, 14; Goetzmann, pp. 233–35; Schafer, p. 294.

78. Johannen, p. 14; Goetzmann, pp. 233, 240–44, 248–49.

79. Billington, pp. 79–81; Walker, pp. 281–82; Frank McLynn, *Wagons West: The Epic Story of America's Overland Trails* (New York: Grove Press, 2002), p. 9.

80. *House Document No. 139,* 20th Congress, 1st Session, pp. 3–5, 25–27 (February 11, 1828).

81. 6 *Oregon Historical Quarterly,* at p. 266; Billington, pp. 70–71; Hall J. Kelley, "A Geographical Sketch of That Part of North America Called Oregon" (1830), in *Hall J. Kelley on Oregon,* ed. Fred Wilbur Powell (Princeton, NJ: Princeton University Press, 1932), pp. 60–61.

82. Weeks, *Building the Continental Empire,* p. 105; 6 *Oregon Historical Quarterly,* at p. 271.

83. *Compilation,* Vol. 4, p. 381; Billington, p. 155 .

84. *Compilation,* Vol. 4, pp. 380–81; Haynes, p. 70.

85. Frederick Merk, *The Monroe Doctrine and American Expansionism 1843–1849* (New York: Knopf, 1968), pp. 65–66; Chambers, p. 296.

86. *Compilation,* Vol. 4, pp. 392–97; Billington, pp. 156–57.

87. *Compilation,* Vol. 4, pp. 394–99.

88. *Congressional Globe,* 29th Congress, 1st Session, p. 259 (January 27, 1846); *Congressional Globe,* 33rd Congress, 1st Session, p. 337 (March 3, 1854); Johannen, p. 16; Wilson, pp. 111–13.

89. Haynes, pp. 98–99.

90. 9 Stat. 496.

91. *St. Louis Reporter,* 18 March 1845 (quoted in Melvin Clay Jacobs, *Winning Oregon* (Caldwell: The Caxton Printers, Ltd., 1938), pp. 37–38 n.4).

92. Stephen Dow Beckham, *Ethnohistorical Context of Reserved Indian Fishing Rights: Pacific Northwest Treaties* (Portland, OR: Lewis & Clark College, 1984), pp. 8–11; 9 Stat. 323.

93. Robert J. Miller, "Exercising Cultural Self-Determination: The Makah Indian Tribe Goes Whaling," 25 *Am. Indian L. Rev.* 165, 189–99 (2001); Robert J. Miller, "Speaking with Forked Tongues: Indian Treaties, Salmon, and the Endangered Species Act," 70 *Or. L. Rev.* 543, 551–63 (1991); Beckham, pp. 15–22, 31, 135–51.

94. *Jones v. United States,* 137 U.S. 202, 212 (1890); Act of Aug. 18, 1856, ch. 164, 11 Stat. 119 (codified at 48 U.S.C. §§ 1411–1419); *Warren v. United States,* 234 F.3d 1331 (D.C. Cir. 2000).

95. *The Island of Palmas Case,* 2 R.I.A.A. 829, Hague Court Reports 83 (1928); Lynn Berat, *Walvis Bay: Decolonization and International Law* (New Haven, CT: Yale University Press, 1990), pp. 118–19; J. Moore, *A Digest of International Law* (Washington, DC: U.S. Government Printing Office, 1906), p. 575.

96. Pratt, *John L. O'Sullivan,* pp. 213, 234.

97. Haynes, pp. 99, 102.

98. *Reprint of Documents,* pp. 46, 70; Horsman, pp. 3, 5, 110, 195, 300–03; Stephanson, pp. 56–57 (quoting statements of the extinction of the Indian and Spanish races).

CHAPTER 7

1. Russell Lawrence Barsh & James Youngblood Henderson, *The Road: Indian Tribes and Political Liberty* (Berkeley: University of California Press, 1980), p. 49; Robert A. Williams, Jr., "The Algebra of Federal Indian Law: The Hard Trail of Decolonizing and Americanizing the White Man's Indian Jurisprudence," 1986 *Wisc. L. Rev.* 219, 257; Note, "International Law as an Interpretive Force in Federal Indian Law," 116 *Harv. L. Rev.* 1751, 1753 (2003).

2. *Felix S. Cohen's Handbook of Federal Indian Law,* ed. Rennard Strickland et al. (Charlottesville, VA: Michie Company, 1982), pp. 207–57; Charles F. Wilkinson, *American Indians, Time, and the Law* (New Haven and London: Yale University Press, 1987), pp. 78–79; *Montana v. United States,* 450 U.S. 544, 560 n.9 (1981); Francis Paul Prucha, *The Great Father: The United States Government and the American Indians* (Lincoln: University of Nebraska Press, 1995), p. 671 n.26; *Morton v. Mancari,* 417 U.S. 535, 551–52 (1974).

3. *Cotton Petroleum Corp. v. New Mexico,* 490 U.S. 163, 192 (1989).

4. *United States v. Kagama,* 118 U.S. 375, 381 (1886).

5. *Seminole Nation v. United States,* 316 U S. 286, 297 (1942); *United States v. Mitchell,* 463 U.S. 206, 224–26 (1983); *Cherokee Nation v. Georgia,* 30 U.S. (5 Pet.) 1, 17 (1831).

6. *Cherokee Nation,* 30 U.S. at 17; Tim Alan Garrison, *The Legal Ideology of Removal: The Southern Judiciary and the Sovereignty of Native American Nations* (Athens and London: The University of Georgia Press, 2002), pp. 235–37.

7. 118 U.S. 375, 383–84 (1886).

8. Robert A. Williams, Jr., *The American Indian in Western Legal Thought: The Discourses of Conquest* (New York and Oxford: Oxford University Press, 1990), p. 103; *Laws of the Colonial and State Governments Relating to Indians and Indian Affairs, from 1633 to 1831* (Washington, DC: Thompson and Homans, 1832; Reprint, Stanfordville, NY: Coleman, 1978), pp. 12, 16–17, 22, 37, 45, 59, 136, 142, 146, 150, 154; *Cherokee Nation,* 30 U.S. at 17.

9. Robert J. Miller, "Economic Development in Indian Country: Will Capitalism or Socialism Succeed?," 80 *Ore. L. Rev.* 757, 767–69, 781–85 (2001); *Cohen's Handbook,* pp. 229–32; *Talton v. Mayes,* 163 U.S. 376 (1896).

10. *Johnson,* 23 U.S. at 573–74; *Cherokee Nation,* 31 U.S. at 17–18; *Worcester v. Georgia,* 31 U.S. (6 Pet.) 515, 542–43, 546, 549, 555, 561 (1832); *Cohen's Handbook,* pp. 23.

11. 435 U.S. 191, 208, 210 (1978).

12. *George Washington Writings,* ed. John Rhodehamel (New York: Literary Classics of the U.S., 1997), pp. 540–41; *The Adams Jefferson Letters,* Vol. 2, ed. Lester J. Cappon (Chapel Hill: University of North Carolina Press, 1959), p. 308.

13. Robert J. Miller, "American Indian Influence on the U.S. Constitution and Its Framers," 18 *Am. Indian L. Rev.* 133, 138 (1993); Francis Paul Prucha, *American Indian Policy in the Formative Years: Indian Trade & Intercourse Acts 1790–1834* (Cambridge, MA: Harvard University Press, 1962), pp. 1–3, 43–50.

14. The General Allotment (Dawes) Act, ch. 119, 24 Stat. 388 (1887) (codified as amended at 25 U.S.C. §§ 331–334, 339, 341, 342, 348, 349, 354, 381); Prucha, *The Great Father,* pp. 140–43, 595, 659, 667–68, 671, 746–47, 754, 867–69, 896; *Cohen's Handbook,* pp. 128–38, 613, 617; John Collier, Memorandum, *The Purposes and Operation of the Wheeler-Howard Indian Rights Bill, Hearings on H.R. 7902 Before the Senate and House Committees on Indian Affairs,* 73rd Congress, 2nd Session (1934), pp. 15–18.

15. Prucha, *The Great Father,* pp. 668, 867; Michelle Tirado, "The Lay of the Land," *American Indian Report* 12, 13 (August 2004).

16. Prucha, *The Great Father,* pp. 513–19, 609–10; 25 U.S.C. §§ 280–280a; Vine Deloria Jr., *God is Red: A Native View of Religion,* 2nd ed. (Golden, CO: Fulcrum Publishing, 1994), pp. 238–41; Robert J. Miller, "Exercising Cultural Self-Determination: The Makah Indian Tribe Goes Whaling," 25 *Am. Indian L. Rev.* 165, 199–206 (2001); Robert J. Miller & Maril Hazlett, "The "Drunken Indian"—Myth Distilled into Reality through Federal Indian Alcohol Policy," 28 *Ariz. State L.J.* 223, 231–33, 235–38 (1996); Robert J. Miller, "Correcting Supreme Court Errors: American Indian Response to Lyng v. Northwest Indian Cemetery Protective Ass'n," 20 *Envtl. L.* 1037, 1039 (1990).

17. Prucha, *The Great Father,* p. 1111; "Message From The President of the United States Transmitting Recommendations for Indian Policy," *H.R. Doc. No. 91–363,* (1970), p. 1; 25 U.S.C. § 450(a) (2000).

CONCLUSION

1. *Johnson v. M'Intosh,* 21 U.S. (8 Wheat.) 543, 572–73, 588–90 (1823).

2. *Beecher v. Wetherby,* 95 U.S. 517, 525 (1877); *United States v. Sandoval,* 231 U.S. 28, 39, 42–44 (1913); Tzvetan Todorov, *The Conquest of America,* trans. Richard Howard (1982; New York: Harper & Row, 1984), p. 45; "The History and Influence of the Puritans," *The Miscellaneous Writings of Joseph Story,* ed. William W. Story (1852; Reprint, New York: De Capo Press, 1972,), pp. 460, 464–65; Steven T. Newcomb, "The Evidence of Christian Nationalism in Federal Indian Law: The Doctrine of Discovery, Johnson v. McIntosh, and Plenary Power," 20 *N.Y.U. Rev. L. & Soc. Change* 303, 308–09 (1993).

3. *Johnson,* 21 U.S. at 562–67, 588, 591.

4. Eric Kades, "The Dark Side of Efficiency: Johnson v. M'Intosh and the Expropriation of American Indian Lands," 148 *U. Pa. L. Rev.* 1065, 1078 (2000); *Johnson,* 21 U.S. at 574.

5. David H. Getches, "Conquering the Cultural Frontier: The New Subjectivism of the Supreme Court in Indian Law," 84 *Calif. L. Rev.* 1573, 1581 (1996); Robert A. Williams, Jr., "Columbus's Legacy: The Rehnquist Court's Perpetuation of European Cultural Racism against American Indian Tribes," 39 *Fed. B. News & J.* 358 (1992); Charles F. Wilkinson, *American Indians, Time, and the Law* (New Haven, CT, and London: Yale University Press 1987), p. 79; *compare* Ward Churchill, *Perversions of Justice: Indigenous Peoples and Anglo American Law* (San Francisco: City Lights Books, 2003), pp. 21–22; David E. Wilkins & K. Tsianina Lomawaima, *Uneven Ground: American Indian Sovereignty and Federal Law* (Norman: University of Oklahoma Press, 2001), p. 63; Newcomb, pp. 308–09; Vine Deloria Jr. & David E. Wilkins, *Tribes, Treaties, & Constitutional Tribulations* (Austin: University of Texas Press, 1999), p. 83; Robert A. Williams, Jr., *The American Indian in Western Legal Thought: The Discourses of Conquest* (New Haven, CT, and London: Yale University Press 1990), p. 326; Elizabeth Cook-Lynn, "The Lewis and Clark Story, the Captive Narrative, and the Pitfalls of Indian History," 19 *Wicazo Sa Rev.* 21, 28 (2004).

6. 25 U.S.C. § 450(a)(1) (2000); 25 U.S.C. §§ 450–450n; 25 U.S.C. §§ 458aa-458-hh.

7. *Morton v. Mancari,* 417 U.S. 535, 555 (1974); *United States v. Mazurie,* 419 U.S. 544 (1975); *United States v. Lara,* 541 U.S. 193 (2004).

8. 25 U.S.C. § 81(b) (2000), Pub. L. No. 106–179, § 2, 114 Stat. 46 (2000).

Selected Bibliography

Only my primary and most significant sources are listed in this bibliography. Please refer to the chapter notes for citations to all the materials relied on.

ARTICLES

Cohen, Felix S. "Original Indian Title," 32 *Minn. L. Rev.* 28 (1947).

Jefferson, Thomas. "The Limits and Bounds of Louisiana," in *Documents Relating to the Purchase & Exploration of Louisiana* (Boston and New York: Houghton, Mifflin, 1904).

Miller, Robert J. "American Indian Influence on the United States Constitution and its Framers," 18 *Am. Indian L. Rev.* 133–160 (1993).

Miller, Robert J. "The Doctrine of Discovery in American Indian Law," 42 *Idaho L. Rev.* 1–122 (2006).

Pratt, Julius. "John L. O'Sullivan and Manifest Destiny," 12 *New York History* 213, 220 (1933).

BOOKS

American State Papers: Documents, legislative and executive, of the Congress of the United States, Vol. 1–6 (Washington, DC: U.S. Government Printing Office).

Billington, Ray Allen. *The Far Western Frontier, 1830–1860* (New York, Evanston, IL, and London: Harper & Row, 1956).

Circular Letters of Congressmen to Their Constituents 1789–1829, Vol. 1–3, ed. Noble E. Cunningham, Jr. (Chapel Hill: University of North Carolina Press, 1978).

A Compilation of Messages and Papers of the Presidents, Vol. 1 and 4, ed. James D. Richardson (Washington, DC: Bureau of National Literature, 1913).

DeVoto, Bernard. *The Course of Empire* (Boston: Houghton Mifflin, 1952).

Early American Indian Documents: Treaties and Laws, 1607–1789, Vol. 1–20, ed. Alden T. Vaughan et al. (Washington, DC: University Publications of America, 1998),.

Foundations of Colonial America: A Documentary History, Vol. 1–3, ed. W. Keith Kavenagh (New York: Chelsea House, 1973).

Goetzmann, William H. *Exploration and Empire: The Explorer and the Scientist in the Winning of the American West* (New York: Knopf, 1966).

Horsman, Reginald. *Race and Manifest Destiny: The Origins of American Racial Anglo-Saxonism* (Cambridge, MA, and London: Harvard University Press, 1981).

Indian Affairs: Laws and Treaties, Vol. 2, ed. Charles J. Kappler (Washington, DC: U.S. Government Printing Office, 1904).

Jackson, Donald. *Thomas Jefferson and the Stony Mountains* (Chicago and London: University of Illinois Press, 1981).

Kennedy, Roger G. *Mr. Jefferson's Lost Cause: Land, Farmers, Slavery, and the Louisiana Purchase* (Oxford and New York: Oxford University Press, 2003).

Laws of the Colonial and State Governments Relating to Indians and Indian Affairs, from 1633 to 1831 (Washington, DC: Thompson and Homans, 1832; Reprint, Stanfordville, NY: Coleman, 1978).

Letters of the Lewis and Clark Expedition with Related Documents 1783–1854, 2nd ed., Vol. 1 and 2, ed. Donald Jackson (Urbana, Chicago, and London: University of Illinois Press, 1978).

Merk, Frederick. *The Oregon Question: Essays in Anglo-American Diplomacy and Politics* (Cambridge, MA: The Belknap Press of Harvard University, 1967).

Onuf, Peter S. *Jefferson's Empire: The Language of American Nationhood* (Charlottesville: University Press of Virginia, 2000).

Pagden, Anthony. *Lords of all the World: Ideologies of Empire in Spain, Britain and France c. 1500–c. 1800* (New Haven, CT: Yale University Press, 1995).

Peterson, Merrill. *Thomas Jefferson and the New Nation* (New York: Oxford University Press, 1970).

Reprint of Documents Manifest Destiny and the Imperialism Question, ed. Charles L. Sanford (New York and London: John Wiley, 1974).

Ronda, James P. *Astoria & Empire* (Lincoln and London: University Nebraska Press, 1990).

Ronda, James P. *Lewis & Clark among the Indians* (Lincoln and London: University of Nebraska Press, 1984).

Salish-Pend d'Oreille Culture Committee & Elders Cultural Advisory Council Confederated Salish and Kootenai Tribes. *The Salish People and the Lewis and Clark Expedition* (Lincoln and London: University of Nebraska Press, 2005).

Seed, Patricia. *Ceremonies of Possession in Europe's Conquest of the New World, 1492–1640* (Cambridge, England, and New York: Cambridge University Press, 1995).

Select Charters and Other Documents Illustrative of American History 1606–1775, ed. William MacDonald (London: MacMillan, 1906; Reprint, Littleton, CO: Rothman, 1993).

Sheehan, Bernard W. *Seeds of Extinction: Jeffersonian Philanthropy and the American Indian* (Chapel Hill: University of North Carolina Press, 1973).

The Definitive Journals of Lewis & Clark, Vol. 1–13, ed. Gary E. Moulton (Lincoln and London: University of Nebraska Press, 1987–2003).

The Writings of John Quincy Adams 1816–1819, Vol. 4–6, ed. Worthington Chauncey Ford (New York: Macmillan, 1916; Reprint, Westport, CT: Greenwood Press, 1968).

The Writings of Thomas Jefferson, Vol. 1–19, ed. Andrew A. Lipscomb & Albert Ellery Bergh (Washington, DC: Jefferson Memorial Assoc. of the U.S., 1903).

Tucker, Robert W. & David C. Hendrickson. *Empire of Liberty: The Statecraft of Thomas Jefferson* (New York and Oxford: Oxford University Press, 1990).

Van Alstyne, Richard W. *The Rising American Empire* (New York and London: Norton, 1960).

Wallace, Anthony F. C. *Jefferson and the Indians: The Tragic Fate of the First Americans* (Ann Arbor: University of Michigan Press, 1999).

Weeks, William Earl. *John Quincy Adams and American Global Empire* (Louisville: The University Press of Kentucky, 1992).

Weinberg, Albert. *Manifest Destiny: A Study of Nationalist Expansionism in American History* (Gloucester: Peter Smith, 1958).

Williams, Jr., Robert A. *The American Indian in Western Legal Thought: The Discourses of Conquest* (New Haven, CT, and Oxford: Yale University Press, 1990).

Index

About the Author

ROBERT J. MILLER is Associate Professor at the Lewis & Clark Law School in Portland, Oregon, and Chief Justice, Court of Appeals, Confederated Tribes of the Grand Ronde Community of Oregon. He is a citizen of the Eastern Shawnee Tribe of Oklahoma.